101
Inspirational
Stories
of the
Power of
Prayer

Father John Vaughn ☺

Happy 60th Anniversary of Entrance into the Order! Much love & Blessings from all your Poor Clare Sisters in Spokane!

101
Inspirational
Stories
of the
Power of
Prayer

Sister Patricia Proctor, OSC

A Called by Joy Book

Franciscan Monastery of Saint Clare
Spokane, Washington

www.calledbyjoy.com

101 Inspirational Stories of the Power of Prayer

> Sr. Patricia Proctor, OSC
> The Franciscan Monastery of Saint Clare
> 4419 North Hawthorne Street
> Spokane, Washington 99205
> (509) 327-4479

Printed in the United States of America.

ISBN-10: 0972844775
ISBN-13: 978-0972844772

First Printing May, 2008

ATTENTION SCHOOLS, UNIVERSITIES, COLLEGES AND CHARITABLE ORGANIZATIONS:

Quantity discounts are available on bulk purchases of this book for educational, gift purposes or as premiums for increasing magazine subscriptions or renewals. For information, please contact:

St. Anthony Messenger Press at 1-800-488-0488.

Ave Maria

This book has been placed under the special care and protection of our loving and kind *Blessed Mother*.

It is in loving memory of our dear

Sister Eileen Lillis, OSC

Sister Eileen's spirit of joy, laughter, courage and inspiration is a lasting legacy to all of the Poor Clare Sisters who will follow her. She was always ready to try something new and to move forward as the Spirit guided her. Although we always pretended to "groan" when she would announce to all, "I have a new idea!", in truth we were inspired and emboldened by her in many, many ways!

If you are in need of heavenly help…she is only a prayer away!

With Prayerful Thanks

To the many friends who have made this book possible. To those who shared their beautiful stories—especially those whose stories space did not permit us to include—your generosity and kindness are so appreciated. May God reward you each and every day.

To my wonderful co-editors, Anne Marie Lillis, Kristina Ries and Michael Ross, who came through with joyful and expert help to make this book the best ever!

To my dear friend Virginia Schmuck for her super job of proofing and fine tuning and always saying "YES" to one more story that I need right away!

To Dale Duncan who not only does a superb job of layout for each of these books but provides constant help, advice and consultation for every technical, logistical and problem I seem to come up with.

Great thanks to Barb Ries who is a great friend, support and co-worker in each book from start to finish!

To Kathy Czeck and the entire dedicated staff at POS printing, and to the wonderful friends at Saint Anthony Messenger Press—GOD BLESS YOU!

AND of course...before, after and during this whole project, the greatest thanks and appreciation to my wonderful sisters with whom I have the joy of living in our Spokane community. THANK YOU!

Sr. Patricia Proctor, OSC

Contents

Appendices

Foreword

One of my theology professors at Franciscan University of Steubenville once told our class, "If you want to lose your faith, just stop praying, and breathe." His statement initially seemed rather odd, since I assumed that falling away from God would take a bit more effort than simply not spending time with Him in prayer. It turns out what he said can almost serve as a one-line summary of the Christian faith. In reality, prayer is the sine qua non of our relationship with the Lord, the essential element without which we would, indeed, soon fail to even think of Him, let alone love Him.

Understanding prayer strictly in that way, however, results in an incomplete appreciation of its power and importance. If we pray merely to avoid losing our faith in God, that's a sort of *white knuckle* approach to seeking salvation, a kind of insurance policy by which we hope to make it to heaven by tossing up an occasional prayer. But God wants prayer to be so much more than that for each of us. Prayer is the means by which we build our relationship of love with the Holy Trinity, how we share everything with God, and receive all that He has for us.

It's often said that prayer is a two-way conversation. Yet, one of the most common mistakes we make—and I've been as guilty as anyone—is forgetting to give God His time to speak. That's understandable, since we can't see Him and, barring a special grace from on high, we can't audibly hear His voice. But there's so much He wants to say to us. And he longs to have us place our prayers before Him and answer them in a way that's in our best interests and according to His perfect timing.

A book of this nature is a wonderful testimony to the efficacy of prayer, an inspiring collection of personal accounts of how God has not only heard people's prayers, but answered them in an amazing variety of ways. Reading such stories can only help us develop a greater trust in God and an eagerness to approach Him with our own heartfelt intentions and petitions.

Being frail human beings wounded by our own sins and the sins of others, there can be any number of obstacles in the way of our entering into a fruitful life of prayer. Perhaps you feel that God couldn't possibly answer *your* prayers. Or maybe you don't think you should bother Him with your petitions. You might even have an unhealthy fear of God because of some hurt you suffered earlier in your life. Each of us likely has something standing in the way of our prayer life reaching its full potential.

If you sense any fear, hesitancy, or other impediment to praying, then the place to start is to ask the Lord to remove such barriers and grant you the freedom to become the trusting child He has created you to be. There's nothing God wants more than to communicate closely with you, for you to share every single aspect of your life with Him, and to bestow upon you "every spiritual blessing in the Heavens," as Ephesians chapter 1 says.

For most of us, finding the time to pray well can be a challenge in today's world. But that just gives us more opportunities to be creative and, if necessary, to make the appropriate changes in our lives that will afford us adequate time to spend in the Lord's presence. Nothing could be more necessary. Nothing could be more rewarding.

As your heart is moved by the stories of the power of prayer compiled in this book by Sr. Patricia, make a new resolution *today* that you are going to make your whole life a prayer, and that you will devote at least a small amount of time each day to conversing with God. He's waiting to hear from you. And he's waiting to pour out His blessings in return.

Jerry Usher

Creator and radio host of Catholic Answers Live, www.catholic.com, and co-author of Called by Name: The Inspiring Stories of 12 Men Who Became Catholic Priests

The Power Of Prayer

By the Most Reverend William S. Skylstad
Bishop of Spokane

Prayer means so many things, to so many people. I have been a priest now for nearly fifty years. Some of those years were spent in parish ministry; other years, educating and forming seminarians as they discerned their call to priesthood. As a spiritual director, I have walked with some remarkable individuals, humbled by the opportunity to share their quest for greater unity with God. In several parts of the country, I have had the honor of leading retreats, especially for groups of priests.

When all is said and done, in all of these circumstances, a fundamental question is asked and seeks a definitive answer: What is prayer? Closely following that is a second question, just as important: How do I pray?

In one sense, the answers are intensely simple. In another sense, the answers are as varied as the rich diversity of God's creation that is manifested in humanity itself.

What is prayer?

Prayer is a relationship. It is the relationship between an individual and God, and it is the relationship between a group of individuals with one another as they seek a relationship, together, with God, in community.

We know that God wants this relationship with us. When people asked him how to pray, Jesus didn't dismiss the question. He gave them—and gave us—a model of prayer that evokes familiarity and respect, that acknowledges our dependence on God while it gives us an opportunity to express our joy in speaking candidly with the One we call Father.

If prayer is a relationship, how do we actually do it?

Remember that prayer is an invitation from God to us—an invitation to spend time with him, to speak with honesty about our joys and our sorrows, our gratitude and our needs. Prayer is the activity that lets us reach out and touch God, and be touched in return.

The most important thing to remember is: To try to pray is to pray.

Keep in mind that there are as many ways to pray as there are people. Each of us speaks with a unique voice, whether we use our vocal cords or a computer keyboard. Some might place themselves before God with a full heart, brimming over with expressions of love, of gratitude, of need. Others come before God with a heart full of sorrow that simply cannot be articulated. They place themselves in God's presence, offering up the feelings that they cannot put into words.

For prayer is not necessarily about words, or even an abundance of words. Sometimes it is enough to say, "Help," and at other times, to say, "Thank You." To say, "O Lord, I love You. Help me love You more."

It is the attempt to pray that is the prayer. It is the desire for union with God, put into action, that is prayer.

There are as many styles of prayer as there are people who pray. Whether we meditate or contemplate, recite or extemporize, pray with friends or alone, in a church or on a street corner: the important thing is to accept God's invitation. In whatever way we choose to accept that invitation—that is prayer. And it is powerful.

Sr. Patricia has assembled another collection of stories about the power of prayer, how prayer has touched people's lives. All of these people have been touched by the power of God's grace through prayer. I know that you will be, too.

The Down Syndrome Miracle

One afternoon while walking through the lobby of a hotel in Grand Rapids, Michigan, I became aware of a disturbance in one corner of the room. I walked in that direction in that casual way we use to check out disturbances in public places without announcing our curiosity. A boy of about four was screaming and rolling around on the floor in some kind of a fit.

Several people were trying to help the parents control the child. A crowd was gathering. It was a bad situation.

Then the Lord spoke to me.

"I want you to pray with that boy for a complete healing," he said. It wasn't an audible voice. But I *heard* the Lord say this as clearly as I have ever heard anything.

I suspected that the boy had Downs' Syndrome. I was astonished. Down's Syndrome is a genetic defect that always causes moderate to severe mental impairment and physical disability. Every cell in that boy's body had an extra chromosome. Every one of the billions of cells in his body was defective, and I was supposed to pray for a complete healing.

But I had heard the Lord. I took a deep and uneasy breath and went over to the parents; I told them that I wanted to pray for their son. I wanted to imply that the idea was mine, not the Lord's, in case nothing happened when I prayed.

I put my hands on the child and prayed. He calmed down immediately. I was filled with a sense that at that moment the Lord began to restore him completely.

He was. In the weeks and months following that event, the boy's development accelerated. The doctors could not find any explanation for it. When they ran the tests they could find no trace of Down's Syndrome. I still hear from the parents telling me how well he is doing.

Michael Scanlan, TOR   *Steubenville, Ohio*

This is an excerpt from the book, *Let the Fire Fall*, by Michael Scanlan, TOR, Servant Publications.

I would advise those who practice prayer, especially at first, to cultivate the friendship and company of others who are working in the same way. This is a most important thing, because we can help one another by our prayers, and all the more so because it may bring us even greater benefits.

St. Theresa of Avilia

The greatest privilege God gives to you is the freedom to approach Him at any time. You are not only authorized to speak to Him; you are invited. You are not only permitted; you are expected. God waits for you to communicate with Him. You have instant, direct access to God. God loves mankind so much, and in a very special sense His children, that He has made Himself available to you at all times.

Wesley L. Duewel

How Mother Teresa Lived

*This following story was told to me (Sr. Patricia) by Fr. Langford,
the cofounder of the Missionary of Charity priests in a radio
interview I was doing with him for my program, "Faith, Hope
and Action." I was so moved by his story that I asked him for
permission to include it in this book and he graciously agreed.
This story is the transcription from that interview:*

One day in the mother house in Calcutta there were about three
hundred novices and they were all out for the morning. One of the
novices working in the kitchen came up to Mother Teresa and said,
"We've planned poorly; we have no flour to back these chipaties for
lunch." Chipaties are little flour and water pancakes. The situation looked
bleak—three hundred plus mouths are coming to be fed in about an hour
and a half and there's nothing to cook with. There's no food.

"What I would expect Mother Teresa to do," Fr. Langford explained
to me, "was that Mother would pick up the telephone and call some of her
benefactors and mobilize them to find some way to feed her daughters.
Instead, her reaction—her spontaneous reaction—was to say to this little
one, 'Sister, you're in charge of the kitchen this week? Well then, go into
the chapel and tell Jesus we have no food. That's settled. Now let's move
on. What's next?'"

Lo and behold, ten minutes later there was a ring at the door and
Mother Teresa was called downstairs. A man she had never seen before
was standing there with a clipboard. He addressed her saying "Mother
Teresa, we were just informed that the teachers at the city schools are
going on strike. Classes have been dismissed and we have 7,000 lunches
we don't know what to do with. Can you help us use them?"

God provided for the needs of his children.

Mother Teresa's sanctity was built on a very simple foundation of deep faith and trust in God. Mother Teresa turned to Him in prayer, not only in need, but also to rest in the arms of the Father—body and spirit.

That is how Mother Teresa lived each day of her life.

Fr. Joseph Langford, MC   *Mexico City, Mexico*

Note from Sr. Patricia: The interview I was doing with Father Langford was about his book, Mother Teresa: In the Shadow of Our Lady. *It is published by Our Sunday Visitor and I highly recommend it. Not just to learn more about Mother Teresa, which you will do, but what Father's book really does is guide you in developing a deep and prayerful relationship with God through our Lady.*

Published by Our Sunday Visitor. Available at www.osv.com, 1-800-348-2440

The mere act of prayer is abhorrent to the forces of evil, and you will find that there will be all kinds of hindrances (depression, doubt, frustrations and so on). Many of those hindrances will have the smell of sulphur smoke about them.

Steve Brown

The devil is not terribly frightened of our human efforts and credentials. But he knows his kingdom will be damaged when we begin to lift up our hearts to God.

Jim Cymbala

Tehilim Psalms

At seven a.m. on Thursday, I got a call from Susie, my father's wife. She blurted out, "I don't think Sid is going to make it."

"What?!" I responded, panic settling in. "What do you mean?"

"The surgery went all wrong," she said. "The doctors don't know if he's going to make it. They really don't know. I bet they didn't want me to call you yet. It hasn't been twenty-four hours."

"Should I come now?"

"No, wait until I can tell you something more definitive."

An hour later Susie called again and told me that the doctors were not happy at all that she called me. They really didn't know what was going on with my father, but he wasn't in immediate danger. No, I shouldn't come yet. He coded (died) on the table and they revived him. They didn't know whether or not his brain was damaged. They had put a defibrillator in his heart and they had thought it went fine, but he was in a permanent state of tachycardia—his heart beating wildly. He had inhaled saliva, so he had pneumonia with a high fever. His blood oxygenation was low. He was on a breathing tube, so he was under heavy sedation in a medically induced non-responsive state.

She said she'd call me later with more information.

I don't remember how many times we talked that day, but in the evening I decided that I had to fly out the next day. I got there as soon as I could, which, because of the flight availability, was not soon enough— something like 4:30 p.m. By this time, my father had been in the same state for at least forty-eight hours.

I didn't know what to do.

But I'm a Jew. What do Jews do at the bedside of someone who is sick? We recite or sing Tehilim psalms. My father is an atheist, but I'm not. In fact, I'm a rabbinical student. I decided that he'd forgive me for doing the only thing I could figure out to do. Besides, he is a musician. Maybe he'd like the music.

I sang psalms. With all my heart and with all my soul and with all my might, I sang.

It wasn't long—a few minutes only. My father, whom the nurses said was non-responsive (meaning that he would have no awareness of what was going on around him due to the deep sedation), turned his head to face me and stretched out his neck as if to get closer to the song. I was heartened. For three hours, until they kicked me out of the ICU, I sang. And while I was there, over three hours, I watched the monitors surrounding his bed. I sang Psalms and his fever went down from 103 to 102 to 101 to 100 to 99. I sang psalms and his blood oxygenation came up from 80% to 85% to 90% to 95%. I sang psalms and his heart rate stabilized.

The next morning when Susie and I returned, his temperature, heart rate and blood all remained in good shape. I continued to sing.

One of his doctors came in. He explained that he had lowered the sedative dosage enough so that my father could hear his voice, and if my dad still had his mind, he could respond to a simple request. The doctor came back a bit later when my father's fog was only partial. Watching him contort and struggle with the pain and discomfort of the thick respirator tube was almost impossible to bear. Then the doctor asked him to stick out his tongue. I was holding my breath. Was his mind there? What would happen? Never would I have thought that the sight of my dad's tongue would bring such exultation, but there it was, and there were my tears.

Even with this progress, with a normal temperature and a stable heart rate and a solid oxygenation level, the doctors weren't sure that my dad was strong enough to come out from sedation. They kept him under for another ten days! When they brought him out he went through several days of predictable physical weakness and sedation induced dementia. After that his health returned to the same state he was in before the surgery. He had lost no heart strength, his mind was 100% whole, and he regained his muscle strength very quickly. He doesn't recall my singing; he doesn't remember anything from that time, but he likes to hear the story.

Debra R. Kolodny   *Silver Spring, Maryland*

It Was All Right

From the moment our little daughter, Karen Sue, came into the world, she lived in a world of pain. We did not know what was wrong. The assumption was that perhaps she had a congenital heart defect. This was in the early 1950s when they did not have the medical tests and equipment to diagnose such things. All I knew was that things were not right with my tiny little daughter. She cried and cried and nothing that I or anyone else could do seemed to help. Night after night and day after day I would hold her, rock her, and try to soothe away her pain.

During the eight months of her time with us there were only a few days during which she seemed to be without extreme suffering. There were few golden moments of experiencing joy and delight in her small life and a handful of precious memories of her three-year-old brother playing with her and bits of laughter and giggles.

It was a hard time for all of us. Stanley, her small brother, pretty much had to fend for himself as I spent every moment trying to help Karen Sue. She was never strong, she could not hold down food, and all the time she cried and cried.

I could think of little else but coping through the day, struggling to keep Karen Sue alive. I lost a lot of weight, became dazed and numb with lack of sleep and exhaustion I struggled to keep going. Finally one night, when she seemed to be particularly bad, I whispered tearfully to Jesus, "I can't do this anymore."

That night we took her to the hospital and found she had developed pneumonia. I stayed with her through the long night as she gasped and coughed and struggled. Later the next morning, I went home to catch a few hours of sleep so that I could spend another night with her in the hospital.

I fell onto the bed, totally spent and drifted into an exhausted sleep. I awoke to the ringing of the phone. It was the hospital. Karen Sue was dying, they said. I did not drive at that time but I quickly called my husband and he drove immediately from work to pick me up and we rushed to her bedside. When we got there, the little bed was empty and I knew she was gone.

I remember the moment hazily as if I was in a dream. I just looked at that little bed, dazed and numb and whispered to Jesus, "It's all right." I felt that God had given me the grace to accept this loss. "It's all right." My heart was broken, my heart was crushed, but "It was all right." I did not want her suffering to continue. I knew she was better with Jesus. The grace to accept this I think was what kept me going.

I do not remember now if it was that night or the next night that I went to sleep in total anguish. I woke up in the middle of the night and saw something that until now, I have shared with only my husband and a few others. I guess I felt that no one would believe me. From my bed, I looked into the hallway and clearly and distinctly as could be, I saw Our Lady standing in the hallway between two bedrooms holding our little girl in her arms.

I was so comforted; I just lay back down, rested my head onto the pillow and went to sleep. It was all right.

Kathryn Rohr   *Hays, Kansas*

Holy Communion keeps me full of joy. Without the constant presence of our divine Master in my humble chapel, I should never have been able to continue to link my life with the lepers of Moloka'i.

Blessed Damien Joseph De Veuster of Moloka'i

A Silly Prayer Story

My husband and I are seniors and not up to snuff when it comes to technology and all those new gadgets. Our children, God bless them, try to keep us up to date by gifting us with machines that perform all sorts of wonderful things.

On a hot day last summer, the power went off for about an hour. Then everything came back on except our TV. One blank blue screen was all we got. We called the cable company and they said everything was fine at their end. The neighbors TVs on the same system as ours were also working fine.

We pushed buttons and read and reread the manual. Nothing worked and we got frustrated and even a bit angry at our seeming incompetence. Finally, we decided to let the TV rest for awhile and try later. Four hours later we tried again but still saw nothing but the blue screen. We pushed more buttons, uttered some nasty words and looked at each other. There was nothing else that we could do except sit and stare at the blue screen.

Oh great, we thought: now we will have to call some repair person and it will be expensive!

Then in the same instant my husband and I had this wonderful idea! Why not ask St. Benedict for help (we heard somewhere that he was quite good at solving this kind of problem). So we silently asked (I guess what could qualify as a prayer) for help.

We did nothing else after that but stare at the blue screen. Then unbelievably the screen got lines and twirls on it and in less than a minute, everything was back on track.

I got goose bumps because I am a real doubting Thomas when it comes to praying. I am still in a state of disbelief but there is no other explanation why this happened. I know it is rather a silly prayer story but it is a true one, and if nothing else it made me a believer in the power of prayer. I know now, without a doubt, that no request is too small or too big for God to answer.

Laurie Obidowski   *Brampton, Ontario, Canada*

Satan has in fact a plan against the saints of the Most High which is to wear them out. What is meant by this phrase, "wear out"? It has in it the idea of reducing a little this minute, then reducing a little further the next minute. Reduce a little today, reduce a little tomorrow. Thus the wearing out is almost imperceptible; nevertheless, it is a reducing. The wearing down is scarcely an activity of which one is conscious, yet the end result is that there is nothing left. He will take away your prayer life little by little, and cause you to trust God less and less and yourself more and more, a little at a time. He will make you feel somewhat cleverer than before. Step by step, you are misled to rely more on your own gift, and step by step your heart is enticed away from the Lord. Now, were Satan to strike the children of God with great force at one time, they would know exactly how to resist the enemy since they would immediately recognize his work. He uses the method of gradualism to wear down the people of God.

Watchman Nee

He Messed With Me

I used to feel quite lonely in my prayer life. Even though I felt I was praying very piously and with great reverence on a daily basis, it did not seem to be making a big difference in my life. I participated in Eucharistic Adoration and Scripture study on a weekly basis. I prayed the Scriptural Rosary daily. I prayed the Liturgy of the Hours regularly. But even with all these opportunities to be closer to the Trinity, I felt quite often that my prayers were not satisfying or even noticed by God.

Last year, without warning, I went from being fairly healthy and active to being disabled due to illness. I had to medically retire from my occupation/vocation of thirty years as a paramedic and paramedic instructor. During those years, I had been awarded and honored numerous times for my teaching and clinical skills, but now it was all over. *Forever!* I was angry at everyone: myself, others, and especially God for letting this happen to me.

I went to church and prayed to God, *hard* and *loud!* My dialogue with him would have been considered "for mature audiences only." I asked God, "Why are you doing this to me? I was good at my job, and I have helped many people in their times of distress! What am I going to do to support my family? God, you are unfair!"

All I *heard* or *felt* for an answer to my prayers was, "Thank you for talking to me. Come back and let's talk again tomorrow."

"What!? Tomorrow? Oh, I'll show you," I said. I went back the next day and the next. I kept going back, again and again. I started reading books, including the Bible, in earnest. I began listening to pod-casts and trying anything and everything to figure out why this was happening to me. I went to confession for the first time in about ten years.

Slowly, over this past year, I have pretty much moved through my anger. I have asked for forgiveness from everyone, especially God. I

11

realize now that my suffering was, and is, a necessary component in my life. I needed to be humble instead of proud and boisterous in my prayer. I needed not only to talk to God, but also to listen to Him.

I still pray and attend all the church activities as before, but now I can honestly say that I have never been more Catholic, and possibly happier, in a long time. God definitely works in a mysterious and unorthodox way. He *messed with me*, and I love Him more now than I ever have.

Daniel E. Halley   *Hazelwood, Missouri*

Prayer is the raising of the mind to God. We must always remember this. The actual words matter less.

Blessed John XXIII

Here are four ways God answers prayer:
1) No, not yet;
2) No, I love you too much;
3) Yes, I thought you'd never ask;
4) Yes, and here's more.

Anne Lewis

God commands you to pray, but he forbids you to worry.

St. John Vianney

Ten Minute Meditation

Imagine that you are in a beautiful garden on a warm, sunny day. The birds are singing, a bee is buzzing from flower to flower, and a small stream nearby is bubbling a gurgling melody. In this garden are two chairs, both empty. You walk over and sit in one. In a little while, you know that Jesus will be coming and sitting in the other one.

You have never met Jesus in this garden before.

This is your Prayer Garden—a place just for you and Jesus to meet and spend time together. You don't know exactly what this first meeting will be like. While you are waiting, think about what questions you might have for Him.

After a few minutes, when Jesus comes and sits in the chair next to you, ask Him your questions. Know that the answers may not come right away, but it is important that you take time to ask Jesus the questions.

Prayer when time is completed:

Thank you Jesus
for coming
to share with me.
I look forward
to spending
more mini minutes
with you.
Amen

M
E
D
I
T
A
T
I
O
N

Notebook of Miracles

One day, while I was sitting in my car, a song came on the radio. It is called "I've Always Loved You" by Third Day. I had heard the song many times before, but this time, the words spoke to my soul:

Don't you know I've always loved you
Even before there was time
Though you turn away
I'll tell you still
Don't you know I've always loved you

There, still in the parking lot, I realized that song was the long-awaited answer to one of my prayers. It was a prayer that began a long time ago when I begged God to show me the way to deal with a troublesome relationship—one that I had endured for many years—as it slowly but continuously ate away at my self-esteem. I had just left an appointment with my spiritual director at church and was feeling down about the direction my life was heading. But the words from the song began to make sense. How could God ever explain His love in words if I regularly ignored His miracles, signs and wonders? I mean, if they weren't enough to prove God's love for me, then what would?

Just then, a soft, gentle rain began to dance on my windshield. I watched and cried as the droplets hit the glass and rolled down. I had been so caught up in my own world of pain and my loveless marriage to an alcoholic that I rarely noticed the rain or any of the other small wonders of my daily life.

Less than an hour earlier I was telling my spiritual director how I felt I had traded years in a no-win relationship for bits of my soul, and in the process, I lost so much of who I was and all that mattered to me. He listened compassionately and then gently asked, "If God could give you anything right now, what would you ask for?"

Without hesitating, I replied, "I want God to give me a miracle."

My desire was for God to wave some sort of magic wand and say "poof" to solve my problems and to fix my husband and take away his addictions. I wanted the "happily ever after" that we are promised as little girls. I wanted to love and be loved in a healthy relationship. I wanted my husband to find God, or at least for God to find him. I wanted everything to be perfect without my having to do all of the work.

My spiritual director smiled and asked me to be on the lookout for my miracle. He asked me to make a list of all the miracles I encounter each day and to keep praying to God for what I needed. We prayed together and as I left, he reminded me, "Our God is a God of miracles."

So there I sat in the church parking lot, his suggestion of a miracle list still fresh in my mind and a song playing on the radio. The song continued, "I don't know how to explain it, but I know that words will hardly do if miracles, signs and wonders aren't enough for me to prove to you...."

The rain kept falling. A little miracle perhaps? Was it God's way of starting to cleanse my soul?

It occurred to me that if I did focus on seeking out the little miracles and tiny wonders that are all around me, I might learn a bit of the lesson I needed before my life and relationship could change.

So I found a piece of paper and wrote "one gentle rainstorm and a perfect song."

I decided that I would identify just one little gift from heaven each day and spend a few minutes thanking God for it. I recorded my little miracles in a notebook. Each has a date and inscription such as "saw a butterfly" or "my daughter has the most beautiful blue eyes." It didn't take long before I realized that as I looked for little signs of God's love for me, I found more than I could count, and many of the signs were not so little. My notebook of miracles was quickly filled.

God never did *fix* my husband or solve my problems for me, but He has been changing me. He has been working on me and rebuilding me over these last few years so that now I can deal with the relationship differently. I got my miracle. The one I needed instead of the one I prayed for. I came to see that God shows His love for me all the time. He never stops loving us and He never tires of showing us the depths of His love. As the song says, "Don't you know I've always loved you and I always will?"

Susan M. Walker   *Wheeling, Illinois*

This is our Lord's will,... that our prayer and our trust be, alike, large. For if we do not trust as much as we pray, we fail in full worship to our Lord in our prayer; and also we hinder and hurt ourselves. The reason is that we do not know truly that our Lord is the ground from which our prayer springeth; nor do we know that it is given us by his grace and his love. If we knew this, it would make us trust to have of our Lord's gifts all that we desire. For I am sure that no man asketh mercy and grace with sincerity, without mercy and grace being given to him first.

Julian of Norwich

Prayer means a launching out of the heart towards God; it means lifting up one's eyes, quite simply, to heaven, a cry of grateful love, from the crest of joy or the trough of despair; it's a vast, supernatural force that opens out my heart and binds me close to Jesus.

St. Therese of Lisieux

Only God Knew

As I was preparing to travel to Brazil, I was praying for all the people I would encounter and the word "more" kept coming into my head.

"More?" I thought. "I've given everything I have and am continuing to give…I don't have any more to give."

Touched with a bit of self-pity, I repented and said to the Lord, "Okay, if You really want more from me, I need You to show me what You want. I will trust You."

From the beginning of the trip, I was amazed at the lavishness of the care I received from the people I met. For a few days, I mistakenly attributed it to being just a series of coincidences. Then, as my every need and every wish continued to be effortlessly granted, the sister accompanying me looked at me wide-eyed and asked, "What is God doing?"

Her question rang like a bell in my head. Maybe this was God at work here. Maybe the "more" I kept hearing in prayer was Him teaching me that He has "more" blessings for us than we can imagine. I had been thanking Him for all of His blessings, but now my heart soared with a real hymn of praise.

Soon after my revelation, a young mother walked up to me holding her ten-month-old baby boy. "Joao Paulo has something he wants to give you, sister," she said. The little guy looked at me solemnly for a moment, and then reached up and pulled off what I learned was his favorite bib. It was beautifully embroidered with his name and little animals, and he held it out to me.

"Oh, I couldn't take this from you," I said. But the mother smiled and said, "Sister, we all need to learn to give. We practice that here by trying to anticipate the needs of others, or what we think God would want us to give. It is most often something little, but, given with a whole heart, it becomes a sign of God's love for His people."

That generous way of serving God and His people is what I had been receiving for days. As I accepted the bib, the little boy reached his arms out and hugged me. I felt like I had been visited by the child Jesus!

Being the skeptic that I am, I asked the Lord for a sign that this was truly the message He was sending me. "If all this kindness and generosity is really from You, and if You want me to see and experience first-hand how You are more attentive than I ever knew to all our needs—great and small—then Lord, grant me this sign; have someone give me an embroidered altar cloth for the little altar on which the Blessed Sacrament sits in our convent back in Michigan." It was something I had wanted to buy for several months, but could not find the one I had in mind.

The next morning, a very poor woman in the neighborhood came to me with a gift. When I opened it, there it was! It was the exact altar cloth that I had been looking for. Only God knew I wanted an altar cloth like this; I had never told a soul I was looking for one. As I looked at the woman's face, I saw her joy in my obvious shock and delight. It was a wonderful moment!

This experience taught me that the Lord has *more* blessings for us than we can imagine. I felt like He said to me, "Nothing in your life goes unnoticed by me. I did this because I want you to tell my people it is true that, 'Eye has not seen, ear has not heard, nor has it entered into the heart of man to conceive what God has prepared for those who love Him.' What I have prepared for you in heaven is beyond anything you can imagine, trust Me!"

Sr. Ann Shields   *Ann Harbor, Michigan*

The Fragile Sand Dollar

I was not raised in any faith, Christian or otherwise, and did not have any idea of how much God loved and cared for me, for all of us, so what happened came as a total surprise.

It seemed that I had failed at everything I ever tried in life. I dropped out of high school with learning disabilities. I was not able to hold a job because of emotional outbursts and disorganization. I had so much emotional pain bottled inside of me that I could see no way out.

Then I made a horrible decision to start using drugs. Crack cocaine. A guy gave it to me saying, "It's not like heroin, you won't get addicted." Stupidly, I believed him. Within two days, I was addicted and became violently ill if I could not smoke it. My raging outbursts became worse, not better. I could not sleep.

It was not long before I was unemployed, homeless, and involved in crime. I was always freezing cold, starving, and thirsty. Every year I would get pneumonia. I was frequently in jail, dirty, or in the emergency room from violent assaults. I was so miserable; I was literally losing my mind. The world hates you when you are in that state, but it did not compare to the self-hatred I felt.

Crack cocaine was a life-controlling obsession. I could not go three minutes without thinking about it. Even after it burned my lungs and I had to have lung surgery to remove a lobe of one lung, I still craved the drug. The minute I was released from the hospital I went right back to chasing it.

I was full of despair, seemingly cut off from the world and any chance of a normal life. Every day I experienced violence, hatred and meanness in the streets. I wondered if there was any hope for anyone.

My first ray of light came in November of 1999 when I had a friend who actually lived in a house with a mailing address. This was very important to me because now, in the rare instance that someone needed to contact me, they could reach me using her address.

For many years, I had not heard from my identical twin sister who had moved to Tennessee. Then suddenly, out of the blue, she sent me a Mass card with a picture of St. Therese on it. The card said that Masses would be offered for my healing.

I found out that my sister had gone through RCIA (Rite of Christian Initiation for Adults) and was now in the Catholic Church. I loved that card because it was a sign that someone cared about and loved me. I had my friend keep it for me. However, although I loved receiving the card and thought it was very nice, I had no idea what healing Masses really meant.

Exactly four months from the day I received my sister's card (this was after six nonstop years of being drug addicted, homeless, hopeless, and in and out of jail hospitals), I caught a terrible case of pneumonia. My temperature rose to 108° and my oxygen dipped so low that I fainted in the streets. I woke up in the ambulance, once again on the way to the emergency room.

I was hospitalized for weeks and was so sick and weak I could hardly move. One day while I was there, a few of Mother Teresa's nuns (Missionaries of Charity) were making their rounds at the hospital. Two of the sisters stopped in to see me. What compassion I saw in those two women! It made me cry with happiness. They were so kind to me, and even had a sense of humor, which surprised me.

Later, I was transferred to a skilled nursing facility to recuperate. The doctor there told me I was in a very fragile state. Although I was extremely weak, they allowed me to have a two-hour leave one day so I could go with a friend to get documents from the social security office and the DMV for disability help. While we were out, I asked my friend if he would take me to the ocean. I have always loved the ocean and was afraid I would not live to see it again.

When we arrived, it was windy, cold, and overcast. My friend had to hold me tightly because I could not stand or walk on my own. As we made our way along the beach, I started looking for a sand dollar. The ones I found were all cracked and in shards, broken up from rocks and the crashing waves. I kept looking though, almost desperately, to see if I could find a whole one, knowing it was unlikely. Then, lo and behold, at my feet was a tiny, almost transparent, fragile-looking sand dollar! There was not one crack in it, nor any chips on its sides. It was perfectly shaped, round and smooth. This little sand dollar had survived when the thick big ones had not! I took it back to the hospital with me, holding it carefully as my little treasure. This small, beautiful gift of the sea gave me renewed hope for my own situation.

I was released, only to end up in the emergency room yet again. It was an infected blood clot in my chest, a stroke in progress, and I was admitted back into the hospital.

This time I asked to see a priest. I wanted to join my sister in the Catholic Church. I wanted to be close to Jesus and not alone anymore. The next day Father Vitale came to see me. He asked lots of questions and I answered them as carefully and truthfully as I could. After that I was able to receive my sacraments right there in the hospital—including my first Communion!

I was so filled with joy! It was indescribable! I was flooded with deep peace in spite of all the pain and sickness I felt physically. The priest was so compassionate, so filled with light. I knew right then and there that I was home. I was not lost anymore.

I knew God loved me. Today, almost eight years later, I never miss Mass, I love praying the rosary, and I still have that special Mass card and sand dollar. I believe God was speaking to me through that little sand dollar. I also still feel that deep sense of peace, after all these years.

Oh, and I have no more drug addictions! I have a nice apartment and still have my good friend, St. Therese. I am still in awe of the ability of Jesus and the saints to love us in whatever state we are in, and His ability to heal so thoroughly. Prayers are definitely answered. There is no doubt left in my mind.

Sharon R. Friel   *San Francisco, California*

Miracle After Miracle

I have experienced so many miracles in my life that I could sit you down and talk for days about them. Miracle after miracle. Some people may say they are just coincidences, but to me they aren't. I will share two of them with you, both of them having to do with home heating oil.

One evening when my finances were at a very low point, I was deeply discouraged and didn't know what to do. I went to a prayer meeting that night and Father Bob approached me. He must have noticed how low I was feeling.

"How are things going, Lill?" he asked.

I half mumbled a discouraged reply. "I need oil and I don't know how to get it."

I was expecting a few words of consolation but instead he laughed! Just laughed, right out loud. That made me mad; I mean, I sure didn't think this was funny.

Then he told me the good news. That very afternoon a gentleman had come to him and said he wanted to give a hundred gallons of oil to someone in need. "Lill," the priest said, "That oil is for you."

Another time, soon after having heart surgery, my finances and my spirits were the lowest they had ever been. My husband had just been fired from his job because of his drinking, and I had quit my job because of the heart operation. We had no income. On that cold winter night, I sat at the kitchen table with my checkbook, trying to figure out how to pay the electric bill, and how I was going to get some oil. I had received a notice that the electricity would be shut off the next day, and I had no oil to heat our home. I only had enough money to pay for one or the other. Everything seemed totally overwhelming. We had two small children, and I knew they would freeze without heat in the house. But I knew that even if I did get oil, I wouldn't be able to use it because I needed electricity to start the heater. I had to have the electricity. I sat there for hours trying to figure out what to do.

Around eleven o'clock that night, I finally gave up. I took the checkbook, threw it in the drawer, and shouted at the Lord, "You said you would take care of us, so do it!" and went to bed.

The next morning, around eight thirty, I got a phone call from my ex-boss. He said he had a check waiting for me and told me to come pick it up. It was from profit sharing, and because I had worked there in January, they had to give it to me. It was for $1,777.68.

I was so excited I could hardly believe it! I knew it was a miracle. It had happened so quickly, so fast. Part of me was upset that I had gotten angry with God, but a bigger part of me was filled with joy that He took care of us so promptly!

I must have floated on air for months. Never had I felt God so near, so caring. It made a wonderful difference in how I faced the weeks of recovery, taking care of my kids, and staying with my husband through very hard times.

The Lord rescued me even though I was angry, and He gave me more than I needed. I was able to pay the electric bill, get oil, and even had some left for groceries.

So you see, once I turned my troubles over to God, He worked them out. I have never forgotten those miracles, and I know that God is always there for us. Not that I don't have bad times—I could share a lot of those with you too—but time after time I continue to receive miracles, small ones and big ones, that see me through life's challenges.

Lillian J. DeOliveira   *East Providence, Rhode Island*

God's word is light to the mind and fire to the will so that a person may know and love the Lord.

St. Lawrence of Brindisi

A Challenge to Trust

During a transition period in my ministry as a nurse and teacher, I experienced a prompting from the Holy Spirit that took me completely by surprise. At the time, I was not working because I was undergoing intensive therapy for a back injury. Physical pain and fatigue prevented me from taking on a consistent work schedule, so I prayed for God to show me what His will was for me during this period.

Soon I began volunteering at a soup kitchen in the basement of an old abandoned school in a neighboring parish. While I was there, I decided to re-open the clothing dispensary room that had been closed because of a lack of volunteer help. The need for clothing was so great that I began working more hours there each day.

One Friday afternoon the director approached me and asked if I would consider opening a family resource center in the room next to the clothing room. However, there would be no allocation of funds for this project—nothing for construction and no operational or program budget. I wondered how I could even consider saying yes to something as big as this.

Part of me wanted very much to do this but I hesitated, concerned that I would begin the project and not be able to keep it up because of my back problem. I told the director that I would pray about it and consider his proposal over the weekend.

As soon as I returned to the convent, I went to the chapel and asked God to make it clear to me what I should do. Aside from communal prayer and Divine Office, my usual way of praying was to sit in silence and pray contemplatively. However, this was becoming more difficult because sitting for any length of time caused the pain in my back to become more severe.

As I prayed, I united my pain with the passion of Christ and asked Him to accept the pain as prayer. My awareness of the pain dimmed as my mind focused on the many needy people of St. John Parish.

God's answer was yes, a resource center would open in this inner city parish. It would provide information and referral services for housing, jobs, and alcohol and drug programs. Emergency assistance and health resources would be available, as well as peer group support in the areas of family violence, women's self-esteem, and counseling. The center would offer special programs for nutrition education, parenting, stress reduction, and spiritual resources.

But I still wasn't convinced that God was calling me to coordinate this project. I asked God for a clear sign of His plan, one that I could not mistake. Then the thought came to me that there would have to be a doorway in the wall that separated the clothing room from what would be the resource center. Plus we would need to build a small office in the room for private consultation. All this would cost money.

At the very moment that the need for a doorway came to my mind, the telephone rang. The voice on the other end said, "Hello, this is Frank. You don't know me, but I was talking to the director at St. John's Soup Kitchen and he told me that you were considering opening a family resource center there."

"Frank, I'm just thinking about it but haven't decided yet," I said.

"Well, if you should decide to accept the position, the first thing you will need is a doorway in the wall between the two rooms."

I couldn't believe my ears! This had to be my answer from God!

"That's a great idea, Frank, but we have no money for construction or anything else."

Frank then went on to inform me that he was a retired construction worker and would gladly put in the door and build whatever else was needed. He could get all the supplies donated and he would do all the work without cost.

"Frank, can you meet me at the resource center in an hour?"

"Sure," he said.

So there we were together planning the layout of the future resource center. Every time I reminded him that we had no money he would say, "Not to worry, we'll have all that we need."

Within two weeks, we were ready to open.

The next thing we needed was a volunteer coordinator and volunteers. God sent Priscilla to me the very day that I was wondering where I would find someone willing to volunteer to coordinate all the volunteers we would need. This woman had all of the necessary gifts for this role, and was a delight to work with four days every week.

From humble beginnings, God's work in this poor inner city neighborhood flourished. Every time we needed supplies or equipment for a special project, it would arrive and it was often entirely unsolicited. As long as we trusted in God's providence, we never lacked the resources we needed. Children's furniture and toys were donated the week we considered opening a children's playroom and reading room. With the expansion of the "Women's Empowerment Group", once again, all that we needed was supplied without cost.

This is just one scenario that demonstrates how God can bring into being more than we can ask for or imagine. As a result of one "Yes" to God's will, jobless people became employed, others continued their education, and women were empowered. All received hope!

Pray, pray, pray in any way you are led, but be careful. The next time your phone rings a special challenge may await you!

Marcella E. Kiesel   *Tampa, Florida*

What did our Lord do during the last hours before his arrest and the beginning of his passion? He went apart alone to pray. So we, too, when we have a grave trial to undergo, or danger or suffering to face, should spend the last moments, the last hour separating us from it in prayer, solitary prayer.

Venerable Charles De Foucauld

Ten Minute Meditation

Imagine that you are in a beautiful garden on a warm, sunny day. The birds are singing, a bee is buzzing from flower to flower, and a small stream nearby is bubbling a gurgling melody.

In this garden are two chairs, both empty. You walk over and sit in one.

In a little while, you know that Jesus will be coming and sitting in the other one.

Today you are going to let Jesus speak first. You don't know what He will say. Perhaps He will say nothing and just be content to sit quietly next to you. You sit quietly waiting.

Prayer when time is completed:

Dear Jesus,
Sometimes it is hard
for me to believe
that you really have
things to say to me.
That you really
want to spend time
with me.
Sometimes it's hard
to believe you really
love me,
especially on days
when I don't love myself.
Jesus help me
to be open to your love.
Amen

M
E
D
I
T
A
T
I
O
N

The Perfect Arrow

My twenty-first birthday was the worst day of my life. Craig, our little baby boy was only three months old that morning when I took him to the pediatrician for a check-up. The doctor did not like what he saw. He called in another doctor. They looked him over, shook their heads and took some more tests. Finally, very somberly, they told me that our little boy's head was growing too rapidly.

I did not know what this meant, but I knew by their demeanor it was not good. My whole world began to turn upside down. I found it difficult to breathe as I tried to comprehend what this might mean. Then they told me we needed to take him immediately to Chicago University for further evaluation.

It was a very sober trip. My husband's parents accompanied us on the long one hundred and fifty mile trip. We were in shock as we drove down the highway, praying for a miracle, praying that the doctors would be wrong and everything would be okay.

But the news they gave us there was even worse. "Craig," they quietly told us, "has less than a year to live." We looked at them in disbelief. We looked at one another in disbelief. We looked at our little baby boy, so small and still in the incubator where they had placed him. "It would be best for him if you leave him with us," they continued. "He will need special care. We have the equipment, the technology, and the knowledge to keep him comfortable and without pain. You will not be able to care for him adequately."

This we had not expected. We were not prepared for such harsh news. Leave our child in the hospital? Until he died? We did not know what to do. Finally, we told them we would go home and decide what we were going to do. For the time, baby Craig could stay with them.

I don't know how we found our way to the car. I don't know how my husband was able to keep his hands steady on the steering wheel as he made his way through the maze of streets and traffic of Chicago until we got back on the highway towards home. It was like a long, gray nightmare in which each of us was screaming with anguish on the inside but barely able to whisper a word on the outside.

I was sitting in the back seat of the car with my mother-in-law and was praying every prayer I could think of asking God for guidance. My eyes were shut tightly, my hands clenched in prayer, and my face was a contorted mess of pain and tears as I begged God to tell us what to do.

Something told me to open my eyes and look up. I looked into the sky. A small white cloud had formed into a perfect arrow. It was as straight and sharp as if it had been chiseled by a knife. The arrow was pointing back to Chicago. I stared at it for several seconds trying to comprehend what it meant.

Then I told my husband to pull over to the side of the road and stop. He did. I told them all to look up into the sky. The cloud was still perfectly solid and formed in the shape of an arrow; an arrow pointing back to Chicago.

We looked at that cloud—we looked at each other. Each of us knew this was a sign from God. There was no question in our minds. If Craig had only one year to live, then God wanted us to give him all the love and care that we could with him at home with us. The minute we made that decision, the cloud disappeared.

My husband, with tears in his eyes but hope in his heart, turned the car around. The doctors were not happy to see us. They were not happy when we bundled up our baby and took him back home with us. A home where he would be loved and cared for in the best way two parents, grandparents, and a loving family could possibly provide.

We drove home where little Craig would live that remaining year and the next year and the next until he celebrated his fourteenth birthday. They were not easy years, but Craig never complained. The doctors told us he would be mentally impaired and a vegetable, but he wasn't. He was so smart that he spoke in sentences by his first birthday. Then, by the time he was seven he prayed for everyone who asked him, and many of his prayers were answered.

Craig's closeness to God was unbelievable. When he was six years old, Sister Caritas came to prepare him for his first Communion. She told us she had never felt so close to Christ as she did when she was with my son.

Craig continued to influence many people, and they came to him for special concerns. He was wheelchair bound, but was not bound mentally or spiritually.

At his funeral, Monsignor Blaecky ended his beautiful eulogy with, "Craig was a jet going to heaven—do not pray for him—but pray to him." We knew this was true. Craig's heavenly flight was as straight and swift into the arms of God as that perfect arrow was that once pointed us back to Chicago.

Eleanor E. Waeyaert   *Moline, Illinois*

Our problem is that we assume prayer is something to master the way we master algebra or auto mechanics. That puts us in the "on-top" position, where we are competent and in control. But when praying, we come "underneath," where we calmly and deliberately surrender control and become incompetent... The truth of the matter is, we all come to prayer with a tangled mass of motives altruistic and selfish, merciful and hateful, loving and bitter. Frankly, this side of eternity we will never unravel the good from the bad, the pure from the impure. God is big enough to receive us with all our mixture. That is what grace means, and not only are we saved by it, we live by it as well. And we pray by it.

Richard J. Foster

A Total Offering

Several years ago, our twenty-five-year-old son was diagnosed with very serious stage-four cancer. He had become very weak and thin before the diagnosis, so his condition was critical as he began receiving chemotherapy.

Our son had married just six months before this, and his wife was distraught. We all prayed on a daily basis that the doctors would have the wisdom to prepare the right treatment, and that his body would respond well to it.

In about twelve months, he was in remission and was very thankful. He and his wife moved to the mountains in Colorado because he had always wanted to live in snow country and the cancer made him driven to accomplish that.

Unfortunately, the cancer soon returned in his hip, and more treatments began that lasted for another year or so. Again, he went into remission, but the cancer returned a third time with a great ferocity. We were called several times to get to Colorado immediately because they thought he might not live more than a few days.

As we sat by his bedside in Denver, the doctor looked at him and then us and said, "This chemo I'm about to start as a drip may either kill or cure, but I have no other options."

During my son's two previous battles with cancer, a priest who was also battling cancer was living temporarily with our pastor in the rectory. As his cancer became progressively worse, he had to leave our parish and move to a retirement facility in California. Each week I called him to see how he was doing, and each time we spoke he would say, "I'm offering my suffering for the healing of your son; he is young and I'm not." My heart broke for him, and I was filled with gratitude for what I knew was a very sincere offering.

This special priest told everyone in the home he was in, in addition to his family back in India, that he was making this offering. My son continued to battle the cancer, and sometimes hope seemed very faint, but we all continued to pray. In the back of my mind I always remembered Father's offering.

After many, many months, I received a call from my son one morning saying, "Mom, I'm free of cancer!" My heart leapt with joy once again.

The next day, my pastor called to tell me that after many months of extreme suffering including going blind, our dear priest friend had died that morning.

I believe in my heart and soul that the priest's offering was acceptable to God. It is now six years later and my son is still in good health, praise God! I give thanks each day for this priest and his willingness to suffer for the sake of my son's healing. God responded to his offering. May we never under-value the powerful prayer of suffering!

Jo Ann Mason   *Temple, Texas*

Heaven is full of answers to prayer for which no one ever bothered to ask.

Billy Graham

Make time to pray. "The great freight and passenger trains are never too busy to stop for fuel. No matter how congested the yards may be, no matter how crowded the schedules are, no matter how many things demand the attention of the trainmen, those trains always stop for fuel."

M. E. Andross

My Sister and Mother Teresa

My sister JoAnne and I have been close all our lives. We were the oldest two girls of five children and, being close in age as well as temperament, we developed a deep friendship.

This friendship continues despite the fact that as adults we live on opposite sides of the country. JoAnne, her husband, and twelve children live in southern California and my family is settled in northeastern Florida. We visit one another as frequently as time, finances, and family obligations permit.

One of our treasured times together was a whirlwind two weeks of visiting various points of interest in California. I was happy to enjoy the company of my many nieces and nephews, including several who are grown or almost grown. We spent hours listening and sharing each others lives, dreams, and aspirations. Then, all too quickly, the time ended and we returned to our routine lives and responsibilities. At no time during our time together was there the slightest hint that disaster was lurking.

I had been home about a week when I received a frantic call from my niece and godchild, Rebecca. "Mom has been rushed to the hospital and is very sick!"

In shock, I listened as she described the symptoms that JoAnne had developed. Rebecca was saying something about chest congestion and a cough, and that her mom was struggling to breathe. She said that her dad was taking my sister to the hospital as we spoke.

I learned later that JoAnne had been unable to sleep or lie down that night, yet she managed to remain as calm as possible so as not to disturb her family while waiting and praying for morning. That so describes my sister.

Her husband, Hilton, who was always an early morning person, noticed JoAnne's condition immediately when he woke up. The first words out of his mouth were, "Do you need a doctor?"

She was so weak she could only nod. Immediately they left for the closest emergency center that would be open.

She was promptly seen, blood was drawn, and oxygen was administered along with emergency medication injected into an intravenous line. The lab results came back quickly and listed the oxygen level in her blood at near zero.

The doctor immediately called the closest hospital for admittance while another staff member called for an ambulance with full life-support on board. There was the usual argument with the insurance company demanding that the patient be taken to one of their facilities. The doctor firmly stated, "She will not live to make it to one of your facilities; she's being sent to the closest facility as fast as we can get her there." JoAnne was being placed in the ambulance as the doctor finished his call.

At the hospital emergency room, she was stabilized as much as possible and transferred to the ICU (intensive care unit). As her husband filled out the admission papers, the rest of her family gathered to be at her side. Soon neighbors heard the news and they came, as well as friends and many people from their church. The halls of the hospital were filled with people who were concerned and praying for her.

JoAnne was well aware that she was fighting for her life. Nothing the hospital staff did seemed to improve her condition, and she continued to struggle to breathe. For the remainder of the day and into the night there was no change. One of her favorite priests came, and during his brief visit, he anointed her. His caring personality gave her the spiritual strength to continue fighting. He spent a good amount of time comforting her family whom he had known for a long time. It was impossible, though, for him to hide his own worry and concern.

The long sleepless night continued, and in the early morning, the hospital chaplain, in making his rounds, anointed JoAnne again with the sacrament of the sick, formerly known as extreme unction or the last rites.

Still there was no change, and JoAnne struggled for each breath throughout the morning. At noon, another priest who had known the family for years came, and JoAnne was anointed for the third time.

Thousands of miles away, I prayed like I had never prayed before. I fell to my knees on my living room floor and talked to God as I had always done, as if He were right in front of me. Weeping, I told Him that I could not imagine not having my sister. I pleaded and begged that, if it be His will, that my sister please be spared and not taken from me. I stood on the promise that, "If you ask anything in My name, it will be given you."

Through my tears, I clung to those words and held them in my heart while I continued my conversation with God, and waited for further word of my sister's condition.

It was around the supper hour that JoAnne, overwhelmed with exhaustion, reached the point of giving up. She prayed to be accepting of whatever God should want of her, even if it meant Him taking her very life. In total submission, she closed her eyes.

The image of Mother Teresa came to her mind, and as JoAnne mentally clung to that, she prayed with her last bit of physical strength, "Mother, your last words were, 'I can't breathe.' Well, Mother, I can't breathe—help me!"

Instantly her breathing changed to the slow, deep, natural rhythm that it should be.

When I called later that night, I already knew that my sister had been restored. I knew because a simple peace and inner knowledge told me that she was going to be okay. Later her family confirmed the reality. I continued to pray, but now they were words of praise and thanksgiving for giving me back my beloved sister.

Afterwards, JoAnne explained to us that later in her distress she could feel the prayers, thousands of them, from everywhere. Pennsylvania, Arizona, Ohio, Florida, the list went on and on, from wherever the prayer group from St. Luke's could reach and unite in their communal petition.

JoAnne was fully aware that she could no longer breathe on her own and the minute she asked Mother Teresa to intervene and intercede for help, she described a gentle hand resting upon her chest, working her lungs for her. She knew her own physical strength was gone and there was nothing left that she could do. She had totally given up other than the simple plea, "Help me!"

By the grace of God, her life was spared. JoAnne and I have been blessed with special times together since that incident, and we are fully aware of the power of prayer and the value of a second chance. Most of all, we know that we have been touched through mercy and love, by the miraculous hand of God.

Mary L. Palmer   *Orange Park, Florida*

In our praying, we should speak to God about Himself - that is praise; or about His gifts - that is thanksgiving; or about other people - that is intercession; or about our sins - that is confession and penitence; or about our needs - that is petition. Prayer has five fingers, like a hand, and each in turn must be pointed to God, that our prayer may be full and complete.

F. W. Kates

The more you pray, the easier it becomes. The easier it becomes, the more you'll pray.

Blessed Teresa of Calcutta

" GOD BLESS WHAT IGUANA ? "

Do Not Forget the Holy Spirit

In my late twenties and early thirties, I taught part time at a nearby university. My classes were in the late afternoon when my husband could care for our four young children. While I was confident about their care, I was feeling increasingly uncomfortable about spending so much time in a chaotic, secular environment that was both mentally and emotionally demanding. Despite praying before leaving the car to walk across campus, I was not able to preserve a sense of peace and found it difficult to even remember God once my foot touched the campus pavement.

One Saturday, early in the fall semester, I went to the local church where I knew a priest would be available for spiritual direction. After waiting in line, I walked into the room where Father Grace was sitting at a table. He gestured for me to sit across from him and I began to share my concerns. I told him how saddened I was that I wasn't able to remember our Lord during my working hours, how discouraging it was to feel so alone while walking across the big campus and teaching, and how even the briefest thought of God was immediately whisked away the moment a student caught my eye or stopped to chat. I knew that my students suffered from the lack of a faith-filled professor and my own children suffered because of the lack of peace that I brought home with me.

Father Grace listened patiently and then offered some advice that dramatically changed my life. He told me to select a prayer to the Holy Spirit, memorize it, and say it daily. He said that people often forget the Third Person of the Blessed Trinity. He believed that they didn't know Him and usually didn't honor Him in their prayers or their lives. The prayer itself didn't matter, he said, but rather that my honoring the Holy Spirit with love and devotion each morning was what was important.

I went home, selected a prayer and set about memorizing it. Monday morning rolled around, and while saying my morning prayers, I added the new prayer to the Holy Spirit. Later in the day, I parked my car in the campus parking lot, turned off the motor and closed my eyes to concentrate on praying to the Holy Spirit. At that moment, I had a strong sense of the presence of God. I knew that sometimes God gave that grace to encourage people, but I was surprised that the sense did not leave me while walking across campus, teaching, chatting with students, or returning to my car. How easy it was to teach and counsel students when I was strengthened by the magnificent presence of God. I continued to pray to the Holy Spirit daily. During the rest of that year, I had a strong sense of the presence of God whenever I went on campus. The presence was so strong that I was able to effortlessly think deeply about God while at the same time performing my duties as a professor. I was also able to maintain a sense of peace at home with my children, and I know I served as a better witness to others, particularly when students would approach me after class to question me about my religion, as they often did.

While there was nothing earth shaking about my prayer experience, it was soul shaking. My faith in God and the truths taught by the Catholic Church were strengthened. My prayer life became deeper as did my love for reading the Bible and the lives of the saints. I also developed a deep love for my vocation as wife and mother and now stay home to care for our children full time.

While I still have to work at keeping myself in the presence of God, I am grateful for the gift given to me by the Holy Spirit, and I pray that others too may honor Him in their lives.

Anonymous   *Binghamton, New York*

Pray at all times in the Spirit, with all prayers and supplication. To that end keep alert with perseverance, making supplication for all the saints.

Ephesians 6:18

Thank You, Josie

A number of years ago, I was privileged to meet a woman who greatly impacted my life. Her name was Sister Josepha McNutt of the Child Jesus, a Missionary Servant of the Blessed Trinity. She lived and worked at Blessed Trinity Shrine Retreat in Alabama.

This wonderful woman was filled with a love of life and of others that was amazing to see. Just being around her was an inspiration. Sister Josepha eventually became my spiritual advisor. I met with her once a month and grew to greatly love her.

During the next few years, Sister Josepha helped me through difficult times and rejoiced with me over the happy ones. Her presence and guidance became a major part of my life. With her encouragement, I felt that I could do anything, and after a while, decided to become a lay member of the Missionary Cenacle Apostolate.

One day upon returning from a trip out of town, I came into my house to see the answering machine blinking with a huge number of messages. When I punched the play button all the messages were from people who were associated with the Missionary Cenacle family asking me to call them!

I knew it couldn't be good. Before answering any calls, I went to my e-mail. There I read the tragic news that my dear Sister Josepha had been killed in an automobile accident. A large truck carrying a full load of logs had struck her car as she turned onto the road near the retreat house. She had been killed instantly.

While mourning the death of my dear friend, I knew that I would continue to have her help through prayer. I asked Sister Josepha to intercede with God for me and for my family and placed myself under her protection, asking her to somehow continue to guide me from her place in heaven. Little did I know how she would come through!

Sometime during the first year after her death, I was driving through the parking lot of a local store. The lot led out into a major highway through a traffic lighted intersection. Lost in thought, I noticed the light change to green and started into the intersection without looking to the right or left.

Suddenly, I felt this presence to the left of my shoulder and heard a voice speaking in my mind saying, "Stop, look! Stop, look!"

I turned my head to the left. Two huge, heavily loaded lumber trucks were racing through the red light. I stomped on the brake in heart stopping panic, barely missing them.

Now the strange thing is that at the time I thought nothing of it. I drove out onto the highway and simply said aloud, "Thank you, Josie," as if it were the most natural thing in the world.

It wasn't until I was a bit further down the road that the full impact of what had happened hit me. Had I not heeded that voice, I would certainly have been killed. Sister Josepha was still on the job.

Emily A. Whitley   *Dadeville, Alabama*

Let yourself be charmed by Christ, the infinite who appeared among you in visible and imitable form. Fall in love with Jesus Christ, to live his very life, so that our world may have life in the light of the gospel.

Pope John Paul II

The time we spend in having our daily audience with God is the most precious part of the whole day.

Blessed Teresa of Calcutta

Life Changing Experience

I would like to share how the power of prayer brought me freedom from twenty-two years of living in darkness. Years of drug and alcohol abuse along with leading a very promiscuous life brought me to the brink of suicide in January 1997. Though I didn't realize it then, even through this difficult time God was never far away from me. Many times I would suddenly get an overwhelming urge to pray and turn my life over to God, but I could not bring myself to do it. I could not even bring myself to think of the words to pray. It was as if something inside of me, beyond my control, would not let me.

One day I hit absolute bottom. My marriage was in ruins; my husband was seriously addicted to pornography; our financial life was in ruins; and my older children were in constant trouble with the police and involved with drugs. I was so totally sick and ashamed of myself, and what I had become, that one morning I fell down on my knees and, between sobs of remorse and repentance, gave it all over to God. I literally put it all in His hands, and at that moment, it was as if the darkness departed from me.

After that life-changing experience, my cravings for drugs and alcohol simply disappeared. I quit cold turkey and never did suffer through any type of withdrawal symptoms or cravings. Unfortunately, my marriage did not survive, but I am proud to say that I am happily remarried and have had no desire to resume my former promiscuous behavior.

I feel so blessed to have had prayer work such a miracle in my life. God's mercy and His love for us are truly incredible. They brought me out of a life of darkness and into His light.

Donna L. Skipper   *Mena, Arkansas*

Ten Minute Meditation

Imagine that it is early morning. The sun is just starting to come up over the horizon. A bird starts to sing. You go to your special place in your garden and you have a surprise. There is already someone sitting in the chair waiting for you.

It is Jesus. He is smiling, and He wants to tell you how much you mean to Him. He wants to tell you of some of the special hopes and dreams He has for you.

It doesn't matter how far away you have been from Him. It doesn't matter that you don't know how to talk to Him or how to be in His presence. Jesus is not concerned with that. He just wants to tell you some beautiful things about how special you are to Him. He wants to share how He created you to be just who you are; how totally you are in his Father's hands, that you are loved and very special.

This is a beautiful day for you. Take ten minutes to let Jesus smile at you.

Prayer when time is completed:

Jesus,
I hardly can believe that you love me,
I thank you.
I want to accept your love.
Show me how to be at peace
in the thought and knowledge
of your love for me.
Everything will be okay.
Amen.

What Are You Waiting For?

My friend Sarah and I had developed the practice of praying the daily rosary for many intentions. Strangely, it was hardly ever for ourselves or our families.

Sarah's daughter had married a Protestant years back, and at the time of the wedding this had been the cause of a great disagreement between mother and daughter. Sarah couldn't understand why they couldn't be married in the Catholic Church, but the son-in-law to be would not have it, and after much discussion and tension, the daughter finally just decided to have her wedding in Las Vegas. End of story.

Years passed and my friend and I, through the daily praying of the rosary, continued to grow through our own conversion. One night she impishly delighted in sharing with me that her grandchildren from said daughter had taken to playing with the rosary that hung from her bedpost. Sarah asked me if she ought to buy some for them, or would this cause friction?

I thought about it for a moment and then suggested that she could buy them each a rosary, but have them keep them at her house. That way they could have the best of both worlds.

Another night she mentioned that it really bothered her that her grandchildren were being brought up outside the faith and worse yet, now they had even stopped going to church at all.

Since we had not yet prayed our rosary, I said we should pray for their conversion; put it in Mary's hands.

I had just recently received the book *To The Priests, Our Lady's Beloved Sons* by Father Gobbi. In the book, it had an insert that said that many mothers worried about their children falling away from the Church. They begged Father Gobbi to ask Our Lady what they could do. In answer, Our Lady had told Father Gobbi that these mothers were

44

to pray the rosary daily and say: "With this rosary I bind my children to the Immaculate Heart of Mary for her guidance and protection." Mary promised Father Gobbi she would see to their conversion.

So I told my friend, "Tonight, let's pray the rosary for their conversion and use the words of Our Blessed Mother!" Sarah thought this was a great idea and so we did.

The very next morning Sarah's daughter called her very agitated. The school district had announced that it was going to become very strict about children going to any other school other than the one in their neighborhood. Her daughter felt that the one in her neighborhood was not as good as the one they were currently attending, so she had decided to send them to Catholic school.

We were so excited! It was already working! We continued to keep this special intention during our daily rosaries, always using the special prayer of binding them to Mary's Immaculate Heart.

Sarah's three grandchildren started going to the new school. A couple of weeks later, her daughter called again. She wanted to know if Sarah had a spare rosary that the older son could have. He was complaining that everyone at school had a rosary except him!

Of course, Sarah was glad to comply. She provided a rosary, not just for him but for each of the children (we were going through what St. John of the Cross describes as the "gluttony" part of our conversion and we easily had some thirty rosaries each).

Every day we continued to pray the rosary, keeping Sarah's family in our intentions and binding them to the Immaculate Heart of Mary.

A short time later, the daughter asked her mother to take the children to Mass, since she and her husband had long since stopped attending services at their own church. Another breakthrough for the Blessed Mother!

We continued praying. Then soon enough the children brought up the question of first Communion. After some debate, it was agreed that they would receive the sacrament in the Catholic Church. That, it turned out, required a letter of permission from the parish priest. Father told them that in order to do that, he would have to sanctify their vows of matrimony on the altar before God.

The son-in-law initially agreed but as the time neared, he began to have second thoughts. He continued to have misgivings right up to the eve of the agreed upon date. In the end, though, he gave in and they were shocked to find that it was not just a quick informal exchange of vows but the whole wedding Mass with my friend's whole family in attendance!

Sarah thought that her son-in-law had balked because he didn't know how his family would take to the news that he had wound up exchanging vows in the Catholic Church. Well, a couple of days after the *wedding*, his mother came to visit. He told her about the wedding vows ceremony. She asked if he was thinking of converting. He hesitantly answered: "Well maybe." She replied: "What are you waiting for?"

It turned out that his widowed mother was dating a wonderful Catholic gentleman, and she herself often went with him to Mass. After that, Sarah's son-in-law couldn't convert fast enough. In fact, he was so impatient that he got irritated that he had to attend classes.

Tonie E. Tellander   *Laredo, Texas*

We must pray not first of all because it feels good or helps, but because God loves us and wants our attention.

Henri J. M. Nouwen

It is good to give thanks to the Lord, to sing praise to they name, O Most High, to declare they steadfast love in the morning, and they faithfulness by night.

Psalm 92:1-2

He Is So Close to Me

My niece is the mother of two boys, Zachary and Cody, both now deceased, who suffered from a genetic disease, San Filipo Type A. Those afflicted with this disease are not expected to live beyond their early teens. Zachary was turning thirteen in March of 1987. His brother, Cody, was six years younger. Their mother's grief while watching the steady decline in their health was heart wrenching, especially as she knew that nothing could be done medically to help them. Science offered little or no help for a possible cure. The San Filipo disease was not one that was given much public attention, and so little funding was allotted to research for a cure.

On March 15, 1987, a Mass was offered on behalf of the older brother, Zachary. His thirteenth birthday was the previous day. Being acutely aware that his entering the teen years was a warning that death was close, I had arranged for a Mass for Zachary, hoping and praying for a miracle to spare his life.

I had read *Miracles Do Happen* by Sr. Briege McKenna. In the book, Sr. Briege states that the best time to ask the Lord for a favor is during the Eucharist. After receiving Communion that day, I returned to my pew and immediately knelt and asked, "Lord, please heal Zachy."

Now, as with most people, I was certain that I would have to wait to see how the Lord would answer me. I hoped for an instant cure, of course, but didn't really expect one. What did happen took my breath away. I heard a beautiful baritone voice say, "But he's so close to Me. Would you take that away from him?"

This was our Lord, Himself, speaking to me. I took a deep breath and answered, "No, I wouldn't, but what about Cody?" This time there was no answer. I knew that Zachary would not be long with us, but I had the assurance of Jesus, Himself, that he would be with the Lord. Who could really ask for more than that?

That event happened more than twenty years ago, but to me it's as if it happened yesterday. Who could ever forget that the God of Abraham, the Creator of the universe, the Jesus of the Cross, entered time to spend a moment with me? It's both exhilarating and humbling at the same time.

There are many who hold in faith all their lives that there is a God. Many simply say there is no God. When God speaks to you, and He leaves no doubt that it is He speaking, you no longer depend on faith to tell you He's real. You simply know it. How I wish that everyone could experience His presence. What a different world this would be.

Prayer can and does produce results. In the case of my nephew, the answer to my prayer was instantaneous. I have prayed for many years for other favors, with no apparent answer, but I never doubt that the Lord hears me and will answer in His way, in His time. I must be patient.

Ann M. Sabocik   *Hobart, Indiana*

You don't need to use many or high-sounding words. Just repeat often, "Lord, show me your mercy as you know best." Or, "God, come to my assistance."

St. Macarius of Alexandria

Be wise, my soul, and trust in God alone, cling to him alone, and cast all your cares on him alone.

St. Robert Bellarmine

Tom's Promise

My story is about my son, Tom, for whom I had been praying for years. Tom had always been a wonderful, happy child, but when he was nine years old my husband and I made the decision to end our marriage. The divorce affected him deeply. It was a difficult divorce—a divorce that resulted in deep wounds and hurts for Tom. He continued to be outgoing and popular in school, but it was obvious that he was also holding inside a lot of hurt.

Alcohol became his friend, his support. He started in high school and got his first arrest for drunken driving as a teenager. He continued drinking and getting into more and more trouble. During the next ten years he was ordered to go to rehabilitation three times, including a session in a state boot camp. After that he was picked up three more times as an adult for driving under the influence. Once he took that first drink, he told me, he was just unable to stop until he passed out. Finally he was sent to the federal penitentiary in the state where he was living.

All through this time I was on my own journey with God. My journey led me to visit different churches and places of worship. After the divorce, I had moved to the Los Angeles area and taught at a Catholic school, Our Lady of the Rosary in Paramount, California. I attended the Catholic Church with my cousins. The sisters were always encouraging me to join the Church but I wasn't quite ready.

After a time I moved back to Fresno, California, and started working in a public school. It was there that a friend invited me to talk to someone at St. Anthony Parish about the RCIA program (RCIA = Roman Catholic Initiation for Adults). The Holy Spirit gave me a final push and I made the call. Soon I started instruction at St. Anthony, and at Easter, I was confirmed in the Church. Shortly afterwards my director for initiation at St. Anthony took our small group to celebrate a Mass of St. Anthony.

During the homily I heard about the wonderful miracles that St. Anthony had performed during his lifetime.

I was so touched by the homily that I felt my prayer for my son would surely be heard. Our director gave each of us a candle to light at the altar. As I lit mine I prayed to St. Anthony to intercede for Tom. I begged St. Anthony to ask God for a miracle in his life. I left the service with a lighter heart than I had had in years.

Less than two weeks after that I got a call from Tom in the penitentiary. He told me that he had turned his life over to God. He was, he said, going to work hard to serve God from that day forward. I was so excited when I got off the phone that I was laughing and crying at the same time.

Tom kept his promise. He started teaching others about God while still in prison. A year or so later, when he finally came home, he immediately found a church and continued to study the Bible and help troubled youths.

Tom is now married and has three beautiful children. His strong Christian family is united in loving and serving God.

Marilyn L. Larson   *Fresno, California*

> *The Lord of the universe is more splendid than the sun and the stars. He will never leave me!*
>
> St. Agnes

> *When I am incapable of praying, I want to keep telling him that I love him. It's not difficult, and it keeps the fire going.*
>
> St. Therese of Lisieux

Through Thorns, The Roses Bloomed

When I was twenty-three years old, I married a very kind and loving man. We talked and laughed and had fun together, but unknown to me, he was an alcoholic. I found this out three weeks into our marriage when I realized that after work he would routinely go to the bar, come home drunk, and cause trouble. This happened every night, and I wondered how I got myself into this. I kept thinking he would change, but he never did. He was like Dr. Jekyll and Mr. Hyde. When he was sober, he was the nicest guy in the world, but when he was drunk, he was horrible.

I felt like I couldn't divorce him because I had made a vow to God that I would be there for my husband, for better or worse. I resolved to myself that I had to do my best and live with it.

After many years, we had four children. I struggled to meet our financial needs, keep food on the table, and heat in the house as my husband wouldn't allow me to work. With him drinking and coming home at two or three in the morning yelling and throwing things around, life in our home was a nightmare that affected not only me, but the kids as well.

My oldest daughter got married when she was nineteen years old, and my son started using drugs when he was eighteen. I was extremely worried about my two younger daughters who were only ten and five years old.

When my son was on drugs, my home was like a horror show. It was especially bad when my husband and son were together. Doors and windows were broken, holes were punched in the walls, and things were thrown everywhere. And just like his father, my son yelled and cursed me, saying all kinds of rotten things to me.

I was totally exhausted, both mentally and physically. I couldn't sleep at night because I was overwhelmed with not knowing what I was doing wrong and why they treated me this way. I really believed our problems were my fault because they both said the same awful things to and about me.

Then I went into a deep depression. I kept the shades down, did only the things I absolutely needed to do, and lost myself in television programs. The house was falling apart, but I didn't care. I kept my youngest daughters in the house after school and on the weekends. I only answered the phone when they were in school in case it was them and they needed me. If anyone else called, even if it was one of my sisters, friends, or my oldest daughter, I would hang up on them. When they came to the house, I wouldn't let them in. Everyone I knew tried to help me, but I pushed them away.

One night I kept thinking that if this marriage and family life were what love is, I wanted no part of it anymore. I got a razor blade and tried to get the courage to kill myself, but every time I tried, I thought about my girls. I worried about what would happen to them if I wasn't there for them and realized that it was my responsibility to care for them until they were older, so I put the razor away.

I continued to do only the necessary things in life and barely spoke to my kids. In my excruciating pain, I didn't care about the people I was hurting. I was determined not to love them because, in my mind, love hurt too much and I'd had enough pain. When my husband or son would start yelling and screaming, I would just sit there quietly, not allowing it to affect me. When they were done, I went to bed. Nothing seemed to matter anymore.

Eventually I had to go to the doctor because I was having problems with my stomach and I couldn't stand it anymore. When he finished examining me, he told me to come into his office. After I sat down he said, "Okay, Lillian, what is going on?" I told him things were fine, but he kept pressuring me and before I knew it, I told him everything.

He helped me see that how I was coping with my pain was wrong. He said that even though I was hurting, it wasn't fair to hurt others, especially my kids, and that I needed to be strong for them. I realized that my behavior was wrong, and it was not only affecting the kids, but everyone I knew. Finally, someone had gotten through to me. He helped me so much that day, and I will always be grateful to him for helping me get my life back on track.

That very day I went home, raised the shades, and cleaned the house. The girls were surprised when they came home from school—their mother was acting normal again. I called everyone I knew and apologized. I found out what true friends I had, for they had prayed and stood by me even though I had hurt them so much. My situation with my husband and son didn't change, but my attitude did. I could cope with my life once again.

Finally, my son went for help and got his life back to normal, but my husband refused to get help and continued to drink. After living like this for twenty-six years, I had a call from my sister**,** Dot**,** who invited me to go to a charismatic prayer meeting with her. She told me what they did and said she got a lot of strength and peace from attending. It sounded weird to me, but I was curious and said I would go.

Two people greeted us at the door. They were very friendly, but there was something about them that was different, and I couldn't figure it out.

After the meeting ended, they invited anyone who had questions to go to the next room. I had a pile of questions and got answers to all of them. It all made sense to me, so I thought that maybe there was something to the charismatic movement after all.

Week after week I went back, and what they taught me was a different kind of love than I had known. They accepted me just as I was, and I even started to like myself! Through their love, they taught me who God really is and that His love doesn't hurt. It is real and everlasting, and He loves me in spite of my many faults.

I learned to pray from my heart and how to talk to Jesus as a friend, thanking Him for all His blessings. What a close friend Jesus became to me. I finally felt that I was worth something and that I was never, ever alone. He completely understood my pain and He lifted my burdens, replacing them with peace and comfort. My life changed.

I am now seventy-six years old and have been married for fifty-three years. My husband stopped drinking and is back to being the man I married. It has been a difficult journey, but, you know what? I have come to realize that it was through the thorns that the roses bloomed in my life, and I would go through it all over again to be where I am right now.

Lillian J. DeOliveira   *East Providence, Rhode Island*

Keep Your Eyes on Me

In 1995, I was fifteen weeks pregnant with my third child when I realized that something seemed different about this pregnancy. I visited my doctor and told him that something just wasn't right, but when he was able to find the baby's heartbeat, he assured me that everything was okay.

The doctor had us schedule a routine ultrasound for a different day, and when we arrived for our appointment, the technician was having trouble with the machine. She called the doctor in and he suggested that we go to another facility where a better machine was available. We went there and had a very short ultrasound. Then we were asked to go back to the doctor's office where we were informed that our unborn baby was not alive. We were crushed as we made arrangements for my labor to be induced the next day.

After our stillborn daughter was delivered, I had some post delivery complications that ended up with me in the operating room for a dilation and curettage procedure. I refused to stay in the hospital and was released at around one o'clock in the morning.

The next few days were the worst in my life. I had no will to go on. That is when I started praying. I didn't really pray the formal prayers of our faith; I just talked to God, repeating things over and over to Him. It was very disorganized prayer. After a few weeks, I started to feel better. After two months passed, my doctor told us that in another month we could try to conceive again. He warned us that since our daughter's autopsy had not shown a clear cause of death, there was a chance that we could face similar results with another pregnancy. Again, I prayed and prayed. Some were formal prayers, but mostly I was just in constant dialog with God. It was at this point that God answered me.

He told me that I would conceive another child, and that though things might seem rocky, if I kept my eyes on Him and followed His commands, the baby would be fine. A month later I conceived and the pregnancy was rocky indeed. Five weeks into it I had complications.

I called the doctor and he felt sure I was miscarrying. He told me that if I didn't miscarry within three days I needed to come in for an ultrasound. I remembered God's promise, and for those three days, I prayed in the same constant and disorganized way I had before.

When my husband and I went for the ultrasound, the same technician who did our previous one took care of us again. I think she was more nervous than I was! I asked her to promise to be honest and tell me the truth about what she would see. She said she couldn't tell me, but when she placed the probe on my belly, the baby's heartbeat echoed through the room. The technician cried out, "Yes!"

In tears, I thanked God and continued praying for my unborn baby's life. My doctor put me on high-risk status and did ultrasounds every month to make sure that everything remained okay. I kept praying, and when I was just short of thirty-four weeks along I went into labor and my little miracle was born by cesarean section.

This sweet time turned rocky when my son was unable to breathe. He was taken to the neonatal intensive care unit where x-rays showed that his lungs were fully developed. Despite that good news, his breathing was still labored. My husband and I prayed and prayed. The doctors did not know why he couldn't breathe and prepared me for my child's death. Both my husband and I continued praying and believing in the promise that God had given me.

Three days later the doctors were still unable to find what was causing my baby's breathing problems, and my son and I were released from the hospital. His breathing started to level out when he was three weeks old, but he was unable to keep breast milk or formula down and was losing weight fast. The doctor sent us for tests and to a specialist. Again, nothing showed up and both doctors thought he would die.

It was recommended that I admit my baby to the hospital and get him hooked up to feeding tubes. I prayed about this and it became clear that I would not bring him to the hospital. He had been diagnosed with gastrointestinal reflux, and one night the solution to his condition came to me in a dream. "Put some cereal in his bottle to thicken up his food" was my answer. I called the doctor and asked if this were a good idea.

"No way," the doctor told me. "It will make things worse." I prayed about this. Should I go against the doctor and keep my eyes on God like I was told to do? I knew the answer and started adding cereal to his bottle. Unfortunately, it didn't help much and I felt frustrated and scared.

For a few days the only answer I got to my prayers was, "Keep your eyes on me." Then one day I had an idea. Forget the formula and add cereal to his diet or better yet, give him fruit because it has more calories. This started to work.

My son, who was down to four pounds when he was just over two months old, gained a couple of ounces. With time, he gained more. The gastroenterologist was amazed and the pediatrician asked what I was doing. When I told them, they shook their heads and said it made no sense. I told them that with God everything can make sense.

I was instructed to continue doing what I had been doing, and my baby thrived. Other problems cropped up like speech issues and more breathing difficulties, and with each situation we just prayed and prayed and received instruction after instruction. My son is now eleven years old and is the picture of health. I know whole-heartedly that God has answered my prayers and that He is the reason my little boy is still alive.

Diane Parkhurst   *Boardman, Ohio*

When a Christian shuns fellowship with other Christians, the devil smiles. When he stops studying the Bible, the devil laughs. When he stops praying, the devil shouts for joy.

Corrie Ten Boom

God Heard Me

When I was about seven years old, my mother became extremely ill with lung problems. I was unaware of the exact diagnosis but I knew it was something very serious.

One afternoon she was lying in bed and I was alone with her because my father had taken my two brothers out for groceries. After a time, my mother became very pale and tried to tell me that she was unable to breathe.

She started to gasp and panic. Immediately, in a reassuring voice, I tried to calm her by asking her to relax and just breathe, very slowly and evenly, which she proceeded to do.

I then thought that I must do something more to assist her. But what? I was alone and helpless. These thoughts were instantaneous and occurred as I left her bedside and walked quickly into my own room.

I stood in the middle of the room, closed my eyes tight, clenched my fists with my arms at my sides, and with every inch of my being, I silently prayed as I shook from head to toe with the extreme effort: "Dear God, please help my mother!"

Right then the phone rang and I ran to my mother's room to answer it. I heard—almost as if I expected it—the voice of our family doctor who said, "This is Dr. Reames and I am just calling to see how your mother is doing."

"She's not doing well!" I said, and handed my mom the phone.

The rest is a fog because I was lost in the warmth of gratitude that God heard me and answered so swiftly.

My mother relaxed as she softly spoke to the doctor. I felt assured that everything would be fine. My father and brothers came home while the doctor was still on the line.

The doctor had never called our home before that time and he never called after it. I thank our loving God again even as I write this down. My mother recuperated within a short time.

Mary Louise Noroski   *Woodland Hills, California*

Reading is good, hearing is good, conversation and meditation are good; but then, they are only good at times and occasions, in a certain degree, and must be used and governed with such caution as we eat and drink and refresh ourselves, or they will bring forth in us the fruits of intemperance. But the spirit of prayer is for all times and occasions; it is a lamp that is to be always burning, a light to be ever shining: everything calls for it; everything is to be done in it and governed by it, because it is and means and wills nothing else but the totality of the soul -- not doing this or that, but wholly...given up to God to be where and what and how He pleases.

William Law

It matters little what form of prayer we adopt or how many words we use. What matters is the faith which lays hold on God, knowing that He knows our needs before we even ask Him. That is what gives Christian prayer its boundless confidence and its joyous certainty.

Dietrich Bonhoeffer

Ten Minute Meditation

Today you are` going to visit your house—your spiritual house. What is it like? Is it big or small? Does it have many doors, many windows? Is it light or dark? Invite Jesus to walk with you into your house. Explore it together. Are there rooms you do not want to enter? That's okay. Today, just go where you want to go and do what you want in your house.

What are you feeling?

Happy or sad?

Excited or apprehensive?

Whatever you feel is fine, but share your house with Jesus.

Prayer when time is completed:

Jesus,
thank you for coming to my house.
Thank you for spending time
with me,
without words
or thought
or judgment of any kind.
Thank you Jesus for coming to my house
just as it is.
Amen.

Stubborn Excuses

One day I woke up and realized my life was not what I thought it should be. I had stopped using drugs, but alcohol remained in my life. Of course, that was not what was wrong with my life, I rationalized to myself. After all, alcohol was legal and everyone drank, right? I had taken a friend to a rehabilitation center and she was getting better, but I knew I didn't need treatment that extreme. After all, she always did more drugs and drank more alcohol than me.

Oh, those stubborn excuses I had, and the awful denial (isn't that a river in Egypt?). But slowly and surely the river of addiction I was swept up in started to veer off into a canal and I started to examine the people in my life who were overcoming their drug and alcohol dependencies. They were obviously feeling better, and I watched as they laughed and lived their lives in a much happier way. I was so jealous.

I wanted what my friends had, but how could I go to an Alcoholics Anonymous (AA) meeting if I was not an alcoholic? That would not be right now, would it? My brother-in-law suggested that I go to an open meeting and just listen to the stories people told and see what I thought. Well, I did, and their stories were all horrendous—they had lost everything and I hadn't. So how could I possibly be an alcoholic?

Then someone said that maybe if I started to pray God would give me an answer to my question of whether or not I was an alcoholic. I kept going to AA meetings and prayed every day, asking God if I was on the right path or not. I begged Him for an answer that I could not deny, something tangible. Then I soon learned that you have to watch what you pray for! You just might get it!

My answer came one evening when I was having dinner with my sister. The two of us were listening to a new and very angelic song by Enya when she left the room for a minute to do something in the kitchen.

I was alone at the table eating when all of a sudden everything in the room went blank. I saw myself in a field of beautiful flowers, and I was on a path headed into a beautiful light. The light was everything that I ever dreamed of, all the unconditional love and acceptance one could ask for. It was an indescribable feeling.

The vision took place very quickly, and when it was gone, I burst into tears. My sister came to me asking what was wrong, and I was so very grateful it was she that I had this experience with. She understood. We realized that my prayer had been answered and that I was on the path God wanted me on to become what He intended me to be.

God knew my soul was dying, and in answer to my prayers, He gave me the gift of light. It has been fifteen years since my last drink, and I am eternally grateful, happy, and free.

Leigh Ann M. Woodin   *Georgetown, Delaware*

Seeing the sun, the moon, and the stars, I said to myself, "Who could be the Master of these beautiful things?" I felt a great desire to see him, to know him, and to pay him homage.

St. Josephine Bakhita

Prayer is any converse between the soul and God. Hence it is that state in which the soul looks wordlessly on God, solely occupied with contemplating him, telling him with looks that it loves him, while uttering no words, even in thought.

Venerable Charles De Foucauld

Bobby's Miracle

Our much-loved eight-year-old golden retriever Bobby was diagnosed with inoperable cancer last February and was given very little hope of survival. Although it was recommended that he be put to sleep immediately, we refused and were referred to a special animal hospital miles from our home.

On the day we arrived, we learned that a cancer research program was beginning that used experimental electro-chemotherapy and the doctors in a large general hospital wanted to take that further step. Our dog was the fifth of twenty needed to conduct the experiment.

The chemotherapy lasted four months. Every night I put holy water on my sick dog and blessed him with a little cross and a relic of St. Pio. After the chemotherapy ended, the doctors gave us the news that it had not been successful and he only had days or maybe weeks left to live. They were so disappointed.

I refused to give up and asked the doctors to scan him again in two weeks. They agreed to just to pacify me, so we took him home, and for the next two weeks while we waited for the second scan we prayed over our beloved dog and cried many tears for him.

After that scan, the veterinarians and doctors told us to bring him back in another two weeks. After that one, we continued to return to that research hospital for scans again and again until our last visit on August thirtieth. This was the last big scan of him, and I was confident that the outcome would be good. To use their own words, the doctors were confounded by the results. They said the tumor was dormant and had been since last May.

Today Bobby is in the fullest of doggie health. We walk three times daily and he is keeping me fit. I have continued to pray over him each morning and evening, and he even sits down ready to pray the minute

I say, "Let's say the Bobby prayers!" His next visit to the veterinarian is not until November thirtieth, and I think the success of his treatment demonstrates the power of prayer and the power of faith in God.

Helen M. O'Leary   *Munster, Ireland*

"Thy kingdom come... on earth" is what we are saying. And if that were suddenly to happen, what then? What would stand and what would fall? Who would be welcomed in and who would be thrown the Hell out? Which if any of our most precious visions of what God is and of what human beings are would prove to be more or less on the mark and which would turn out to be phony as a three-dollar bill? Boldness indeed. To speak those words is to invite the tiger out of the cage, to unleash a power that makes atomic power look like a warm breeze.

Frederick Buechner

What seem our worst prayers may really be, in God's eyes, our best. Those, I mean, which are least supported by devotional feeling. For these may come from a deeper level than feeling. God sometimes seems to speak to us most intimately when he catches us, as it were, off our guard.

C.S. Lewis

He Is Waiting For Us to Ask

As I was growing up, my parents had a nightly ritual of kneeling down beside their bed to pray. Even when they got older and this was difficult, they continued to pray this way. When I was a young child, they taught me how to pray the Our Father and the Hail Mary, and they also taught me the importance of praying by simply talking to God. I learned that God especially appreciates prayers that are spoken from the heart.

When I was in about fourth grade, one of my brother's close friends and classmates at the seminary he attended was involved in a terrible car accident and had a life-threatening head injury. My brother called home very distraught, and asked our family to pray hard. They didn't think he was going to make it.

It was a custom for our class to attend morning Mass before school began. I recall being very upset that morning after hearing the news about my brother's friend. I had met this young seminarian a few times and recalled that he was such a handsome, friendly boy with so much going for him. I couldn't bear the thought that he might die.

During the entire Mass, I focused my thoughts on this young man and pleaded with God to have mercy and spare his life. I was entirely transfixed by the crucifix behind the altar and I kept a running dialog with Jesus the whole time. There were moments that I recall imagining that Jesus was actually moving on the cross while we spoke. I knew in my heart that He heard me, and when I left the church, I was certain my brother's friend was going to live.

A few days later, we heard that the young man was now out of danger. They said his improved condition was nothing short of a miracle. I know that I was not alone in praying for him. His faith-filled family and the entire school of seminarians had also sent many prayer petitions to God.

He had a long and hard recovery ahead of him, but by the grace of God, his life had been spared.

That memorable experience at such a young age convinced me even more of the power of prayer. Since then, as I have gone through the ups and downs of life, I have never had any doubt that God hears and responds to every single one of our prayers. As my teenaged daughter recently said, "God already knows what we want and need—after all, He is God. He is just waiting for us to ask Him, plain and simple."

Regina M. Sabadosa   *Oak Lawn, Illinois*

Listen, my friend! Your helplessness is your best prayer. It calls from your heart to the heart of God with greater effect than all your uttered pleas. He hears it from the very moment that you are seized with helplessness, and He becomes actively engaged at once in hearing and answering the prayer of your helplessness.

Ole Kristian O. Hallesby

What an extraordinary thing it is, the efficiency of prayer! Like a queen, it has access at all times to the royal presence, and can get whatever it asks for.

St. Therese of Lisieux

He Was Watching Me

A few years ago, when I was about eight years old, I was in one of my Communion classes preparing for my first holy Communion. These classes help you to become closer to God in the weeks leading up to your first holy Communion. I was in a particularly special class that day as this was the day I made my first holy confession.

As my friends and I sat in St. Roberts Church (my parish church), ready to make our first confessions, we were all very nervous. After about the second person had gone into the confession room, I heard some really loud footsteps at the back of the church. Everyone looked, and when I turned to look, I saw a real live image of Jesus!

He was *very* real, and He was just standing there in red and white clothing, looking *as if He were* watching me. Everyone else turned back around to face the front of the church, so I presumed they didn't see Him. I kept watching, and a few moments later, He half faded as He floated up and out of the church. I turned back around and sat there in the pew thinking about it.

Finally, it was my turn to make my first confession. I was very nervous, but as I walked into the confession room I became really confident, and I think I made a very good confession. When the Communion class ended, I told all of my friends what I had seen and they didn't really believe me. They didn't think it was true because when they turned around they didn't see anything. I know it was true, though. Now I am twelve years old, and whenever I feel nervous, I always think of what happened on that day.

Bridget A. M. Donaldson   *Morpeth, Northumberland, England*

Headed For Trouble

The story of my life of prayer began a long time ago when I was a child. I can still remember my father kneeling at his bedside in prayer and my mother teaching me through her words and actions that God always hears us when we pray. My parents were quiet and thoughtful people who treated my brother, sister, and me with great love and respect. They went about their conscientious lives with a beautiful blend of humor, faith, and love.

Despite my solid Catholic upbringing, after my divorce I fell away from the Church, God, and prayer. I rejected God in many ways and proceeded down a path without Him where I thought I would find adventure, excitement, and true happiness. I can't believe how stupid I was in not realizing that I was headed for trouble. Not only did I put my own life in jeopardy, but I did the same to my innocent one-year-old daughter.

During this turbulent time, I enrolled in college and worked hard at sometimes more than one job. I found a good daycare center for my daughter, had friends, and believed that if I worked hard, happiness would follow. I had given up believing that God listens to our prayers and that He actually cares about us. And so, even though I loved my daughter, I did not give her the most precious gift of all—faith.

As a little girl, my daughter had always been a kind, thoughtful, obedient kid, but when she was a teenager, this changed. She started rebelling, partying, and drinking. It was my wake up call. Deep in my heart I realized that she was headed to a precipice over which she would surely fall, and I knew I couldn't save her. It was then, the moment I feared for my daughter's life, that I knelt at her bedside in her dark room and prayed to God, begging Him to help my precious Jennifer and me. I knew He would help.

The very next day, I went to the parish rectory and found a priest who would hear my confession. As soon as I started telling him my sins and about how my attitude and actions over the years had affected my daughter, I started sobbing. Trying to handle life without God did nothing but lead me to a life filled with anger, pride, hate, resentment, and jealousy.

The kind priest listened to me for about an hour and then said something I will never forget. He said, "When you are a saint, you will look back on this day and remember it as the day you turned the corner and got onto the right path."

I thought to myself, saint? Me? Is he kidding? But then I remembered the Jesus in the Scriptures whom I loved dearly as a child. He healed and forgave sinners, and he brought the dead back to life, just as He would do for my daughter and me through the power of heartfelt prayer.

That night was the first step on a journey that has led to what I now know is the path to true love and happiness. It was far from easy though, and through our struggles, I learned to embrace many types of prayers. Perhaps the most instrumental prayer tool I used was a prayer journal where I would spare no thought or concern in telling God, who was my new and trusted best friend, everything that was on my mind. I held nothing back and felt nothing but His peace in return.

From the very beginning of my desperate return to God, Jennifer and I started to slowly change and felt God's healing grace. I found a good therapist who helped her to work through her problems and encouraged her to make good choices in her life. When she graduated from high school, Jennifer was awarded with $500 for being the most improved student. It is so true that prayer is powerful and that His peace surpasses all understanding.

Jackie M. Farrell   *Ft. Washington, Maryland*

Ten Minute Meditation

Many times we don't quite believe that Jesus is truly interested in our personal happiness. We let creepy feelings in that tell us that following Jesus is hard and lonely and full of suffering.

I think the truth is that life *without* Jesus is all those things and it is the trick of the devil to try to get us mixed up!

The truth is—with Jesus, even the worst hardship can become Joy and without Jesus all the money, fame and fortune in the world becomes blah!

So…today…go to your special place in your garden and talk to Jesus about some negative thoughts you have about your Christian walk.

Bring them out in the open. Let Jesus know your fears, doubts and questions.

Prayer when time is completed:

Jesus,
thank you
for letting me discuss
everything
and anything with you.
I know you are Love
and that you desire
only Love and goodness
for me.
Help me to accept your love
more completely in my life.
Amen.

MEDITATION

Not Staying Home

When I was a young novice in our community, I became familiar with the Chaplet of Divine Mercy devotion that our Lord gave to St. Faustina. I prayed the chaplet daily and came to personally embrace the deep meaning of the words our Lord revealed to Faustina.

Our Lord promised that anyone who prayed the novena prayers and chaplet beginning on Good Friday and ending on the first Sunday after Easter would be granted his request, provided it was His will for that person's life. One Easter season I had a very large favor I desperately needed to have granted.

It all revolved around my father who had been away from the Church for many years. I learned from my mom that he was a very religious person when they were first married and while I was a young child. Being a proud and honest man with a *tell-it-like-it-is* personality, my father could not tolerate hypocrisy of any sort, so when some people in the Church hurt him, he stopped practicing our faith altogether.

My mom and I always prayed that one day he would return to his faith. Then, when I entered religious life at the young age of fifteen, I made it my mission to pray him back to church. The Chaplet of Divine Mercy became my major source of prayer, but as time passed and the months turned into years, I began to wonder if God was really listening.

This particular Easter season I was stationed in a school in Wisconsin when I once again reflected on the promises of our Lord in regard to the Chaplet of Divine Mercy Novena. Then, for nine days straight, from Good Friday until the first Sunday after Easter, I earnestly prayed the novena and chaplet each day, and desperately pleaded to Him in prayer, "Mom and I have been praying for a long time, and only You can perform a miracle. Please bring my dad back to the family of faith."

On the last day of the novena, which is now officially called Divine Mercy Sunday, I felt at peace. As the days went on, I remained in a state of hopefulness.

Three weeks later, I visited my home in Pittsburgh, Pennsylvania. My mom and I went out for the day and returned home late in the evening. I knew my father would be worried because we were so late in getting home. As we came in the door, I heard him say, "I am not staying home anymore!" Thinking he meant that he regretted staying home for the day and wished he had gone with us, I told him that he could have come with us.

He emphatically said again, "I am not staying home any more. I am going back to church!" Well, I looked at my Mom and she at me as if we were not hearing right. Then I exclaimed, "Praise the Lord!" It was an evening of joy!

Dad went back to church that following Sunday, and two weeks later my parents renewed their marriage vows in the same church where they were married thirty-five years before, by the same priest who joined them in the holy sacrament of matrimony. I cannot describe the happiness I experienced and the joy I felt knowing firsthand the fruits that come with the gospel words, "Pray without ceasing!"

Sr. Georgene M. Golock   *Akron, Ohio*

Do not be troubled if you do not immediately receive from God what you ask him; for he desires to do something even greater for you, while you cling to him in prayer.

Evagrius Ponticus

Two Angels

Over the Memorial Day weekend in 2007, two friends and I went on retreat in Ann Arbor, Michigan. It was held by the Dominican Sisters Mary Mother of the Eucharist. As we prepared to leave Ann Arbor on Sunday afternoon to head back to Cleveland, we realized that we didn't have directions for the way home. Rather than try to guess the correct exits and highways, we decided to use the Global Positioning System (GPS) my mother had insisted I take with us. The GPS directed us home through rural areas instead of sticking strictly to the highways, but at least we knew we would not get lost.

Half an hour out of Ann Arbor, and a few minutes after leaving the freeway, I noticed that the battery icon light on my dashboard was lit. Never having seen that icon before, I asked the friend who was in the front passenger seat to get the owner's manual from the glove compartment and see what it meant. Then I asked my other friend to grab the holy water from my purse so we could bless the car. We started praying that we would be able to make it home.

We found out that the symbol meant the car had a broken or torn alternator belt and that I should pull over immediately so the engine would not overheat. Being in the middle of the country with no gas stations in sight, we were a little nervous about stopping on the side of a two-lane road, yet we definitely did not want the engine to overheat either. We could see that about a mile down the road there was a dirt pull-off area that was just past an intersection with a flashing light. We decided to stop there, feeling that we would be safer on the pull-off area than the side of the road.

When I was growing up, I read many of Guideposts *Angels on Earth* magazines and enjoyed the stories where people would be in need and a mysterious stranger or two would show up to help them, and then disappear without a trace. So as we got out of the car, I told the Lord we could really use two angels to help us now, please.

We popped the hood open and peered under it, but we had no idea where to find the alternator belt, and nothing looked wrong to us. However, when we tried to start it again, it was clear that something was definitely wrong. We must have made a pathetic picture, three young women staring helplessly under the hood of our broken-down car. As we stood there, two vehicles slowed down on the other side of the road, each with a man in it. The men asked if we were okay and if we could reach someone to help us. I knew inside that they had only the best intentions to help and not harm us.

When they heard we were from Cleveland and had no idea where the alternator was, they crossed the road to give us a hand. They showed us the broken alternator belt, and when the towing company was completely uncooperative about finding a tow truck to help us, the men volunteered to get the part and fix my car themselves.

We had broken down less than half a mile from their parents' property where they and their families were camping that weekend. So, in their father's barn which had practically every tool known to man, they replaced my alternator belt. These two guys who just showed up on the side of Samaria Road were an answer to my pleading prayer, and they were true Good Samaritans.

Not only did God answer my prayer to fix my car, but He also taught me another lesson through this experience. While I was on retreat in Ann Arbor, each person there picked a verse from a litany out of a bag and we were supposed to pray about what God was saying to us. All weekend I had prayed about mine, but I left the retreat with no greater insight.

As we continued on our drive home, I told my friends I had finally heard what God was saying to me in my litany, and that I had heard it through our broken-down car experience. I had experienced what it meant to truly surrender my trust to God. My litany verse had been, "Most Sacred Heart of Jesus I place my trust in You." God provides, He always provides, maybe not so quickly at times, but He is always with us and helping us.

Katherine M. Komar   *Broadview Heights, Ohio*

"AS NEAR AS I CAN FIGURE SOMETHING BAD HAPPENED AND THEY'RE BOTH IN ON IT."

My Husband's Dream

Our family migrated to Australia last year and we attribute the success of our move to Mama Mary. Six weeks before our migration documents were to expire, we were informed by our local agent that if our permanent resident visa was not released within a month, our documents would expire and we would have to submit more recent documents. We were a bit anxious with our situation because at that time our visa processing had already been delayed by some local agencies.

With anxious hearts, our family prayed for guidance and direction for our situation. That night, my husband dreamt of someone instructing our family to pray the rosary, dedicating each bead to the migration officer who was in charge of processing our application. For the next three days, my whole family gathered and prayed the four mysteries of the holy rosary the way we were instructed to do so in my husband's dream. Towards the end of the third day, we received news from the migration officer who we had been praying for that he would release our visa within the week!

The manifestation of the power of the holy rosary did not stop there. We immediately made a short trip to Sydney, Australia, to scout for schools for our children and to find ourselves a new home before we permanently migrated there. Our friends referred us to the schools their children attend, but unfortunately the classes were all filled and the schools could not take our children.

We again prayed the holy rosary the way we were instructed in my husband's dream, but this time we dedicated each bead for Mama Mary to show us the schools and the suburb that would be best for our family. The following day, a former co-worker showed us around his suburb and told us about the Catholic schools nearby. We took the chance and inquired at these schools, and not only did they graciously answer all of our questions, but they also accepted our application and enrolled our children.

At the end of the day, we thanked Mama Mary for answering our prayers, and we were not very surprised when it turned out that our children will be attending St. Mary's Primary School and Marist High School, and our new parish will be St. Mary's.

Grace R. Vega   *Cammeray, New South Wales, Australia*

If a man wants God to hear his prayer quickly, then before he prays for anything else, even his own soul, when he stands and stretches out his hands toward God, he must pray with all his heart for his enemies. Through this action God will hear everything that he asks.

Abba Zeno

Make your requests with definite earnestness if you would have definite answers. Aimlessness in prayer accounts for so many seemingly unanswered prayers . Be definite in your petitions . Fill out your check for something definite, and it will be cashed at the bank of Heaven when presented in Jesus' Name. Dare to be definite with God.

Anonymous

Taking My Own Advice

Like many others, my story begins with disappointment. I was disappointed at work, because I did not get to do what I wanted to and everything I laid my hands on was a failure. I was disappointed at home because I could not spend enough time with my four-year-old daughter. I felt that my relationship with my family was suffering. I had dreams and ambitions that I felt I would never be able to fulfill.

My mind was filled with doubts when a person I knew very well started at my work. This person was a Hindu and had a lot of questions about Christianity. As a good Catholic, I began telling him about Jesus and my relationship with God. Eventually, he began turning to me for spiritual support. As I guided him, I came to realize how important it was to submit to God.

One day he was really down and low with plenty of personal problems, I told him to submit to God and that everything God gives us is for a reason. All pain and suffering is for a reason and all joy and happiness is for a reason. No matter what, God will never forget us. I quoted my own version of a passage in the New Testament, "Do the lilies worry about their clothes or the birds about their food?" I told him to leave everything to God and watch how He takes care of things.

After this, I felt that the same applied to me. Not only did my conversation with this person increase my awareness of God, I also started doing the things I advised him to do. I had no set time for prayers; I began regular conversations with God, even at times when I was in conversation with people. I included Him in every part, every conversation and every decision I made in my life. For me, prayers are no longer just the Our Father and Hail Mary. They are thanking, consultation, and seeking advice from the Father (who I lovingly call Papa), Jesus (my loving brother who never lets me down) and the Holy Spirit whose guidance I seek when I have to say or do something. I found more meaning in every prayer. I had never before concentrated on our Lord's Prayer but now I can say it from my heart and mean every word of it.

I told God about my passions and interests, told Him that I would leave everything to Him and submit to His will. I left my job to start something on my own, so I could spend more time with my daughter. Our salaries were not enough to support us, we paid a high rent, we had a lot of financial commitments. God took care of things so beautifully and we somehow managed everything. Although we were on pins and needles many times, we stopped worrying, concentrated on what we could do and God took care of the rest.

It has been six months since I left my job and now I own a training institute. Projects come to me without my having to seek them. Every now and then, I receive a pleasant surprise from Papa. I am not much of a marketing person, but God markets for me, He manages my finances and gives me what He thinks is right for me. Sometimes, if I listen, I can hear him speak to me and tell me, "Don't worry, Rowena, I will take care of you." I know that as long as I trust Him, and remain happy and thankful for what He does for me each day, He will continue to guide and support me. I now spend a lot of time with my daughter and my relationships have become stronger. I am truly happy.

Rowena S. Glasfurd   *Bangalore, Karnataka, India*

Silence of Mary, speak to me, teach me how with you and like you I can learn to keep all things in my heart as you did,... to pray always in the silence of my heart as you did.

Blessed Teresa of Calcutta

Everything Changed

My twenty-fifth anniversary was supposed to be a special one, but the marriage ended a week before we reached it. I prayed for my husband who did not have any religious affiliation. I prayed that he would love me and show his love as described in the Bible. I had two beautiful boys who were raised Catholic. They were and still are a gift from my Creator.

I often look at the life Mary and Joseph had, and how they overcame their suffering. I believe in prayer and became involved in prayer meetings at a very young age. I had a beautiful house and a nice job. My parents lived close by. The only thing I didn't have was the love of my husband. He looked for love outside the marriage and we became even more distant. I still prayed, but I was losing hope. I decided that I must end the marriage because he loved the other women. When I left, everything changed. My financial security, my lifestyle, my family, and my heart were broken. I had also lost my mother to a heart attack during this time. It was very difficult to go through this period of my life, but I still prayed and attended Mass and received Communion.

I became very sad and hunted for love to fill my void. I had several boyfriends. Because of my hurt and pain, I had no appetite, and at the age of 46, I looked like a 36-year-old. I was attracted to any man who would show me attention and love, but I paid a heavy price. I felt like a traitor to my Catholic faith on the inside and justified all my actions because of my losses. I still prayed and did the best I could at the time, but I was unhappy because I did not wait for Jesus to answer my prayers. I rushed ahead and did it my way, the wrong way.

Eventually, after many mistakes, I decided I could not find love on my own. I prayed to God our Father to show me His will. At this time, I was living alone in a basement apartment, losing my business, and becoming very dependent on God. I was very sad and I started to go to daily Mass, say the rosary, and to go to adoration and confession regularly. I prayed with many people and said many novenas. I was at the lowest point in my life. I felt as if I were a failure and that my life was over. I was trying to live day to day, but I cried a lot. I also prayed a lot, and Mass brought peace and Christ into my heart. I was talking to God frequently. I told Him that I would suffer if this is what He wanted. I surrendered totally to His will and way.

Finally, I met a wonderful man. He, too, was suffering from the loss of his spouse. We met at St. Joseph the Worker Parish in Oshawa. We became friends and fell in love. My prayer was answered because I never gave up on God. I am now in a beautiful house, married in the Catholic Church, and work at a job in the hospital close to my home. My husband loves me and we share our Catholic faith and our love for Jesus daily. We say the rosary and go to Mass together. He was put in my life because I prayed and God took care of all my needs. I thank God everyday for the suffering I went through because it changed my life. I just had to be patient and wait for God.

Heather J. Toutant   *Oshawa, Ontario, Canada*

Prayer...vanquishes all the strength of the tempter, and it changes men from blind into seeing, from weak into strong, from sinners into saints.

St. Alphonsus Liguori

There are more tears shed over answered prayers than over unanswered prayers.

St. Teresa of Avila

My Kitchen Prayer

Ever since being saved, I have been a person of much deep prayer both day and night. I try to attend Mass as much as possible since we live five minutes away from church. I read my Bible regularly and I play my songs of worship every now and again when I am alone at home. I can remember that ever since I lived with my aunt after my stroke, I cooked for her children, her husband, and my son.

One morning, while I was cutting up the chicken to prepare lunch, I discovered that the knife was dull. Since only my left hand had the strength to cut this chicken, I was devastated.

I remembered when I was in Guatemala, that there were men who went around blowing their flutes and shouting, "Do you need to sharpen your knives? We sharpen knives and scissors."

I said to myself, "Oh God, if only one of those men would pass right now, that would be so good. I could get my knife sharpened and our scissors too. I would use my little money from my pension to pay for it because my aunt does not even have a knife sharpener and I just cannot cut this chicken. The children need to eat when they get home from school. What could I do, Oh God?"

My mind was filled with my own self-pity and my dull knife when I heard the exact same flute all the way from Guatemala in our own little country of Belize!

I heard the flute but I couldn't believe it was one of those men from Guatemala. It took me about two minutes to get myself to the door and check if what I heard was really true. By the time I got to the door, because I walk with a limp, the man I saw looked exactly like the ones from Guatemala with their equipment to sharpen knives, but he was already turning the lane across the street. I cried out to him but he did not hear me, so I cried out to God, "Oh God, I was so stupid for not checking immediately, please send him back, please?"

I went back to fighting with the chicken when in about five minutes, I heard the whistle again. This time with a big smile on my face, I strutted as fast as I could to the door. I stopped the man. He set up his equipment and started sharpening my knife and scissors.

What a view for all my neighbors. They all stared as if it was the first time they had seen this man as well. I was so happy. The man spoke Spanish. He charged me $16.00. I gave him a $20.00 bill. He didn't have change, so he asked me in Spanish where was the nearest shop. I pointed one out to him. He went to change the money leaving his equipment with me. When he returned, he gave me my change and bid me a good day. That was the first and last time I saw one of those men or heard his whistle in Belize.

Was this man an angel of God, sent to me when I was in real need of help? Of course, I thanked my Heavenly Father and Jesus right away. All I knew was that the food was ready for the kids when they got home from school for lunch.

Maria M. Fabro   *Buttonwood Bay, Belize*

Learn to love the Creator in his creation, the Worker in his work. Don't be so fascinated by things created that you forget the One who created them all.

St. Augustine

Speak now, my heart, and say to God, "I seek your face; your face, Lord, I seek."

St. Anselm

Ten Minute Meditation

Take a moment to visit your beautiful garden. Look at the flowers. Are there any new ones blooming today? Can you hear the waterfall over to the side? Listen to the birds singing in the trees. Spend a few minutes thinking what a beautiful and restful place this is.

Now think of someone that you are having difficulty with today or in your past.

When you have the person in mind, notice that Jesus is walking towards you and He is talking to that difficult person in your life. It actually looks as if He is enjoying being with your problematic person! Oh my goodness! How could that be?

Now the difficult person is walking out of the garden. Your garden! Jesus continues to walk towards you. He smiles at you and you know He is glad to see you and wants to spend time with you.

Did you stop breathing for a few seconds when you saw Jesus with this difficult person? Let your breath out now…slowly and easily. It's okay that Jesus loves you and the difficult person in your life as well.

Talk with Jesus about this or simply let it be and just sit in the garden quietly. Healing comes when we see someone in a new light—even those we have difficulty with.

Prayer when time is completed:

Jesus,
thank you
for opening my heart
to see others
as you see them.
Thank you
for loving all people,
even those I find
difficulty in loving.
Amen.

83

The Abusive Collection

As a corporate credit manager, I have many accounts to manage and collect. Several years ago, one construction account became extremely difficult to handle. Its debt was a large six figures, and the company kept making excuses for not paying. Finally, it got to the point where they started making threats that they were not going to pay at all.

My last call with the man I had to deal with was horrible. He got loud, angry, and verbally abusive. The next day I was supposed to meet with him in person, and even though the prospect of seeing him was not pleasant, I went ahead and followed up with the arrangements because it was my job.

That evening I could not get rid of the sickening feeling in my stomach. I was so nervous and upset that I could hardly eat or think of anything else. I spent a lot of time in prayer asking for the guidance of the Holy Spirit to help me. Over and over, I rehearsed the details in my mind, what I needed to say, and what I needed to accomplish.

Because this account was so big, a lot hung in the balance. It wasn't just my job that was at stake here, but the future of the whole company. A lot of people were depending on me and I certainly did not feel up to the task.

Finally, I felt the nudge of the Holy Spirit urging me to call my pastor and ask him to pray for the meeting the next day. I described the whole situation to him, how I had been working with this client for several months, and how it was getting worse and worse as time went on. I am sure he could tell from my voice just how upset I was.

Father agreed to pray, and I immediately felt somewhat better. I knew he took prayer very seriously and was a very powerful prayer warrior.

The next day I drove to the meeting, nervously praying a rosary on the trip.

When the meeting began, the man was there with approximately eight other people from various companies involved in the project. He started in right away making very inappropriate remarks and comments.

But suddenly, unexplainably, I felt God's presence. A feeling of peace and calm overcame me. A quiet confidence seemed to well up from within me. With every statement that was hurled at me, I knew exactly what to say and how to respond. Slowly the mood around the room began to change.

The meeting continued for about forty-five minutes, and when we reached the end, the man who had been so adamant about not paying looked at me and said, "Come by my office and I will have my secretary cut you a check for ninety percent. I almost fell out of my chair with joy!

I left the meeting practically walking on air. As I drove to the office to collect the money, you can be sure I was thanking God every inch of the way. I called my husband and asked him to find our pastor and tell him I knew he had to be praying because I could feel God's presence so real and powerful in that meeting. I told him what the result was. He was as surprised and amazed as I was!

He started to laugh, and told me that our pastor had already called to see how things went. He told my husband that just before the time I had given him, he felt strongly led to get two other people and make a holy hour before the Blessed Sacrament for this cause!

Even as I write this today, I have goose bumps remembering how powerfully God heard and responded to our prayers. I continue to be filled with gratitude for my busy pastor who took the time out of his packed-full day and the two other prayer partners who went with him to spend a holy hour before the Lord for me.

This pastor soon began perpetual adoration in our parish and it is still going strongly today, "Thanks be to God!"

Jo Ann Mason   *Temple, Texas*

The Dangerous Curve

Three years ago, when my youngest son was eighteen years old, he was involved in an accident on his way home from visiting friends in a neighboring town. He usually came home between eleven o'clock and midnight, but this night was different.

I had gone to bed, but as usual, I would not actually sleep until I heard him come in the door. My heart suddenly became extremely panicked and I knew that his life was in danger. I took my rosary and began to pray fervently. Between my Hail Mary's I pleaded with God to please let him live. "Please Father, please don't take him. You know I am not strong enough for this. Please, I am begging you."

I cried and prayed for approximately fifteen minutes. Then the kitchen door opened and I got up and met my son in the hallway with my rosary still in my hands. Before I could say a word, I knew by the look of pure terror on his face that I had in fact received a premonition.

He started by saying, "Mom, you will never believe what just happened." He explained how he had been driving on the highway, passing a car on a very dangerous curve, when all of a sudden he came upon a very large deer that was dead in the middle of the road. He had no place to go. He was going too fast to come to a complete stop, and there was a car on his right and a barrier on his left. He had to drive over the deer—and the underneath of his car showed us the evidence.

I told him what I had been experiencing at the exact moment this was happening, and it confirmed to my son how much God loves him. There is no doubt in my mind how powerful prayer is, and I continuously thank God for sparing my son's life.

Jo Ann Breau   *Leominster, Massachusetts*

Blessed, Not Lucky

About three years ago I had what I thought was a terrible migraine headache. Little did I know that it was the warning sign of worse things to come. When a mass of tissue was found in my brain, I found myself in such a dark place that I could not pray, so I asked others to pray for me. Catholics, Lutherans, Episcopalians, Methodists, Baptists, Muslims, and even Hindis were praying for me.

Then I went to the hospital to have brain surgery. Throughout my whole ordeal I kept hearing in my head, "Give thanks in all things," so I started looking for things to be thankful for. I gave thanks for my insurance, and for being able to choose my neurosurgeon, who, incidentally, is one of the best in the nation for my kind of tumor and was right in my own backyard!

I gave thanks for the knowledgeable, insightful, and compassionate nurses who took care of me, and I gave thanks for the medicine that relieved my pain. I gave thanks for my family and friends. Then something remarkable began to happen.

People volunteered to feed my family for eight weeks, and my brothers and sisters used their vacation time to stay with me and my daughters, who were only three and nine years old at the time. It opened my eyes to what is really important—your faith, the people in your life, and your health.

I realized that so many things that I once took for granted could be whisked away without a moment's notice. My eyes were opened. Another Catholic told me that what I experienced was called *redemptive suffering*. I don't fully understand what that is or how it occurs, and I certainly didn't know about this type of suffering at the time of my surgery. But I do know that I came through it all with flying colors!

When I saw my endocrinologist after my surgery, he told me I was very lucky. He said that ninety-eight percent of the people he sees with my kind of tumor end up on some kind of hormone, but all of my lab work was normal and I didn't need to take them. When he told me how lucky I was, I corrected him and told him I was blessed, not lucky. It has been three years since I had my brain tumor removed and I continue to remain blessed with normal lab values!

Susan DeFanti   *Euless, Texas*

It is not I who wanted prayer. It is he who wanted it. It is not I who have looked for him. It is he who has looked for me first. My seeking him would have been in vain if before all time he had not sought me.

Carlo Carretto

Is prayer your steering wheel or your spare tire?

Corrie Ten Boom

To pray is nothing more involved than to open the door, giving Jesus access to our needs and permitting Him to exercise His own power in dealing with them.

Ole Kristian O. Hallesby

The Perfect Nursing Home

Shortly before Christmas in December of 2005, I found myself pleading with the Blessed Mother to help me find a nursing home for my grandmother, Mildred, or Gram as we call her. She had been hospitalized during an illness and was not recovering quickly. Sadly, my mother could no longer care for her at home, and we had only a couple of days to find an appropriate facility for Gram.

I wondered how I could find a place in two days that would be good enough for my very special ninety-six-year-old grandmother whom I loved and honored. None of the facilities I looked at could ever be like home for her, yet she had to go somewhere.

I quickly realized that this was too big a job for me. I desperately needed the Lord's help, so I asked His mother to intercede for me. Happily, my prayers were answered. I found a nursing home near her home in Oak Lawn, Illinois, and we moved Gram in the day before Christmas Eve.

The day after Christmas, when I should have been joyful, I was feeling very anxious about my grandmother's situation. I worried about everything. What if Gram is stuck with a difficult roommate who keeps her up all night? What if she falls out of bed or doesn't eat right? It was then that the Lord gave my grandmother her new roommate.

Antonia was the Blessed Mother's reassurance to me that Gram would be all right. She is a quiet, peaceful, and prayerful woman with a strong faith in God. Her Catholic presence in a non-Catholic facility (my grandmother is Serbian Orthodox) also gave me the peace of mind that I needed.

When Antonia's family told me that she likes to pray all day long, well, that was music to my ears! How wonderful for my grandmother to have a roommate who would constantly pray for her intentions. She couldn't have picked a better roommate with whom to spend the rest of her days in the nursing home.

There are many visible signs of our Catholic faith in my grandmother's room. A large crucifix is hung on Antonia's wall above her bed. A Divine Mercy picture is on the wall opposite their beds. They can lovingly gaze at the face of Christ as they wake up each morning and again before they go to bed at night. Statues of saints are everywhere. It no longer resembles an ordinary nursing home room. Instead it looks more like a Catholic shrine.

I have noticed other visible reminders of the Blessed Mother in the nursing home. A small statue of Our Lady is in the main dining room, and out in the courtyard is a large one of Our Lady of Grace. What is so amazing to me is that even though this is not a Catholic facility, reminders of Our Lord and Our Lady's presence are clearly visible for all to see.

My grandmother's road is not an easy one. She is turning ninety-seven in May and is anxiously waiting out her time on earth in a nursing home. Dementia has robbed her of a once healthy mind. The days are long, and she often forgets many things. On days that she can remember, she would rather be living in her own home.

The Lord is with her, walking right beside her. I am grateful to the Blessed Mother for interceding for me. She saw to it that the Lord gave my grandmother a safe place to live and Antonia to keep her company. Antonia is a blessing and a great example of someone who is living out her Catholic faith, even from the confines of a nursing home.

If you are ever faced with putting a loved one in a nursing home, try going to the Blessed Mother first. Ask for her intercession; the Lord eagerly listens to His mother. You, too, may find that your loved one may be blessed with a good facility to live in, staff members who care, and hopefully an Antonia too!

Kathleen Delia Miller   *Chesterton, Indiana*

Saint Joseph's Protection

My mother taught us children to pray at a young age. We often prayed the rosary together while sitting on the back porch, and as we prayed we would look at the sky. Mom would say, "Look at the beautiful sky, it's 'Blessed Mother Blue'." She frequently said, "You know, St. Joseph protected Jesus and His mother. If you pray to him he will protect you, too."

My mom gave each of us a copy of a prayer to St. Joseph and told us to always keep it with us and to pray it often. As the years passed, I gave copies of this prayer to my own children and taught them to pray it often.

When my youngest daughter Eileen was nineteen, she had to take her first long trip to Philadelphia by herself. It was her first time on a major highway. When she returned home safely, we went out for lunch. We sat near a window in the restaurant and watched as a workman removed a curb in the parking lot with a backhoe. At one point in the conversation, Eileen leaned over the table towards me and said, "Boy, Mom, the traffic was really bad on the highway. Did I ever say my St. Joseph prayer!"

At that very moment, the backhoe suddenly slipped off the curb and came through the window. I watched in horror, unable to move as the hoe crashed through the window missing my daughter only by inches. Sharp, wicked shards of glass broke and shattered behind her head.

We jumped up in shock, barely able to breathe or speak. I looked at my daughter in disbelief. Amazingly, not a sliver of glass had touched her. Had my daughter not leaned forward to stress that she had prayed to St. Joseph for safety, she would have been hit in the head and neck by those swords of glass. When we ask him to, St. Joseph truly does protect us as he did Jesus and His blessed mother.

Roberta H. Sefchick   *Prompton, Pennsylvania*

His Grace Every Day

I was my husband's caregiver for the last nine years of his life. During that time, we made many trips to the emergency room, and he was often admitted to the hospital. There were even periods when this happened on a weekly basis. Every time we had to seek medical care, I prayed with my whole heart, giving the situation entirely to God with complete surrender to His will.

In every new crisis I would tell God that whatever the outcome would be, I knew it was in His hands and that I accepted whatever His will was for our lives. I told Him that I knew in my heart He would provide us whatever we needed to deal with each situation we were presented. I kept my heart, ears, and eyes open for His graces every day.

Praying like that put my spirit at ease and kept me calm during each emergency we faced. Among other things, it got me through my husband's heart attack, stroke, and a possible amputation. God, in His mercy, provided us with the right people to help us through each crisis, and also the best solutions for care when my husband was released from the hospital.

Stacie A. Van Deusen   *Norwalk, Connecticut*

As our body cannot live without nourishment, so our soul cannot spiritually be kept alive without prayer.

St. Agustine

Ten Minute Meditation

Push open the little wooden gate that leads into your garden. Notice how easily it opens. A light touch from your hand and it gently swings back so you can enter.

Today as you enter your garden you notice there is a wheelbarrow. There is a small tree in a clay pot in the wheelbarrow. You notice a little tag tied to the branches. Hmmmm. It must tell what kind of a tree it is. Go over and read what the tag says.

The tag says, "This is your tree of Hope. Plant in sunny spot and water it daily."

In the wheelbarrow there is also a small shovel. Take the shovel and look about for a place to plant your tree. Think about an area in your life that you would most like to see a change.

On the tree there is another little tag. This one has nothing on it. Take a pen out of your pocket and write on the tag the hope you are longing for.

Plant your tree. Give it some water. Now leave it to God to bring the sunshine it will need and the rain and the nutrients of the earth to supply its roots. Every once in a while visit your tree and talk to it. Encourage it.

Prayer when time is completed:

Dear God,
thank you for this gift of hope.
No matter how small
my hope may be today,
I know under your love
and care it will grow
as long as I plant it
and let it take root.
Amen.

MEDITATION

Have You Been Saved?

I cannot tell you how many times in my life I have been asked, "Have you been saved?" Of course, along with this I also have been bombarded with the classic fundamentalist Protestant affirmation, "You're a Catholic, so you cannot be a true Christian!" It would be impossible to tell you how upset that used to make me. There were times when I rationalized beating the hell out of the person by thinking I have been confirmed, and am a "soldier of Christ." I thank the Lord that He never allowed me to act on my thoughts at those times.

I grew up in a traditional St. Louis Irish/German inner-city household. My mother is still the *virginal saint* who can do no wrong. She is known to still wear a smock or apron, even though she now resides in a retirement apartment. My father went to church every day of his adult life. He would leave home early in the morning to go to the six o'clock Mass at St. Alphonsus, "The Rock," church prior to going to work. We would go as a family to the six o'clock Mass on Sunday mornings because, as my dad often said, "The first thing you do on the Lord's day is be with the Lord." I now also believe we went that early because everyone fasted from dinner Saturday evening until after Mass and my dad wanted to eat!

My strong family religious upbringing included parochial grade schools; serving at Masses, funerals and weddings; Perpetual Help devotions every Tuesday evening; and of course the Sisters of St. Joseph nuns and my sometimes sore knuckles and ear lobes. Despite all that, I would have considered myself Catholic by association, or a cradle Catholic who had a typical prayer life. I didn't think I was doing anything gratifying, unusual, or even really important.

That is, until I was about seventeen years old. By that time, my father had long since died, and my family had moved from Most Holy Name Parish in north St. Louis to St. Mary Magdalene Parish in south

St. Louis. The pastor at this parish was a true example of the Irish priest (even though I think he was actually German) you may have seen in a Bing Crosby movie. His name was Msgr. Louis F. Meyer. He had white hair, was large in stature, and had a strong voice. When I was twelve years old he scared the holy hell out of me.

After getting to know him, I realized that behind his strong, somewhat serious and stern voice and mannerisms was a man who loved his vocation, his parish, and his parishioners. He actually turned out to be an intelligent, warm, caring and humorous person.

Msgr. Meyer did something else that was surprising. He awakened the Holy Spirit within me and ignited my personal love for Jesus and the Blessed Virgin Mary. Now I pray every day and meditate on the rosary daily as well, and it's all because of his example and what I witnessed on one particular Sunday.

I was seventeen years old. I would sit at Mass with my mother who always insisted on sitting in the first pew. I grudgingly went along and did not complain much because it wouldn't have done any good anyhow. I said my prayers with my usual lack of passion, which in reality was just a function of merely *going through the motions.*

Msgr. Meyer had his usual homily that was interesting and ended with a mind-blowing, open-ended question that actually made you think about the readings of the Mass. He had just started the Eucharist Prayer Number Two. I still remember this vividly, thirty years later, because it seemed like he always used Eucharistic Prayer Number Two.

At the beginning of the prayer, he would always hold both arms up like an umpire calling strikes, with two fingers of each hand out forming the peace sign. While watching him that particular Sunday, in an instant I became aware that "Monso Meyer" was not just reading the prayer, and he was not merely acting out the Last Supper. He was actually living the Eucharistic prayer in his words and actions. You could tell that Monsignor Meyer loved God through Jesus and through the Mass.

I remember getting warm and opening up to what was happening. I felt like a sponge wanting to suck in as much of this feeling and energy as possible. I wanted to learn and understand more about this thing called "Mass" and about God.

To this day, I still have that feeling of wanting to learn more. My prayer life is no longer melancholy, and I pray continuously. I live for Eucharistic adoration at our parish, and, believe it or not, the sacrament of reconciliation.

My Protestant friends would call my relationship with God "being saved," and so be it. I now realize that when they say they are "saved" they are referring to something that Catholics experience every day, although many of us take it for granted these days. Protestants believe that they are saved when they overtly ask for God to come into their lives. Catholics do the same thing at every Mass, every confession, and with every prayer. Catholics are "saved" every day of their lives when they pray and have God in their hearts. Thank you Monsignor Louis F. Meyer. I pray for you every day.

Daniel E. Halley   *Hazelwood, Missouri*

Christians must lean on the cross of Christ just as travelers lean on a staff when they begin a long journey. They must have the passion of Christ deeply imbedded in their minds and hearts, because only from it can they derive peace, grace, and truth.

St. Anthony of Padua

When we are before the Blessed Sacrament, let us open our heart; our good God will open his. We shall go to him; he will come to us...It will be like a breath from one to the other.

St. John Vianney

The Math Challenge

My two daughters, Chivonne and Chantelle, have always struggled in math and in any subjects related to math. Last September as the new school year began, I started praying that they would overcome their weaknesses in those areas, and that the years ahead would go well for them. In the past, their difficulty in those classes sometimes brought their grand totals down, and it often made them nervous and afraid of those types of subjects.

Chivonne, my oldest daughter, is an eighteen-year-old sophomore at American University at Dubai. She is studying business administration and is taking classes such as quantitative analysis and accounting. At first, her quantitative analysis class was especially difficult for her, and she dreaded her first quiz. To her delight, when she actually sat down and took the quiz, everything flowed smoothly and she scored a seven out of a possible ten. This success gave her much needed confidence, and now that her fear is gone, she is finding that she understands the material better.

Fifteen-year-old Chantelle is in grade eleven at a reputable school. Like her older sister, she recently dreaded taking a math quiz that she ended up doing very well on, scoring a sixteen out of a possible twenty. Then, just today, she shut herself in her room and said she had loads to study for a chemistry quiz tomorrow and asked not to be disturbed the whole evening. I could not believe it when twenty minutes later she was in my room grinning from ear to ear, announcing that she had already finished studying. She felt confident that she would retain everything and that she would do well on the quiz but did not have a clue how this came about.

I mentioned to her that I had been praying really hard, and that I was sure that divine intervention made this all possible for her and her sister.

Thank you to the infant Jesus and Our Lady of Lourdes for answering my prayers. And thank you also to Papa John Paul, as I call him. He is very powerful indeed, and I have received many answers to my prayers through him.

Della L. D'Cruz   *Abu Dhabi, United Arab Emirates*

Sometimes people ask me this question: 'If God does not wish us to ask for material things, but for Himself, the Giver of all good, why does the Bible never say: Do not pray for this or that, pray simply for the Holy Spirit? Why has this never been clearly expressed? 'I reply, Because He knew that people would never begin to pray if they could not ask for earthly things like riches and health and honours; He says to Himself: If they ask for such things the desire for something better will awaken in them, and finally they will only care about the higher things.

Sadhu Sundar Singh

What man of you, if his son asks him for bread, will give him a stone? Or if he asks for a fish, will give him a serpent? If you then, who are evil, know how to give good gifts to your children, how much more will your Father who is in heaven give good things to those who ask him!

Matthew 7:9-11

God is Wonderful!

I desperately wanted a baby but it just didn't seem as if I were going to be blessed with a child. Imagine the joy I felt when, after many miscarriages and seeing several doctors, including a specialist, I was pregnant again and this time the baby was thriving inside of me.

Not far into the pregnancy the doctors gave me some upsetting news. They said they believed the baby would be born with severe medical problems because ultrasounds and other tests showed that the baby's stomach was much smaller than his brain. There is only a one-in-a-million chance that a baby will be born with this problem, and when it does happen, the baby usually either dies at birth or has mental problems if it survives.

My faith through prayers and more prayers was so strong that not even for one second during my entire pregnancy did I ever believe that my baby would be born with a problem. Everyone on this earth has a place and a purpose, and I knew that God had sent me this baby for a reason, and that everything was going to be okay.

Well, the time came to give birth and yes, he was born with a problem in his esophagus. Three days after he was born, the pediatric surgeons reconstructed his trachea and attached his esophagus to his stomach. After three weeks of care and recuperation, I took my baby home.

Today my son is a healthy ten-year-old boy who is growing more each day with no problems either physically or mentally. He is my angel sent from above. Each time I look at him I have no doubt that God made a miracle occur in my life, and that the power of prayer and faith can make miracles happen every day.

Josie Zuniga   *Miami, Florida*

The Price of Freedom

My grandson, Russell, had spent time in Kuwait as a scout for the army and was finally back at his base in the United States with only five months left to serve when he was notified that he was being sent to Iraq. After he arrived in Baghdad, the army informed Russell that his service time had been extended for another year. He needed the prayers of the entire family if he were to get home safely. I am a great believer that there is no greater power available to us on earth than prayer, so my husband and I prayed the rosary every single day for his protection and safe return home.

I wrote and encouraged him not to give up hope, and told him to let his superiors know that he would be out of Iraq by Christmas because his grandmother was praying for him to be home by then, and that she has pull with someone a lot higher up than the president of the United States.

All of our prayers were answered and Russell was home for Christmas, and his time in the service was not extended another year after all. I give our Lord and our Blessed Mother all the credit for his return home by Christmas.

After he returned home, Russell told me a story about a night when he was on patrol in Iraq. He said that he and the other soldiers were crossing a bridge in a Humvee (Army Hummer) when they were attacked from the front and rear by the enemy. He said bullets were flying everywhere and there seemed to be no way out. They did get out though, and he did not know how they ever managed to escape that ordeal.

I know how they escaped that enemy fire and I told Russell how he and the other soldiers were saved that night. You see, when it was night time in Iraq, it was daytime in the United States. There were many times when I would be working around the house and I would get a premonition that Russell needed prayers, so I would pray for him as I did my work. I assured him that it was prayer that delivered him out of harm's way that night.

While Russell was in Baghdad he hurt his back. After he received his honorable discharge from the service it was difficult for him to find a job that did not involve lifting, because that aggravated his back condition. Besides that, no one in the family could persuade him to get the psychological counseling he desperately needed after all he went through while in Iraq.

We were all very surprised when he reenlisted in the army within a couple of years after being discharged. A short time later he was sent to Germany to await deployment to Iraq again. We all had an uncomfortable feeling that if Russell was sent to Iraq again he would never return.

Just to show how faithful our Lord and our Blessed Mother are in answering prayers, even though we had become lax in saying the rosary as often as we had in the past, the prayers my husband and I did pray, as well as those of his entire family, prevented him from going back to Iraq.

While he was in Germany, Russell was in a freak accident with a Humvee and broke his leg. Gangrene had set in his leg, and the combination of our prayers and the excellent medical attention he received while stationed in Germany brought him through. His leg healed and he received therapy for it and his back as well. He also received the psychological counseling he so desperately needed. Russell received a medical discharge from the army and is now home safe and sound. He is going to college to get the education he needs to find a job that won't be physically challenging.

Russell told us that the people in Iraq are very grateful to us for freeing them from bondage, and that they too are losing loved ones in the conflict over there due to the actions of snipers in their midst. We need to continue our prayers for the soldiers and everyone involved in the war.

Russell shared this story:

Shattering a Jewel

The dust blew across the surface of the desert in the dark and musty night air. In the distance, the sound of the Holy Koran could be heard soothing the mind over loud speakers from the nearby mosque. It was a relaxing end to a long, violent, and brutally hot day in eastern Baghdad. On the rooftop of the Iraqi police station, the normal temperature could reach to over one-hundred and thirty degrees Fahrenheit.

A soldier who had just finished a guard shift on the roof made his way down to the front gate of the old rustic building. He walked down the stairs to the first floor and passed by the holding cells that resembled dungeons from a medieval story. The grotesque smell of the thirty or so bodies crammed inside the dark cage was unsettling to the stomach. As he headed towards the front door, he walked past some of the Iraqi police whom he was accustomed to seeing. He stopped and greeted them before continuing on to the army hummer parked outside the building.

The soldier began chatting casually with one of his sergeants like they always did on quiet nights like that. Small cackles filled the air as two IPs started to horse play, lightening the mood of the nearby spectators. The two soldiers made their way over to the gate of the building as a couple was being escorted out of the police station with looks of discontent on their dirt-covered faces.

Suddenly there was a loud thunderous scream! It shot through the air as it struck through the heart like a jagged arrow. Vigilance filled the faces of each individual positioned in the vicinity of the entrance. In the distant darkness, the soldier could make out the figure of a woman carrying something in her arms.

As she came within feet of the tentative men they became aware of what the dreadful sound they had heard was. The scream had come from the woman who was holding the limp body of a blood spattered eight-year-old girl.

Speechless and terrified at the sight, the soldier quickly took the child from her mother. His eyes gazed in horror as he tightly held the cold and lifeless body of this beautiful little angel close to his body. "My dear God, why?" he asked himself as a murky stream of tears trailed their way down his sweat-covered face. The soldier pulled himself together as quickly as he had lost control of his feelings, and, in a rage, he stormed inside the building.

As he gently laid her on a couch in the police commissioner's office, a crowd began to gather around the body of the young girl. Tan skin, pink lips and long flowing dark hair. Never would she see another sunrise through her large majestic eyes that remained open. Her violent death was burned into the horrified expression on her sweet, loving face. The sergeant made his way through the crowd and reunited the mother with her late daughter.

Quickly the sergeant began to move clothing to spot the source of the poor girl's demise. He began to slowly and cautiously raise the dress of the girl. Pink and covered with flowers, the dress was made by the girl's mother as a gift. As her daughter's wounds were exposed, the mother gasped in disbelief and instantly fell cold and unconscious to the concrete floor. On the girl's tiny body lay several bullet wounds, marking the point-blank shots of the sniper.

By Russell R. Weller

Coreen V. Marson   *Catoosa, Oklahoma*

Our prayers lay the track down on which God's power can come. Like a mighty locomotive, his power is irresistible, but it cannot reach us without rails.

Watchman Nee

The Difference Was Prayer

On January 24, 2006, the day after his eighty-seventh birthday, a cancerous tumor began to break through the lining of my dad's esophagus. He was rushed to the hospital, listed as critical, and given little, if any, chance to survive. I remember holding him as he convulsed and cried in pain.

We called and e-mailed our families and friends, asking for prayers for his strength and prayers for him to be at peace. My dad had suffered a great deal already with advanced Parkinson's disease, and his mind had not been clear for nearly a year. Now the cancer had taken over, too. We had no hope for my dad. His esophagus had ruptured and he could no longer swallow; his kidneys were failing; he had tumors near his heart, intestines, and brain; and he had pneumonia. I didn't think there was anything in this world that could make him better again, and I prayed God would just relieve him of his pain.

But I was wrong in thinking there was nothing in this world that could make him better, because the thing in this world that made all the difference was prayer. The prayers of our families and friends hit heaven and a miracle happened.

My dad woke up, he could swallow a little bit and his memory returned. He talked of things he had not remembered in years. He sang songs, told jokes and prayed with us. He even complained about the terrible hospital food (because, of course, hospital food was not fitting for a true Frenchman!). His strength increased, and he was able to walk with a walker and eat at the table again. We had our dad back.

Then, on June 8, my dad took a turn for the worse. We all knew it would happen, but it did not make it any easier. One final trip to the hospital and we were told there was nothing more that could be done for him. It was time to let him go. At ten o'clock on June 17, the night before Father's Day, our heavenly Father called him home.

The story of my dad's final days may seem to be over, but his final witness of God's love is not. Many prayers were said for him, and I truly believe that those prayers are what pulled him from the grip of death last February and brought him back to us a hundred percent better than he had been in a long time. Although having him back like that made his death that much more painful for us, it was so worth it.

Sometimes we see people go through tough times and we casually say, "I'll pray for you." Prayer is not a casual thing, and its results should not be taken lightly. What prayer did for my dad is a witness to the power of prayer. The comfort and love that came with each and every prayer gave us the precious gift of four more beautiful months with our dad—months that were considered medically impossible.

God makes the impossible become possible. The powerful gift of prayer not only brings our needs to God. It is what brings God into our lives and lets us know that He is always with us, even until the end of time.

Therese C. Corsaro   *Palmdale, California*

Say alleluia always, no matter the time of day, no matter the season of life.

St. Benedict

I will abandon myself fully to the Holy Spirit, allowing myself to be led wherever and whenever the Spirit wants, accompanying the Spirit, for my part, with effective and strong resolutions and serious discernment. The Holy Spirit descends upon us with great gentleness, never with a racket.

St. Frances Xavier Cabrini

A Sudden Calm

I was fourteen and it was our annual youth service. I had been chosen to lead the service from the pulpit. Scared does not even begin to describe how I felt. I was shaking so much I thought I would faint. In those first few moments of quiet, before I needed to say anything, I prayed that I would do my best for God. A sudden calm came over me and I enjoyed leading the service without any fear. I am sixty-three now, but that experience will live with me forever. If ever I needed proof of God's being, I had it at that moment.

Anne A. Jones   *Rushden, Northants, England*

We must pray without ceasing, in every occurrence and employment of our lives—that prayer which is rather a habit of lifting up the heart to God as in a constant communication with him.

St. Elizabeth Ann Seton

O Lord, come in my heart and soul and mind, guide my every thought, word, and deed.

St. Germaine De Pibrac

Ten Minute Meditation

Today the garden looks as if it needs a little work. Some of the flowers are starting to droop. They must need a drink and maybe even a bit of fertilizer.

You notice that Jesus is over there looking at a little green bush that appears to be wilting.

How can you give a cup of cold water to that little bush? How can you give a moment of help and friendship to someone in your life today?

Ask Jesus, "Who needs my help today?"

Prayer when time is completed:

Jesus,
help me to help someone
who is in need today.
Perhaps write a letter or
give a smile, a hug,
or a chocolate chip cookie.
Amen.

M
E
D
I
T
A
T
I
O
N

The Writing Contest

Back when I was in the eighth grade at St. Stephen's School in Streator, Illinois, I was looking forward to graduation. About a month before graduation, someone came to our classroom to announce that a local jewelry store was holding a writing contest for all the eighth grade graduates. The prize was a new watch! There would be one for a boy and one for a girl.

There was a buzz of excited voices and our teacher, Sr. Servatia, held up her hands for us to quiet down. The person who announced the contest then passed out the information forms that we would take home to our parents.

I couldn't wait to get home to tell my mom and dad and start writing. I read the top line on the sheet that was passed out. "Why do you want to win a watch? Must be fifty words or less." All the way home I thought of what I would write.

When I showed the form to my mom, she did not raise my hopes. She reminded me how many girls were in our eighth grade and the other grade schools in town, and the fact that there would be only one winner! I did not mind, because my mind was set on winning the watch.

The form stated we were each to come into the jewelry store with our entry and select a watch that we would like to win. My mother walked hesitantly, reminding me all the way not to be too excited, should I not win.

Stepping into the jewelry store was an experience I will never forget. The flutter in my heart was intense when I glanced at all the pretty watches in the glass case at the jeweler's. The man behind the counter led us to one case where the watches for the contest were so I could make my selection. My eyes fell on a white gold watch with a black elastic band. Each watch had a name next to the price tag. I asked the man assisting us if I could take a closer look at the watch. My mom whispered, "Be careful when you hold it!" She was afraid I might drop it and, of course, she would be unable to pay for it. I was very careful. In fact, I didn't touch it; I just let the man bring it out of the case and hold it in front of me.

I read the name of the watch, "Princess Anne," next to the price tag, $65.00. I wasn't interested in the price or the name at the time. The watch itself was so delicate and beautiful. I told the man this was the one I wished to win. He smiled, wrote the name on the form, and told me to put it in the box on the counter.

Walking home, my mom again cautioned me about the chance I would have to win with all the others entering the contest. Then she kindly suggested to me, "Let's say a novena to St. Anne to intercede in this." Needless to say, I prayed to God right away and started saying a nine day novena to St. Anne that very evening.

It is my belief that prayer works wonders, especially children's prayers.

I turned the whole matter over to God and put my trust in Him. I just needed to be patient for the time at which He would answer my prayers. For in my heart, I knew my parents could never be able to afford to buy me a watch for graduation. There were seven of us children and they were lucky to keep us clothed and fed in the early 50s. My dad was a simple carpenter by trade and my mom was a stay at home mother who kept busy with all of her children.

The day finally came when the winner of the jewelry store writing contest was announced. I won! I was so elated it felt as if I were on a cloud. I went up to the person and accepted the "Princess Anne" watch and was saying a prayer thanking God and St. Anne all the way home from school that wonderful day. The watch was on my wrist and I couldn't wait to tell my mom my prayers were answered.

To this day the "Princess Anne" watch that I won in eighth grade is still running. Eventually my husband bought me a new silver band with tiny rhinestones around it, replacing the black band. The watch is now fifty-six years old.

This answered prayer years ago taught me the power of prayer and now I pray unceasingly. Also, my devotion to St. Anne increased over the years.

When I was pregnant with each of my seven children, I said novenas to St. Anne and I had seven healthy deliveries and seven healthy babies.

I also have an ongoing 'new baby' prayer list and pray for the moms to be whom I know in my family and friends, and even some others I do not know very well. It is wonderful to see a new baby who was on my prayer list, especially my grandchildren, nieces, and nephews. The wonder is to be able to hold them or receive a photo of them when they are born.

I believe the prayers of children and mothers are very important to God. The last words between my mother and me were these: she looked at me fondly and said, "I'll be praying for you." I looked back at her and said, "I'll be praying for you, too, Mom." She passed away soon after we exchanged those words. Believe me, prayer works wonders!

Evelyn Heinz   *McHenry, Illinois*

Hold on to the staff of prayer and you will not fall. And even a fall will not be fatal, since prayer is a devout, persistent coercing of God.

St. John Climacus

Prayer pleases God, it gets what it asks, it overcomes enemies, it changes men.

St. Laurence Justinian

"This doesn't look good."

My Secret Desire

My miracle is my daughter. My husband and I were blessed with five sons and I tried to be content, but I still had a secret desire for a daughter. I prayed and more importantly I trusted. I said, "God, you have given me five beautiful sons and I should be happy. I will leave this in your hands. If you don't send me a daughter then I will be happy. I believe you know what is best for me." I was finally at peace. Less than two months later I was pregnant again and everyone said it was a boy, but from that first moment I knew this child was a girl. I believe that this knowledge was also from God. Of course, the baby was a girl.

At two months, my beautiful, God-sent daughter Rachel was diagnosed with biliary atresia, a bile duct problem which affects the liver. We went from her doctor to the surgeon in a matter of four days, and on the fifth day, she had surgery. There were so many people praying for her. One lady sent us a priest so that she could be baptized in the room before her surgery. Another lady gave us Halloween costumes so the younger boys could go trick-or-treating. People sent meals for the boys since my husband, Michael, was taking care of them and going back and forth daily to be with Rachel and me. During the surgery, a couple literally driving out of town turned around and came to sit with me because my husband had to leave. They came because they were "called" and not by us.

Now Rachel is four and a couple of months ago she had another exam, like she does every six months. The doctor said "it isn't every day that we see a miracle." Her liver numbers are normal, even though about 80% of these children need to have liver transplants. I knew she would be all right as I placed her into God's hands. Prayer was important in all these events and I will continue to pray for her always.

Susan M. Phillips   *Omaha, Nebraska*

A Friend Who Cares

God is with us and he cares! Emmanuel!

I have come to believe more than ever that God is very near us and shares our every moment. This revelation has helped me to trust and surrender all my cares to Him.

A few weeks ago, I found myself with a huge financial problem which required me to pledge paying a certain amount every month to clear the debt.

I had nowhere to turn for help. I hoped that I would be able to solve my problem as long as I continued to work at my present job and was given at least forty hours of work every week.

The first month things went well and I was able to pay in the pledged amount. As if to check my faith, the following week my hours of work were cut to almost half. Not only that, one day as we worked the manager told me to go home as there was not a lot of work then. This meant that my hours of work were becoming even fewer than earlier predicted.

I was downcast, but I did not reveal my disappointment to the manager. While walking home I prayed with a lot of anguish. I told the Lord of my anxiety about meeting the debt and questioned Him about the way forward.

The following week things were no better; the schedule bore fewer hours than I had budgeted for if I were to solve my problem. I was getting very upset and worried. As I worked, I pondered the circumstances I was in and told the Lord, this time out loud. I do not know whether someone heard me talking alone.

This is what I told Him: "My Friend, you had better find more hours for me; otherwise, things are not going to work out. Well, You know how much I have to pay in this month, don't You?"

Before the end of the shift, the manager called me with the schedule in her hand to inform me that she had changed it and to ask me if I minded covering night shifts for two weeks because the night staff had some problems and would be absent!

This meant doubling my previous hours! I could hardly hold back my joy. My beloved Lord had not only heard my prayers, He had answered them instantly. I thought this was a miracle. Now I tell Him everything because He is really near me and present in my every moment. I have a friend who cares. Talk to Him and you will never be disappointed.

I will praise my God forever. Ps 145: 18-21.

Josephine Stella Namatovu   *Cathays, Cardiff, Wales*

When I speak alone with God and with our Lady, more than as a grown-up, I prefer to feel myself a child; the mitre, the zuchetto, and the ring all disappear. And I abandon myself to the spontaneous tenderness that a a child has for his mamma and papa.

Pope John Paul I

Prayer is nothing else than union with God. In this intimate union God and the soul are like two pieces of wax molded into one; they cannot anymore be separated. It is a very wonderful thing, this union of God with his insignificant creature, a happiness passing all understanding.

St. John Vianney

Yes, No or Not Yet

"According to Your most perfect and holy will, Lord!"

That is how my prayers now begin or end. If God is disposed to answer my prayer, I praise Him and thank Him. And if He chooses not to answer it now, or ever, I thank Him and I praise Him nonetheless.

I have certainly made my share of demands upon God. I haven't always prayed for His will to be done, because at one time I thought I knew best. But, because of God's grace, now I do, and I find it to be so liberating.

We have all heard it said that God answers all prayers. He says "Yes," "No," or "Not yet." When we can just trust in Him, it is all taken care of, whether we believe our prayers were answered or not.

Regardless, I have had many prayers answered. Some have been quite dramatic, while others have been almost unnoticeable. One of each type happened to me on the same day and in the same situation.

At that time, in 1997, I was teaching elementary school in west Texas. Getting everything ready for the first day of school means that teachers invariably have to put in extra work. In fact, the preparation can take up to three weeks.

I had returned on July 31 from a trip, and consequently, I was very behind in preparing my classroom. I should have had at least half of the work done, so I had to go early and stay late.

Unfortunately, Texas can have dangerously high temperatures during July and August, and that year the school district had taken away the teachers' ability to set the thermostats in their classrooms and centralized the control in Dallas, over 400 miles away.

We were understandably quite unhappy with this new policy, but we had no say in the matter. As we tried to prepare our classrooms, the air conditioners came on only from 9 a.m. to 12 noon. As a result, for most of the day I was in a steel building, with outside temperatures hovering at 107º Fahrenheit. My classroom was no cooler, because the windows were poorly positioned, preventing any significant air flow. Even that would not have helped, because there was no breeze outside.

Each day, my classroom quickly became baking hot. After the first day's suffering, I brought three fans from home, and they helped slightly.

But on that particular afternoon, I was feeling terribly hot and nauseated and afraid that I would pass out. Stepping outside for a moment, I sat on a step and said, "Lord, can You just send me a little breeze?"

Immediately the most wonderful cool breeze surrounded me and continued for about four minutes. It was so sweet! I felt the love of God so profoundly at that moment that it brought tears to my eyes. I was truly grateful. But God wasn't finished!

I resumed my work and was so uncomfortable that my work was going badly. So I said, "Lord, if you would just turn on this air conditioner for about fifteen minutes or so, it would cool the room for awhile and I could get the rest of this work done. Just fifteen minutes, Lord, that's all I need. I know nothing is impossible with You."

Within two minutes, my air conditioner came on! Between bursts of laughter and praises to God, I quickly closed the windows and the door, and my room began to cool down. I ran outside to check the rest of the units, and not a single one was on. Mine was the only one running!

When another teacher saw me outside and asked how I was tolerating the heat, I told her my air-conditioning unit was running.

She naturally asked, "What did you do?"

When I told her exactly what I'd done, she asked me to request God to turn hers on as well, which I did. But later she told me hers had never come on.

My unit stayed on for more than fifteen minutes, which was enough to cool the room nicely. It stayed comfortable for a good while, allowing me time to finish the work I needed to do.

Yes, God answers prayers! Sometimes His answer is "Yes," sometimes "No," and sometimes He says "Wait a bit." He alone knows the reason why. He is so good and so merciful, and I never hesitate to share with others the many ways He has answered my prayers—so many I could write a book!

Dora C. Gallardo   *Uvalde, Texas*

One More Hug

In 2003, my husband and I returned to Toledo, Ohio, after living in Gig Harbor, Washington, for three years. It was wonderful to be back with my mom, dad, daughter, sister, nieces, nephews, aunts, and uncles.

My 84-year-old dad, Tony, was still as independent as ever, and full of love for life. He still worked three days a week delivering nuclear medicine to area hospitals, and was still keeping his house maintained— cutting the grass, building decks, painting, and putting in new floors in his home.

However, he began to feel unusually tired, and his doctor recommended a heart catheterization.

On the day of the procedure, we were all laughing and telling stories about how wonderful life was when we were growing up, and how much we loved each other. None of us could imagine that anything might go wrong.

While we were in the pre-op area, we all said the rosary for the doctors and for a successful outcome. We said our goodbyes and asked my dad if he were afraid. He said, "No, I am in perfect health."

During the procedure, we were called into a consultation room and told that my dad had experienced a massive heart attack, that he had flat-lined, and that he was now on a respirator! We were in total shock. My mom put her head down, my sister screamed and walked out of the room, and I felt like all life drained from me.

The doctor asked us what we wanted to do. He said he could let my dad go since my dad was in no pain and because a bypass surgery might not give him more time, due to his advanced age.

We explained to the doctor what a great person my dad was and started listing the countless reasons why he needed to live, including how many people there were who depended on him. We told him to ask my dad's internist what my dad's quality of life was prior to the procedure. We felt as if we were begging and pleading.

Finally, the doctor agreed, and we went in to see my dad before he went in for the emergency bypass. We all hugged him, told him we loved him, and once again prayed—begging for this wonderful man's life to be saved.

The surgery was going to take approximately five hours, so all of us—my mom, daughter, sister, uncle and aunt, cousins, nieces, and nephews—gathered in the waiting room and began praying the rosary repeatedly. We were so intent, so sincere, and so innocent in our prayer. We were praying it out loud, over and over, telling our Lord that we were knocking—asking and seeking—and that we were confident He would not let us down.

Midway through the surgery, the doctor came in to give us an update. He heard us praying and asked that we pray for him to be guided through the remainder of the procedure. So, we prayed more. I cannot remember how many rosaries we prayed. It was a plea for a miracle, and also a comfort to us.

Finally the results came: A miracle had indeed occurred! The surgeon came in, knelt down in front of us, and told us our prayers had been answered and a miracle had occurred! My dad was in excellent physical shape, and the bypass had been successful.

A year later, my dad was diagnosed with pancreatic cancer and told by doctors that he had only one month to live.

Through our family's prayers, a second miracle occurred, and my mom and dad celebrated their 60th anniversary eight months after he was given the dreadful news.

We lost him January 31, 2006, followed by my mom, two months later, on March 24. If there were any way to pray them back, my sister and I would. However, we had the miracle of extra time—of special time, of one more birthday, one more hug, and one more example of unselfish love. All because of prayer!

Betsy J. Jackson

Toledo, Ohio

Faith Peeking Out

Throughout my teen years I lived with undiagnosed anxiety, panic attacks, and depression. My mother and many in her family were also stricken with these sorts of problems, and she personally suffered from depression, panic attacks, and agoraphobia. She had been raised to believe that everyone experienced life this way, and that people simply learned to tolerate it in different ways.

My mother leaned heavily upon the Sisters of the Precious Blood, a cloistered monastery in New Hampshire. She often went to see them and wrote to them and continues to do so.

In 1973, nearing my high school graduation, I was working in a mill and still battling anxiety and depression. My mother requested prayers for me, and the sisters kindly sent me a letter with some prayer cards, which I had opened but not yet read.

On one particular day, while at work, I was in the midst of another dark period of deep depression, and, without fear of being seen or heard, cried out to God to please help me. I asked Him to please tell me what to do and how to stop the torturous pain.

Bending down to grab another spool from my cart, I noticed something had fallen out of my purse. It was a 3x5 card, sent by the sisters, with the word "Faith" peeking out. I stopped and read that card. Standing there on that factory floor, I was suddenly comforted with a sense of total peace.

Shortly after this incident, I joined the US Army. During the years that followed, I kept that card with me, and would always pin it somewhere in the room where I slept—usually where I could see it at night when I laid my head down to rest. Remarkably, no matter where I was staying at the time, some tiny light would find that card. Sometimes it was the only place in the room where the light from the hall snuck through a crack in the door, or a street light from outside shone through a narrow gap in the window curtain.

It seemed God knew that I needed that assurance, that little sign that others might not think anything of, or might even be prompted to complain about, wanting a completely darkened room. But for me, God was telling me that the words on the card were alive every day and every moment. And they all began with "Faith."

I eventually got married and was gifted by God with two children, who are now in college. I have been a teacher of elementary students for over eight years and recently earned a masters degree in education. But much more importantly, my life started on the day that God surprised me with His promise in such a unique way.

Thirty-two years later, I still have this yellowed, wrinkled card, with its thirteen pinholes, representing the many times I hung it by my bed wherever life led me—South Carolina, Virginia, Germany, Texas, and Nevada. No author is listed, and there is no publication company or date. I like to believe that God was the author of this little card, since no one else has claimed it. If there is another author, I am sure these words were completely inspired.

I believe we must keep strict guard over our faith and protect this living, daily gift that carries us through our pilgrimage here on earth. It all begins with faith. I also believe that, had the sisters not shared their faith with me through the simple gesture of including this card, I would not have this story to tell.

Faith

God guide you through
each troubled day,
When all seems dark
and clouds are gray,
God give to you
the blessed gift
Of faith that trusts
till shadows lift,
through each day's length
His love, your comfort
and your strength.

Celeste D. Lovett   *Henderson, Nevada*

Ten Minute Meditation

Today might be a nice day to sit in your garden for a few minutes and think of all the ways that you have been blessed with kindness by people doing *loving* things for you.

I remember my mom used to get us drinks of water when we were sitting watching television or reading a book. We were the lazy ones while she was busy working in the kitchen, but she seemed so glad to do that for us.

I remember when my sister Euli sewed me a Paddington bear for Christmas one year—stitch by stitch, all by hand. She even made him little clothes.

When my sister Barb was eight years old and I was nine, she made me a set of little wooden boxes that fit inside each other. They had little leather hinges. The wood was from a piece of plywood we had which was old and weathered. The only thing she had to cut the pieces with was just a plain wood handsaw, so the boxes were a bit rough but I so loved them! I could not bring many things to the monastery when I entered but I did bring one of those little boxes.

Good memories are like patchwork quilts, no two remembrances alike and yet when sewn together make a very warm and protective comforter of friendship and love.

Spend time today remembering when you have been blessed by others. This exercise will cheer up even the dreariest day!

Prayer when time is completed:

Jesus,
thank you for friends,
and family,
and even strangers
who have blessed me
in so many ways.
Amen.

Please, God, Help Me!

My most memorable answer to prayer occurred when I was fifteen years old. Having been educated in a Catholic school, I knew what prayer was, and like all the other children in my school, I sometimes said my prayers, and always attended Mass on Sundays.

Unfortunately, my family life was anything but spiritual: My father was an extremely abusive alcoholic, and my mother had severe psychiatric problems.

I remember the day so clearly. I had been through a particularly rough time with my father and was hiding under the house, in the dark, hugging my dog. I was crying on the outside, and screaming on the inside. My prayer was a silent scream from the heart: "Please, God, help me! You have to get me away from here! I just want to be loved!"

I was heartbroken. In my pain and anguish, I repeated my prayer over and over again.

About a week later, I met my new religious education teacher for the year. She quickly sensed that there was something wrong with my home life, so she befriended me and took me under her wing. I was delighted to discover that someone actually cared about me!

However, at the end of the school year she and her family moved to a dairy farm about a two-hour drive north of where I lived, so she could no longer be my teacher.

Thinking that I would never see her again, I was inconsolable. But then God answered my prayer completely. My teacher spoke to my mother, and it was arranged that I could go up to the farm for a weekend! This in itself was a miracle, because I was rarely allowed to go anywhere.

The first visit to that farm and the beautiful family living there was wonderful, and it became the first of many visits. They soon became my safe haven.

My prayer had truly been answered. Someone showed me that I was loved, and God rescued me away from a difficult and painful situation, just as I asked!

It is now thirty-five years later, and I love that family—my God-given family—more than ever. They were God's answer to a teenager's cry for help, and I will never stop thanking Him for supplying my needs so abundantly.

Over the years, I have had many answers to my prayers. Some prayers were heartfelt conversations; some were well-known *recited* prayers; sometimes it was the rosary. It doesn't matter to God: He always hears.

He doesn't always give me what I want, but He's always given me what I *needed*. Some of my prayers are ongoing; I've been praying them for years and haven't received an answer…yet.

But God hears and answers our prayers. I know this without a shadow of a doubt, because He blessed me with a sanctuary and a loving family when I was a sad fifteen-year-old child hugging her dog.

Gail L. Creswell   *Brisbane, Queensland, Australia*

Build yourself a cell in your heart and retire there to pray.

St. Catherine of Siena

Prayer is not asking. Prayer is putting oneself in the hands of God, at his disposition, and listening to his voice in the depths of our hearts.

Blessed Teresa of Calcutta

Angels, Air and Green Lights

One chilly night when I left work, I noticed that my tire was low, so I headed for a nearby convenience store to add some air. As I put air in the tire, I could hear a hissing sound as it escaped. I quickly called the tire company and explained my problem. They were closing in ten minutes but would help me if I got there in time.

Rather than drive on the highway that the dealership was located on, I drove on a residential street that ran parallel to it because the highway did not have a shoulder to pull over onto if the tire did go completely flat.

I started praying for angels, air, and green lights. The first light was red, but I continued my prayer, "God I need angels, air, and green lights."

The next light was red. I was at my second four-way stop sign before I realized that there were no more stoplights on this street.

"God, I need angels and air," I prayed over and over. Several four-way stops later, I turned toward the highway, having overshot the dealership by a block, and was stopped at another red light.

"I need angels and air," I prayed, knowing that there couldn't be much air left in the tire.

As I pulled into the dealership, I was waved into an open bay. I let out a big sigh, thanking God. I looked up and saw the mechanic looking at me in a funny way. He held the air hose in his hand and just stood there.

"Oh, no!" I thought. "The tire is wrecked and he's not going to want to stay and put a new one on."

I got out of the car. "Which tire is it?" he asked.

I pointed to the tire. Not only was it not flat, but it had more air than when I left the convenience store. I guess God knew I wouldn't need the green lights, since He sent the angels with air.

Lynda S. Lowin   *Blunt, South Dakota*

My Walk With God as an Advocate

I am an advocate in Nairobi, Africa. I help my clients to resolve their legal problems either in court or with legal advice. I am also a secular Franciscan, which means that I have made a permanent commitment to live a life of penance, sacrifice and service to God and others in the way of St. Francis of Assisi.

As a result, I am often asked how I can marry my private business practice with my spiritual practice. It is not easy, but I try to hold on by prayer, by punctuating my work with moments of prayer, mostly the Divine Office.

I am not very good at mental prayer; I find a few days of retreat far more helpful in keeping my faith alive and putting me back on the right track of trying to live a Christ-like life.

The most trying moments for me are when a client comes to explain his problem to me but has a definite mindset of just what I should do to solve his problem. Ways that are not always legal or moral. At other times, I simply get a sense that something is not right. At those moments, I send a prayer upwards and ask our Lord Jesus not to let me accept a case which may in any way cause scandal to His Holy Name, even when I am in dire need of money.

This is illustrated by a particular incident which occurred when I was completely penniless and didn't know what to do. I needed money to pay for school fees, not only for my own children, but for others whom I had taken into my care. In addition, the office rent was due, among other needs at home and in the office, such as salaries.

This day a new client came into my office. When I listened to the client's story, I realized that I could not help him because there was nothing that I could legally do to assist, despite seeing the injustice to him. The only way I could receive payment would be to lie to him, so I informed him of my opinion, and he left.

I then asked my Lord to provide for all of my needs at the time, in whatever way He deemed fit.

It was difficult, but our Lord helped me through. He didn't give me money, but He gave me the grace to move on and not dwell on what I had lost.

While I was preparing to attend an eight-day retreat, I was questioned by colleagues as to what effect my absence would have on my practice, at a time when all of us were feeling deeply affected by the terrible inflation in the economy.

I prayed for strength, and attended the retreat anyway. On my return, I found that all was in place, and since then I have never hesitated to attend retreats as often as I can.

Nowadays, I pray through the holy rosary most mornings while I go to work, because it is quiet, and it seems more appropriate when not many people like to engage in talk. I also try to attend daily Mass celebrations. In the evening, we gather together as a family—children and employees—and not only pray, but also read the gospel for the next day. This is in the hope that God in His way will talk to each individual. At times we share the word, and at times we listen with a minute of quiet meditation. I end my day with prayer, and meditation with the help of a meditation book based on the next day's Mass readings.

Jane Wangari Muthoga   *Nairobi, Africa*

Hush your tongue that your heart may speak (which is meditation), and hush your heart that the Spirit may speak (which is contemplation).

St. John of Dalyatha

Thanks, God!

For my entire life I have watched my mother remain constant in her steady stream of thanksgiving to God. Whether it's in giving thanks in Russian after every meal, or a hearty, joyful, "Thanks, God!" after hearing good news, or even just a quiet, humble, "Thank you, God," Mom has been a living example of gratitude in every situation.

As a little girl in post-revolution Russia, my mother experienced what hunger was and watched as her own mother miraculously stretched a bit of bread and milk or a small piece of meat to feed her family of seven. It wasn't much, but there was food on their table, thanks be to God.

My mother worked as a forced laborer in Germany during World War II before she began her life in the United States. She has never taken food for granted, no matter how simple or lavish it might be. After she was married, my parents grew many of our vegetables, and nothing was ever wasted. Her gratitude for food fostered in us a profound respect for the earth's fruitfulness, and her feeling of responsibility to care for it was a way she showed her thanks to God.

Her spontaneous, "Thanks, God!" oftentimes includes a huge smile and hands clasped in awe. Whether it's a grandchild's first tooth or the first tomato of the summer, her thankfulness is genuine and contagious. Her appreciative attitude has rubbed off on my son and me, and I see her influence on us in the way we respond to situations as mundane as not running into traffic, to the sublime, like seeing a flock of great blue herons while on a nature walk. Her prayerful gratitude for the littlest of things has been a wonderful gift she has passed on to future generations.

Weakened and aged, my mother still thanks God daily with a humility that deeply touches those who witness it. When she gets to the top of the stairs, or is fresh from a bath, or has had a chance to just talk to someone for a while, there's always a soft, "Thank You, God" that comes straight from her heart. These whisperings of thanks are the most wondrous of all, and they have a way of bringing the hope she has had in the past—and continues to embrace in the present—to the future.

As I reflect on my mother's prayers of thanks, I see how they have blessed so many areas of her life and touched the lives around her. I praise God in gratitude for her thankfulness and the profound positive influence she has had on the world around her.

Elizabeth Goral-Makowski   *Baltimore, Maryland*

The neglect of prayer proves to my mind, that there is a large amount of practical infidelity. If the people believed that there was a real, existing, personal God, they would ask Him for what they wanted, and they would get what they asked. But they do not ask, because they do not believe or expect to receive.

Brownlow North

The Spirit helps us in our weakness; for we do not know how to pray as we ought, but that very Spirit intercedes with sighs too deep for words. And God, who searches the heart, knows what is the mind of the Spirit, because the Spirit intercedes for the saints according to the will of God.

Romans 8:26-27

Places of Prayer

Several years ago I went with one of our Sisters to visit a member of her family. I was so impressed during the visit because of the little prayer corner that she had set up. She lived alone and this prayer place was in a corner of her living room—making the statement that prayer was definitely an important part of her life. From that moment I thought how inspiring it would be to see how others have set up places of prayer in their homes.

Sr. Patricia Proctor, OSC

In my backyard, I have made the Way of the Cross, where anyone can walk around—stop at one of the fourteen spots and meditate. There are benches to sit and meditate if people want to do that. I say people *because, every so often, I look out back and there are people walking around out there, meditating and praying. We live in a normal house with a slightly larger than city lot—not out in the country, with rolling hills or anything fancy. It is just sort of a personal shrine, I guess.*

Carol Gustafson, Erie, Pennsylvania

This corner shelf was made for me by a next door neighbor for my Blessed Mother statue when I was eighteen. He converted to the Catholic faith on his death bed. I am now sixty-nine and have treasured it for more than fifty years. This man's granddaughter, who is a fervent Catholic, will be receiving this corner shelf upon my death.

Bernadette List, York, Pennsylvania

I live on top of a cliff overlooking the Valley of a Thousand Hills. This is my quiet place.

Leanne Delderfield
Kwa Zulu Natal
South Africa.

One of my favorite places to pray is at a little shrine I have in the corner of our bedroom, with the Blessed Mother, the Holy Family, the Crucifix and two of my favorite saints, St. Theresa and St. Anthony.

Teena Marie Smith
St. Augustine, Florida

Here is picture of my shrine I have set up in my bedroom. The three children were a gift from a priest I worked with and the large statue of Our Lady I acquired at a pilgrimage in Fatima. In October 2003, we had a huge wildfire in our area. When I evacuated I took the statues, my husband's memorabilia and a few necessities. I am so grateful that I did take these with me as I lost my home and everything that was left in it when the fire raged through my neighborhood of Cedar Glen, California. Our Lady has always looked after me and continues to. I am surrounded by angels.

Connie Tate, Twin Peaks, California

This statue of the Sacred Heart was given to me from a woman that received many Catholic items from a family of an elderly lady that died and they didn't want any of them. This statue was broken and the arms were off. I repaired Him and He is very special to me. The glass domed Sacred Heart was my grandparents from Belgium. I am sixty-one so I have no idea how old it might be.

Judie Kolloen, Shelby Township, Michigan

Our Lady of Lourdes statue is something I bought in a garden center. It was all grey so I painted it like this. I found the serving tray in a dollar store, would you believe? The Madonna is a music box that my husband gave me.

Judie Kolloen, Shelby Township, Michigan

This statue of St. Theresa was my mom's. I got the "Our Lady of Smile" figure on the right at the National Shrine of St. Therese of Lisieux a year ago.

Judie Kolloen, Shelby Township, Michigan,

I have many places of prayer, mostly all in my bedroom. I come in to my room and say the rosary with the Catholic TV station every day at 6:00 p.m. When I am making certain novena's to my saint buddies *I have places of honor set for them. This St. Jude statue was my mom's and I was named after him (Judith).*

Judie Kolloen, Shelby Township, Michigan

This is a photo of my prayer place on the window sill by my chair which looks out onto the garden. I have the globe to remind me of the needs of the world, and Mary and Jesus to inspire and lead me to God. The hands with the light inside can mean all sorts of things to me, for example, God holding me in his hands, or me holding the light of Christ. It talks to me of peace and security and of the tender loving care that God gives us, and as a well to offer our needs and praises to the Almighty.

Helen Kennaway, Worcestershire, England

The chair is as old as me and was handed down from a friend. Short, squat and comfortable, it's the perfect prayer chair—a bit worn, but absolutely solid.

Janet Smith, Gainesville, Virginia

I find peace and prayer time with my Heavenly Family watching over me while I sleep and pray.

Christine Esteves, SFO

This is my prayer place, a corner away from the world, but not out of the world. It gives me great peace to be in my prayer closet.

Loretta G. Baker

This my humble prayer area. When I kneel at the bedside, I can see a wooden crucifix on the facing wall. (Not visible is a wooden statue of the Blessed Mother and an icon of her and the baby Jesus on the other two walls around the bed.)

Eva, Bern, Switzerland.

I am a Catholic priest from Malta, the Island of the Apostle St. Paul. Here are some photos of my prayer corner.

Fr. Paul Raggio, Malta

*This little corner of
the world is where I like to
pray. Pax et Bonum!*

June Harris, SFO
Coquitlam
British Columbia
Canada

*This picture was
taken in my apartment in
Gloucester Point, Virginia.
It shows the small backyard
where I had a lot of trouble
getting anything to grow.
Even that fact served me as
a point of contemplation.*

Jackie Farrell
Gloucester Point
Virginia

This picture was taken in a town called Orleans and the water is called Pleasant Bay. It is such a heavenly place. I feel, when close to the shore, that I am in the midst of our Lord.

Margaret Gazzola-Eltablawi, Cape Cod, Massachusetts

My prayer corner.

Walter Harris, Coquitlam, British Columbia, Canada

Saint Lucy to the Rescue

We had a power outage at ten o'clock one December morning and were cold all day. That night my husband and I bundled up when we went to bed, and the next morning we were still without power. I wanted to be in a warm and light place, so we decided to go to Mass. Afterwards, the thought of returning to our cold and dark mobile home was too miserable, so we decided to go to the library and check our e-mail.

Since I needed some joy, I opened Sr. Patricia's Joy Notes before I read my other e-mail. Sr. Patricia had a St. Lucy holy e-card available to us that week, so I decided to send it to my friend Luci. When I clicked on the link that had information about St. Lucy, I discovered that her name meant *light*. This inspired me to pray silently for St. Lucy's intercession in restoring light to our home.

My prayer was very simple, but urgent and heartfelt. I was a little doubtful that it would be answered because the last time we were without power, it wasn't restored for eleven days. I was expecting a similar situation.

We finally went home because we were hungry, and we figured we'd better start eating all the food in the fridge before it spoiled. Lo and behold, when we arrived home, the light in the kitchen was on! It was certainly a miracle to me that our power was restored, and that it happened so quickly after I had prayed about it. My husband said he prayed all during Mass for our power to be turned back on and he believes it was his prayer that was answered.

Feeling thankful and satisfied to have light, heat, and water again, we thanked God the next day at Mass and also later that same week on December 13, the Feast of St. Lucy.

The power went out again at eight o'clock a couple of nights after our first miracle. Once again we resigned ourselves to a cold night and went to sleep all bundled up. I decided that, because of my first success, I would say a quick bedtime prayer to St. Lucy, asking for her intercession in getting our power back on again. In the middle of the night I woke up to the sound of the refrigerator running! That sound usually drives me crazy when I have insomnia, but that night it was a welcome sound of relief. I felt very nicely cozy and warm.

The awe and amazement of my *light* miracles renewed my faith and reignited my prayer life.

Margaret A. Jensen   *Stark City, Missouri*

The one concern of the devil is to keep Christians from praying. He fears nothing from prayerless studies, prayerless work, and prayerless religion. He laughs at our toil, mocks at our wisdom, but trembles when we pray.

Samuel Chadwick

If you can't pray a door open, don't pry it open.

Lyell Rader

Praying without faith is like trying to cut with a blunt knife—much labor expended to little purpose.

Anonymous

Tom's Mother

My brother knew exactly who to call—Tom's mother. She believed in prayer, and I needed a miracle fast! I was in a hospital, barely hanging on to life. My spinal cord had been severed by a bullet, and both of my lungs had collapsed. My prognosis wasn't good.

Tom's mother showed up at my bedside and told me to blink my eyes once for yes and twice for no when she asked me if I wanted to be baptized. I blinked yes. With my family around my bed, she gave me an emergency baptism. Two days later, she sent a priest to invest me in the Brown Scapular of Our Lady of Mt. Carmel. It was a miracle that I survived and was able to accept life in a wheelchair.

A couple of years later, my brother again knew exactly who to call—Tom's mother. She believed in prayer and I again needed a miracle fast! It was just hours before the New Year would be celebrated all over the United States and I was in the emergency room at the local Catholic hospital.

She arrived around eleven o'clock that night. My brother told her that I had been diagnosed with an inoperable mass behind my knee. The doctor who examined my x-rays had decided that the only solution was to amputate my leg. Two other doctors confirmed this and I was quickly admitted to the hospital. Surgery would take place in the morning.

I was in a desperate situation and felt I could not face life without my leg. I tried to accept it, but suicide seemed like a better choice.

Tom's mother brought some relics and holy water with her to the emergency room. With all my friends around my bed, she touched the relics to my tumor and said a prayer to the saint whose relic it was. She asked all those present to say "Amen" when she finished her prayer. Then she put water from Lourdes on my leg.

Later she came up to my room and asked if I would sign a paper that would designate her as my medical power of attorney. I did. She spoke to the doctor and then told me that they would call her before they did anything to me. Meanwhile, she told me to believe in the power of prayer and the saints that she had prayed to—St. Theresa, the Little Flower, Padre Pio, and Our Lady.

Although three doctors had recommended the amputation, the following morning I was instead sent home with no explanation. It was January 1, the feast of Mary, Mother of God, and the beginning of a new year!

To this day, no one has told me why I was sent home with no further follow-up. Sometime later, I once again experienced the power of prayer when the *mass* disappeared.

Melvin Perry   *Jacksonville, Florida*

Who could have given me our Lord, but the Virgin Mary. It was easy to pray to her, repetitious though it may seem. Saying the rosary as I did so often. I felt that I was praying with the people of God, who held on to the physical act of the rosary as to a lifeline.

Dorothy Day

My Jesus, how good it is to love you! Let us be as two friends, neither of whom can ever bear to offend the other.

St. John Vianney

Ten Minute Meditation

A new shop has opened. It's called The Miracle Shop.

It's very nice. You go in and there is a kind and smiling clerk behind the counter. You ask for whatever miracle you want and the clerk looks through the catalog for you. Lo and behold, the very miracle you want is available! Not only that—it is *free* with immediate delivery.

So you order it. I mean after all it doesn't get much better than that, does it?

So you go back the next day and order another miracle. Same thing. Pretty soon you just start expecting those miracles to always be there. On time, free, and with immediate delivery.

Then one day you go in and the regular clerk isn't there anymore. Everything has been changed. It's all self service now—virtual shopping. You sit down and look at the computer screen.

Lots of miracles available but, oh my, now they are not free and the delivery is uncertain and the price is really, really high. Even for the little ones. And worst of all there is no one to talk about it with at all, just an empty room with a cold computer screen.

So you leave and go back to your garden. You find your favorite place and you wait for Jesus to come, because you want to talk to him about the changes with this miracle shop.

It's been a long time since you came to your garden—because for some reason you've just been going to that little miracle shop and not spending any time here at all.

Are there times in your life when you want miracles more than you want a Jesus relationship?

Prayer when time is completed:

Jesus,
thank you for the miracles
I have received in my life,
but most of all
thank you for being there
for me
every day,
always and forever,
whether or not,
I get my miracles.
Amen.

M
E
D
I
T
A
T
I
O
N

Father Tom's Blessing

In 1982, at the age of twenty-eight, I had to face the terrible diagnosis of advanced endometrial cancer. My treatments included aggressive radiation and surgeries. I survived the cancer but was left with deep emotional scars from the experience and the painful reality that I would never conceive a child.

As I wrestled with the many physical side effects of my cure, I prayed for guidance on the question of motherhood. I chose my seat at Mass in front of the statue of the Blessed Virgin Mary, and I prayed to her fervently for an answer to my heart's desire to love and raise a child.

Many years later, in 1992, I completed an adoption home study and began to wait and pray that I would be blessed with a child who needed a home. I prayed that my home would be the best and perfect place for that child. The wait was very long, yet I never ceased my prayers for motherhood.

Then, on May 27, 1998, I was at the funeral Mass of Ruth Missett, my sister's mother-in-law. The priest, Father Tom, was a close friend of the Missett family, and during his eulogy he stated that "there's another story I need to tell you today, but it hasn't come to me yet, so I will just keep talking until it does."

Finally, Father Tom said, "Aha, I've got it." He told a story of being lost in a small ocean side community and stopping to ask for directions. He was directed into a house where he met a woman holding a baby. She said, "Father, please give us your blessing; we are trying to adopt this baby and there have been some legal delays." Father Tom obliged and blessed the baby and young couple, got directions to his destination, and was on his way. Several months later, the couple wrote him in praise and thanksgiving because the legal hurdles had been cleared and the adoption was final.

I was sitting next to my mother at this funeral Mass, and after hearing Father Tom's story, she nudged me and suggested that I seek his blessing. So, indeed, I sought out Father Tom after the Mass and received his blessing for *the right child* to be placed in my family for adoption.

Little did I know then that a little girl had been born and placed in a foster home on the very day that I received Father Tom's blessing. When I found out that her birth was on the very day that Ruth Missett had been received into heaven, I just knew in my heart that this was the child who was meant to join my family. I continued my prayers to the Blessed Virgin Mary, endured some false hopes and legal delays, and finally, nearly a year to the day of Father Tom's blessing, had Kayla Elizabeth Grace placed in my arms.

Now Kayla and I sit at Mass in front of the statue of the Blessed Virgin Mary and pray for her light to shine on us. I speak to Mary as any proud mother would of the wonder and joy this beautiful girl, my special daughter, has brought into my life.

MaryAnn Holak   *Beverly, Massachusetts*

When thou prayest, rather let thy heart be without words than thy words without heart.

John Bunyan

It is necessary to rouse the heart to pray, otherwise it will become quite dry. The attributes of prayer must be: love of God, sincerity, and simplicity.

John of Kronstadt

135

Snapshots

"I'm going to say my prayers.
Anybody want anything?"

Accepting God's Will

In December of 1995, I was fortunate to receive a cadaver kidney transplant after almost four years of dialysis. It had been a long haul, and although each dialysis session wiped me out, I always made it to work the next day. My job as vice president for faith formation was to oversee the campus ministry department in our high school of over a thousand students and a hundred twenty staff members.

After a month or two I found out that my transplanted kidney was only working at about twenty-five percent capacity and that it was gradually getting less productive. In June of 1996, the kidney was removed and I went back on dialysis for three to four hours at least three days a week. It was disheartening, but I was supported by prayer and by being driven to and from dialysis by a large number of co-workers.

My prayer throughout this ordeal was that of Jesus in the garden. "Father, not my will but Yours be done." Although it was easy to say this prayer, and it became my mantra, it was hard to really accept it and make those words my own.

In September of 1996, I was blessed again when I received another cadaver kidney. I spent many days in the hospital before I was finally released, and I worked from home as I recovered from the surgery.

Shortly after arriving home, I was chomping at the bit to get over to the school to do some work. I decided to go on a Saturday when fewer people would be there. With my immune system being very compromised, I was fearful of catching a cold or other virus from someone I might meet.

While in school that day, I accidentally bumped my leg on a desk. I thought nothing of it until a day or two later when my leg was infected and swelling by the hour. I immediately went to the emergency room, and by then I had a high fever and was in excruciating pain. Needless to say, the doctors were concerned for me and for the survival of my newly transplanted kidney.

The infection continued to grow and was moving up my leg. I was quite heavily medicated with morphine and other meds when one of the brothers told me that the doctors were going to give me the medication for just three more hours. After that they were going to have to amputate my leg before the infection got to the main part of my body.

In my state of stupor. I began praying as best as I could. I can remember praying, "O Lord, You cured the sick and healed the sinners in Your time; now please heal me." Then I added my mantra, "Father, not my will but Yours be done."

My family, the school community, and the brothers were alerted to the seriousness of the situation. It was a scary time, but I was hopeful that the Lord would hear our prayers, and He did. Within a short while, the infection stopped its progression and things took a turn for the better. After another two weeks in the hospital, I was able to return home to recuperate. Home-visit nurses came twice a day for almost a year to care for the gaping wound in my leg before it finally healed.

To this day I believe the whole experience was a series of miracles.

God worked in my life through the power of intercessory prayers from people who had complete confidence in the Lord. He also guided the hands of the doctors and provided me with the right medicine to treat and heal my infection. Having a strong Irish sense of humor also helped my recovery—it reminded me to not cry in my beer because that would only water it down!

I am forever grateful to the Lord for His intervention in my life. My difficulties have attuned me to His presence in a heightened way, bringing a deeper meaning to His words, "Come to Me all you who are heavily burdened."

Br. Kevin Brutcher, FSC   *Fridley, Minnesota*

The Perfect Home

We had sold our home, and now, after living with my mom and step-dad for a month, we were finally going to settle on our new home. We had been praying for an affordable house near St. Matthew's Church and school in Baltimore for a long time and had finally found the perfect home. My husband Charles and I had three children and I was eight months pregnant with our fourth. We were eager to get on with our lives.

At the settlement table, we were crushed to learn that the seller had accepted cash from another buyer and the house was no longer ours. It was back to square one.

Again we prayed for a home near St. Matthew's Church and school. I talked to Mary and told her she knew how it felt to need a place to be when she was carrying her baby. "Help me, please!" I cried, and she did.

We found a corner row house just two blocks from the first one we were going to buy and were able to get immediate possession. Then I talked to Mary and God a lot about getting settled into our new home before the baby arrived. Have you ever seen Tevye, the milkman in *Fiddler on the Roof* talk to God in his heart-to-heart conversations? Well, that is me when I pray, and I had one of those heart-to-heart talks with God about the whole situation.

The baby arrived three weeks early. Not too long after that, on a lovely fall afternoon, I put baby Joanne in her carriage and strolled past the house we first wanted to buy. I was astonished to see it was for sale again. A lady was sitting on her porch next door, so I asked her about it. She said the house was always being sold because it had a water leak that no one seemed to be able to fix. When it rained hard, water ran between the outer brick walls and the inside walls and the basement flooded. It would cost a fortune to correct the problem.

For eight years we lived happily in the home that God and Mary led us to. The parish was wonderful, and in thanksgiving, for three years I taught art as a volunteer at the school. I really don't know who enjoyed it more, the kids, the nuns, or me! It was a great adventure.

We feel thoroughly blessed knowing that when God said "No" to the first house that our hearts were set on, He was protecting us. He knew what was best for us, and what we first considered a disappointment was actually God looking out for us. Father knows best; we just have to listen to and obey Him.

Norma W. Coffin   *Melbourne, Florida*

By reading the Scriptures I am so renewed that all nature seems renewed around me and with me. The sky seems to be a pure, a cooler blue, the trees a deeper green. The whole world is charged with the glory of God, and I feel fire and music under my feet.

Thomas Merton

If you invoke the Holy Spirit with a humble and trusting heart, filled with good desires, he will descend with his blessed light and inflaming fire. He will come and penetrate into the very center of your heart, purifying it, changing it, enlightening it, inflaming it, and consuming it with the flames of his holy and divine love.

St. Francis Xavier Cabrini

My Prayer Support

In 2001 I had pain in my right arm and had surgery to remove a tumor. I figured it was done and over, so I went back to my normal life. Shortly after this surgery, I received an email from a woman who was Catholic and wanted to know if I would like to join their online support group, a small group of about ten or eleven women. This invitation came completely out of the blue as I did not at the time know the woman who invited me or anyone else in the group, but it seemed like something I should do. I joined the group with no idea of what a strong support this group would be for me in the days ahead. God was looking out for me.

Three months later I had the same pain as before; it was another tumor. When I went back to the doctor, he scheduled me for surgery, and I actually had two tumors removed. I kept my online prayer group informed of what I was going through. These wonderful women were there for me when I felt awful and continuously sent me their prayers of encouragement.

When I went back for my recheck three months later my arm was sore again, and I had surgery for a third time. After the surgery, the doctor told me he couldn't remove the entire tumor and it was possible that I would have to have my arm amputated. He sent me to a radiation oncologist.

This oncologist was the most wonderful person I've ever met in my life. She asked me how I was dealing with this, and I told her that I had friends in my online prayer group praying for me. She asked me what religion I was, and I told her Catholic. She was too, and she hugged me and told me everything would be okay. She told me the doctor I had seen the first three times had messed up all of my surgeries. She told me I needed to see a surgical oncologist and told me which one to go to.

I went to see him and he was a great man too. He scheduled me for surgery. The women at my church prayed for me, the parish prayer group prayed for me, and of course my online support group prayed for me. This was a wonderful thing for them to do and I thanked them. I felt overwhelmed and cared for by their love and support.

The oncologist got negative margins, and I was so happy. Unfortunately, on my third month checkup, the tumors were back, and he told me he had to send me to an orthopedic oncologist to make sure I wasn't going to lose my arm.

The orthopedic oncologist and surgical oncologist agreed that I should have radiation before I had surgery and sent me back to the radiation oncologist who had been so good to me. I had pre-op radiation, and every time I saw this doctor she hugged me, which really helped.

One month later, before I went in for my last and biggest surgery, the women at my church and our pastor prayed for me and anointed me. My online prayer group also prayed.

I had my last surgery on October 8, 2003. When I went into the operating room, I wasn't sure I'd come out with my right arm, but thankfully I did.

I lost half of my Triceps and half of my Deltoid muscles, but I have my arm.

I had post-op radiation, and that wonderful doctor comforted me when the pain was too much to bear. She told me she was praying for me also.

Fortunately, this October 8 will be five years with no recurrence. I know it is the power of all the prayers.

I still have constant pain and nerve damage, but I have most of the use of my arm. I figure the pain is God's way of letting me know I still have an arm, and I'm alive. There is always someone worse off than me.

Linda M. Cass   *Weymouth, Massachusetts*

Three Thirty Three

When I was a little child, my dear mom would often talk to us about how good God was. She would emphasize how great His love for us in that He died upon the cross to save us. I remember many times my mother explaining that Jesus was thirty-three years old when he died. She would tell us that when we died, no matter how old we were at the time, or what condition we were in, when we entered heaven, we would be at Jesus' perfect age. This made a deep impression on me and I started the habit of always saying, "Thank you, Lord," whenever I saw the number thirty-three in honor of Jesus' great sacrifice.

My oldest son is a police officer, as is his wife, and they live quite a distance away from us in the state of Virginia. I pray for them and for all police officers every day. One night something happened. I had gone to bed as normal and was sleeping peacefully when I heard my son, who was well over a hundred miles away, urgently calling out to me, "Mom! Mom!"

I bolted upright in bed and said "What, Joe?" The voice was so real and sounded in such peril that my heart started pounding so hard I felt it would burst through my chest. I knew that my son was in danger and needed help. I looked at the clock. It said 3:33 in the morning. I started praying for him immediately, repeating the prayer, "Jesus, I trust in Thee, Jesus I trust in Thee," over and over until eventually I felt calm enough to drift back to sleep.

The next morning I continued praying for him as I moved about the house doing all the daily things that needed to be done. I would remember again and again his calling out in the night and my heart would quicken and I would renew my fervency in prayer for him.

Later in the day, my son called. He spoke to his dad for a long time. I had told my husband what had happened during that night but he did not seemed that concerned. Now listening to their conversation, I could feel that he too had become convinced that my experience was real. They talked quite intently for some time and I could see that he was shaken. I anxiously waited for my turn while my husband kept holding up one finger as if to say "Wait one minute, wait one minute." Finally, he handed the phone to me.

It was such a relief to hear my son's voice. He quickly assured me, "Mom, I am all right…but…while I was on duty last night someone I had stopped for a violation shot at me…. He missed."

I cannot describe to you the flood of gratitude and relief that I felt. All I could reply was, "Oh, thank you, Lord!"

He told me more of the incident, what had happened, where he was, and many of the details that he was allowed to share.

Then I asked, "What time did it happen, Joe?"

He replied, "About three thirty in the morning."

I think I expected this answer, even before he opened his mouth, but at his words a huge emotion of thankfulness to God arose within me. Every fiber of my being was drenched with gratitude. Our Lord had truly woken me up to pray for my son's safety, and I will forever thank Him.

As soon as the call was over I went into my bedroom and got down on my knees to thank God, over and over. Even now as I write this, every emotion of fear, gratitude and thankfulness to God comes back. I tell others that we are often given clues of when to think of God and that we should always pray and thank Jesus for dying on the cross for us.

Roberta H. Para Sefchick   *Prompton, Pennsylvania*

Prayer is not overcoming God's reluctance, but laying hold of His willingness.

Martin Luther

Prayer Warrior Hit List

My own personal miracle of prayer is the recovery of my alcoholic son, who drank and lived on the streets for thirty-three years. My wise mama said: "It is your responsibility to love your son; it is God's responsibility to save him."

My prayer journey began as a small child through the Baltimore Catechism, and took off when my aunt, Sr. Augusta, stepped in with some prayerful ideas of her own. She taught me that every breath I breathe is an *act of faith*, every tear I shed is an *act of hope*, and every beat of my hear, is an *act of love*.

I took the words of my aunt, and composed a prayer which I say every night:

May every breath I breathe
be an act of faith.
May every tear I shed
be an act of hope.
May every beat of my heart
be an act of love.

Thus no matter what condition I may be in, because I have made this specific intention to God, I am always in total prayer.

I take it very seriously when someone asks me to pray for him. I try to hold that person constantly in my heart in prayer. The list of people I prayed for grew and grew until one day I decided to make it a mission of mine to get these prayer requests out to other prayerful people. I developed a Prayer Warrior Hit List which I email every Sunday to partners all over the USA. This list has even traveled to Fatima, Lourdes, and the holy places in Rome. In return, I have received some miraculous updates of prayers answered.

My own dear husband is a seven-year survivor of cancer, and he thanks God every day. There have also been claims of miracles from dear souls who are battling cancer and other life threatening diseases, but the biggest and best are the ones who have returned to God through their trials.

Molly N. O'Connell   *Mason, Ohio*

Shake off anxiety. Last year it was something that you smile about now. Tomorrow it's about something that will not be serious if you raise your heart to God and thank Him for whatever comes.

Venerable Fr. Solanus Casey, O.F.M., Cap.

Have no anxiety about anything, but in everything by prayer and supplication with thanksgiving let your requests be made known to God. And the peace of God, which passes all understanding, will keep your hearts and your minds in Christ Jesus.

Philippians 4:6-7

Few souls understand what God would accomplish in them if they were to abandon themselves unreservedly to Him and if they were to allow His grace to mold them accordingly.

St. Ignatius Loyola

Ten Minute Meditation

Practice the gift of inward silence. Take ten minutes to sit quietly

not praying

not thinking

just listening

and absorbing

life about you.

Prayer when time is completed:

Jesus,
how much of life
is going about me
that I never seem to notice.
Thank you for
filling my world
with so much.
Amen.

MEDITATION

Answered Prayer

My husband, Patrick, and I have five sons; we will be married thirty years as of October of 2008. When our oldest son, Jon, was in his early twenties, he and his girlfriend, Jill, decided to move in together. Soon they were expecting a child. We joyfully welcomed their beautiful little girl and invited them to move in with us. We wanted to give the young family a chance to save money for a wedding and a home for themselves.

Mitchell, my youngest child, was nine years old at the time. In my wallet, I still carry a picture of the first time we took our granddaughter Rachel Patricia to Mass. In the picture, I'm holding my four-month-old granddaughter, and standing next to her is my son (her uncle) Mitchell.

My husband and I wanted very much to see Rachel baptized, but her parents were on-again, off-again with the idea. In truth, it had been a quick merging of families and everyone had different goals and ideas of what things needed to be accomplished and how. It's a hard thing to start a family in a home where a family is already established. We managed, however, to come together. Little Rachel was baptized when she was six months old and Jon and Jill hosted a lovely baptismal party.

Let me say that, during all this, I had been bugging God. Really bugging God! I was praying for my granddaughter to be baptized and praying for Jon and Jill to be married in the Church. I offered up my communions at Mass, said the rosary daily, made endless novenas, and fasted from little things and prayed the Divine Mercy chaplet.

Rachel's baptism was a major answer to my prayers. My next move I decided was to make a fifty-four day rosary novena. The novena consists of praying a rosary each day, the joyful mysteries one day, the sorrowful the next day and on the third the glorious mysteries. You do this nine times in a row for a total of twenty-seven days for your intention. You repeat the sets of rosaries again, this time in thanksgiving for answered prayers, even if the prayers haven't yet been answered for a combined total of fifty-four days. So I prayed that, plus more rosaries, chaplets, and novenas. The woman in the Bible who kept pestering the judge had nothing on me!

Eventually Jon and Jill could afford a starter home. They moved when Rachel was nine months old and were married in a civil ceremony. Rachel was two when her baby sister Sara Ireland was born and was soon baptized.

Jon and Jill began going to Mass regularly and developed a fondness for their parish priest. They became involved in the parish and were warmly welcomed. Soon they asked their pastor about being married in the Church.

It turns out that the pastor of their parish has a special devotion to the Divine Mercy. He thought Divine Mercy Sunday would be a great time to welcome them into the Church. On April 3, 2005, we attended Mass with them and after Mass everyone went with Jon and Jill into a side chapel where they were officially married in the Catholic Church.

How is that for answered prayers? "Jesus, I trust in You."

Linda J. McCann   *Philadelphia, Pennsylvania*

Men may spurn our appeals, reject our message, oppose our arguments, despise our persons; but they are helpless against our prayers.

J. Sidlow Baxter

Anything big enough to occupy our minds is big enough to hang a prayer on.

George Macdonald

149

God Helped Papa and Mum

Life is a lesson in our daily lives. A young lady I was when family wrangles chunked into my family and I often asked God why some things happen in our life. At first, I thought God was unfair but with time, I came to know that all that we encounter in life is a lesson.

I knelt in prayer every time I got a chance to offer a special novena for my family, especially my mum and dad, who were ever fighting. Years lapsed without any change, no matter how much I devoted my life in prayer and fasting.

At times, I even lost confidence in praying because having finished my catechism and knowing that we have a God who sees us during our suffering and who hears our prayer, I wondered *who* He was because I prayed and no good was happening?

But I came back to my senses and I said to myself, I should not lose hope! I know my God loves me and will hear my prayers. I asked my little sisters to join me in the mission I was intending to make. And so curious they were to listen to their elder sister.

I told them what I was taught at catechism and what our parents were going through was because we were not praying for them to change. My goodness, what a positive response I got from my younger ones! They were very happy with my mission and Michele, who was by then seven years old, said she was the one to start leading the prayers. Her sister boomed at her as she wondered what kind of prayers she could lead.

Never despise anyone because I believe everyone has some thing he or she can offer the society. The small lady told every one to shut up and she started, "God, help papa and mum to love each other and to stop fighting." She repeated these words several times and we made it a daily routine. Days turned into months, but no years, when for sure joy was on our side.

By now, you may already have guessed what happened. My parents stopped their fighting and they became good Christians. We had much joy! This was enough lesson for me, that all that human beings see as helpless is very possible though prayers.

I am narrating this real story after having wrangles in the family. We had no energy to fight them to stop, but dear readers we had energy to pray for them to change! Today, being a student, I go to college, and I attend Mass to pray for several issues because I have known that prayers work.

Let's all pray until something happens. I love you all who believe in the power of prayers. Be all blessed.

Jackline Mukami Nyagah   *Embu, Kenya*

The hope on which my prayer rests is in the fact that it is he who wants it. And if I go to keep the appointment it is because he is already waiting there for me.

Carlo Carretto

When we are linked by the power of prayer, we, as it were, hold each other's hand as we walk side by side along a slippery path; and thus by the bounteous disposition of charity, it comes about that the harder each one leans on the other, the more firmly we are reverted together in brotherly love.

St. Gregory the Great

The Express Novena

My story is about the power of praying the "Express Novena" that has been made popular by blessed Mother Teresa of Calcutta. For us it had to do with getting a job and also jobs for some other people that I am aware of.

Several years ago, while watching morning Mass on EWTN, I was pleased to hear a homily given by Fr. Andrew Apostoli concerning the topic: "God Answers Prayer." He talked about the ways to pray that God hears and answers. Toward the end, he mentioned how Mother Teresa always prayed the "Express Novena," as she called it. It consists of saying the Memorare nine times in a row.

I was so impressed with Father's homily that at noon, when the Mass was repeated, I turned off the phone and forbade anyone to talk so that I could record it.

Shortly afterwards, my husband, Dave, an engineer, lost his job during a time of downsizing. We were on unemployment compensation, and during that time, he went on one interview after another with no results.

Dave joined a group of unemployed people who met weekly to be of help to each other and pass on information about any jobs that they had heard of. One week, when we had just received our last unemployment check and were down to nothing, so to speak, he decided to go to another meeting.

I thought to myself that I might call up a friend to go out for a sandwich while I still had a few dollars in my pocket. But, before calling her, I needed to get refreshed. I decided to take a bubble bath, thinking that would be soothing to my stress. While in the quiet, soaking in the bath, it seemed to me that this would be a great time to pray. My prayer was the "Express Novena," done with great sincerity and interior grace.

Right after I finished praying, I got a severe back pain and barely made it out of the tub to get dressed. "There goes the sandwich and the visit with my friend," I thought. So at that point, the only thing to do was head to my recliner in the hope that I would feel better.

No sooner did I sit down than the phone rang; it was a friend of ours who asked to speak with my husband. I said he was at the meeting and wouldn't be home for at least another hour and would return the call. Just at that point, in walked Dave early! He spoke to our friend who said that he had a job lead for an engineer in a nearby steel mill. Dave took down the number and called the person. After the call, he went for an immediate interview and was hired on the spot!

I *know* it was the Blessed Mother answering my bathtub prayer!

Later that week I was speaking to a nun friend of mine about this *miracle* and she told her cousin about it. He had been out of work for two years and was very depressed. Before the week was over, Sr. Agnes called to tell me that her cousin was hired for the best job that he had ever had. She thanked me for telling her about the novena.

Another time my son-in-law had just left the Army, (he was a captain) and come home to his wife (our daughter) and two little girls. He was working at MacDonald's and as the first Town Crier in Pittsburgh for the local paper. He couldn't find any work for which he had been educated. I told my daughter to give him the "Express Novena." He wanted her to say it, since he was not a Catholic at that time and didn't know the 'Memorare'. She told him it had to come from him and gave him the prayer. And you know the rest of the story. He still has the job after nearly thirteen years.

Elizabeth L. Chabala   *Bridgeville, Pennsylvania*

Remain steadfast in faith, so that at last we will all reach heaven and there rejoice together.

St. Andrew Kim

A Fast Recovery

In 1999, my youngest sister was hospitalized with back pain. The doctors mistakenly said she had different types of illnesses and treated her for them. Her real illness was not diagnosed, and her condition turned from bad to worse.

It was finally discovered that she had a five centimeter tumor on her vertebra. The doctors prescribed an immediate operation but could not guarantee that she would be able to walk after it. They also said it would be several months before she would be able to stand on her leg. The whole family started to call out for God's mighty interference.

On November 7, 1999, the tumor was removed and she was sent to the intensive care unit where the doctors predicted she would stay for at least two weeks. To our surprise, she was released from ICU the very next day and put in a regular hospital room.

On the fifth day after her surgery, my sister stood on her leg. On the seventh day she started walking, and on the nineteenth day she went back to work at the elementary school where she taught. Nothing is impossible with the all powerful God!

Sr. Ambika Mary, F.I.H.   *Kollam, Kerala, India*

Our true worth does not consist in what human beings think of us. What we really are consists in what God knows us to be.

St. John Berchmans

Finding My Son

It began August 6, 1966. I was pregnant with my firstborn son, out of wedlock. At that time, my mom and dad thought it would be best if I gave him up for adoption. I was so torn when I saw him for the last time when he was baptized. My grief was so bad, but I knew in my heart it had to be done. For years I thought about him, wondering who he looked like and if he were in a good family home. In 1993 and 1994 I tried to locate him but I needed special papers that I did not have.

In 1995, I asked God to help me to get these papers. That year my dad passed away, God rest his soul, and two days after the funeral my mom gave me a big envelope with my name on it. I could not believe my eyes. It contained all the papers I needed to find my son!

I thanked God every day. My one goal in life was to see my son before I died. I sent the papers to the appropriate people and the Toronto registrar. Two weeks later I received a letter from Toronto and I was informed that it would take six months to two years to find him. However, I was told that my son was also looking for me.

I prayed and prayed some more. On March 21, 1996, I received notice that I had registered mail. I did not have time to pick it up at the post office that day but went with my husband and picked it up the next day after work. I opened the big, brown envelope and started to cry and cry.

My husband thought someone in the family had died. But it was good news. It was a letter telling me that they had found my son and that he was looking for me. I could not stop crying and my husband did the same.

My husband and I also had a son together, and when we got home he was there and wondering why I was crying. We told him we had found his brother. Then my son, his girlfriend, my husband, and I were all crying.

My firstborn son had been looking for me for nine years. For me, it was nine months to the day since I had sent in the documentation that I received the news.

I thanked God, I do not know how many times, but I know it was a lot! My family was a bit skeptical about my first meeting with my son, but I was not. I asked God to be with me and He was. I knew that God heard me. The meeting went well.

I found out he was married to a wonderful girl, and that his adoptive father had changed his name to Howard. His wife was pregnant for the first time. I was going to be a grandma. Oh! Was I ever thankful!

God gave me back my son and many blessings. I have two beautiful granddaughters and a wonderful daughter-in-law. The girls are now eleven and eight years old.

Sadly, my world turned upside down once again in 2006. On Sunday, March 5, my son was killed while riding his snowmobile. He hit a tree head on and died instantly. I thought I would die. I had lost him for the second time.

We have prayer group every Monday night, and when I arrived at the church, I ran to the altar to speak to God. I did not blame him for the accident or his death. I wanted to thank Him for giving me ten wonderful years with my son and his family. I see my granddaughters all the time and God has given me the strength to be brave and be with my babies and wonderful daughter-in-law. My heart still yearns for him. We all miss him, but God has given me the strength to carry on and to help his family through the pain. I thank God every day. We will someday be together again in heaven.

Carol Lynn Thibault   *Ottawa, Ontario, Canada*

Leap of Faith

The doctors told us I wouldn't be able to conceive the child we had prayed for and recommended that I take medications and receive treatments that are not allowed by the Church. They said they would make us parents if nature wouldn't. We prayed, turned down medical treatments, and waited. We were thrilled when our first daughter was blessedly born!

Before her birth, I had planned to use a daycare for my baby when I returned to work. Then I saw her face. Those sweet eyes and lashes, those tiny toes needing a nibble, those dimples needing a kiss. I needed to be the one to teach her, cherish her, to be there for her. I just couldn't give my blessing away to a stranger. But surely I couldn't quit my job. We needed my salary to pay the mortgage on our large home. What to do? We were afraid, but feeling desperate. So I prayed. And my husband prayed.

As I prayed, I suddenly heard a voice inside me say, "Take a leap of faith!" It was audible, as though the whole world could hear it. I didn't have to stop to analyze this; I knew exactly what God was telling me. He wanted us to trust Him, for me to quit my job, and for us to downsize our home. He wanted us to count on Him to provide great work for my husband's capable mind and hands. So we did just that.

Right after I quit my job and we sold our house and moved, my husband's position was threatened in a bargaining agreement. We panicked! I mean, what, were we crazy? Quitting my job and moving? I worried and fretted, and worried and fretted some more. Then the day came when we would find out if my husband would have a job or not.

As I drove down the road to meet my husband, I glanced at a license plate of a car in front of me. It read "LPofFTH" (an abbreviated version of leap of faith). I kid you not. The bargaining was secured that afternoon and my husband's job remained intact. To think I had done all of that worrying for nothing. Our leap of faith has been an excellent, hilarious, and loving ride. God is great and we are all blessed. Pray everyone, pray!

Lisa Curran-Crimp   *Kennebunk, Maine*

Contemplative prayer...in my opinion is nothing else than a close sharing between friends; it means taking time frequently to be alone with him who we know loves us.

St. Teresa of Avila

I need Thee, O Lord, for a curb on my tongue; when I am tempted to making carping criticisms and cruel judgements, keep me from speaking barbed words that hurt, and in which I find perverted satisfaction. Keep me from unkind words and from unkind silences. Restrain my judgements. Make my criticisms kind, generous, and constructive. Make me sweet inside, that I may be gentle with other people, gentle in the things I say, kind in what I do. Create in me that warmth of mercy that shall enable others to find Thy strength for their weakness, Thy peace for their strife, Thy joy for their sorrow, Thy love for their hatred, Thy compassion for their weakness. In thine own strong name, I pray. Amen.

Peter Marshall

Ten Minute Meditation

Some miracles come when we don't expect them. We may not even be aware of how badly we needed them until they happen.

Know what that means?

It means that someone very special—
Someone very powerful and loving and kind—
is watching out for you.

Today, be filled with *Joy*
because God is there for you
without you

doing anything at all.

Prayer when time is completed:

Jesus,
I wish I would worry less
and trust more.
Thank you
for helping me
bit by bit
to realize that your love
is holding the world
together,
not me.
Amen.

M
E
D
I
T
A
T
I
O
N

Enough

It seems to me that I've always loved to pray. It gives me a feeling of connection to God and I know that He's always paying attention to me. Each morning I find a quiet place to sit and slowly let go of all the worries and concerns of my busy life until I find that still, peaceful place inside where God dwells. That's where I feel safe and protected. I simply sit and offer God my time.

But one morning in 1977, my morning prayer was anything but calm or quiet. We were living in a rural area of Northern Virginia in the foothills of the Blue Ridge Mountains. Scenically beautiful, it is home to horse farms with acres of rolling pastures and endless ribbons of white board fences.

We had moved from the suburbs of Washington, DC to a restored farmhouse in the country because we felt that the smaller, less frantic environment would be a better place to raise our three children.

Our youngest daughter Cathy had just started kindergarten that year, but twice a week I pulled her from class and drove her to an appointment with a speech pathologist thirty-five miles away.

On this January morning, the scenery was like a postcard. The fields were covered with more than a foot of snow from a recent storm. Melting in the sun during the day and then freezing at night had created a glassy crust on top that mirrored and reflected the weak winter sunlight.

Although the roads had been plowed, they were still covered with snow. There were stretches where roadside banks of ice-covered snow piled up—sometimes two feet high—bordering the pavement. And in places where the narrow country road cut through hills, the top layer of snow melted and then froze overnight creating a surface like an ice skating rink.

I had successfully negotiated the drive to school and picked up my daughter. Now we were re-tracing the route to connect to the interstate.

As we started a gentle incline into a curve between hills, the heavy station wagon became a wild beast. Rocketing back and forth from one side of the roadway to the other, we were slamming into a bank of ice on the right—pow!—then catapulting across the roadway into the snowbank on the left—pow! Frantically, I twisted the steering wheel to counteract the skid, as we ricocheted left and right from one snowbank to the other, until we finally emerged from between the hills. Suddenly, the vehicle spun a hundred and eighty degrees and, like a bullet, shot sideways toward the edge of the roadway above a sheer twenty-five foot drop, where there was no bank of snow to stop our fall.

I threw up a desperate mental prayer: "Oh, Lord. Don't let us be hurt too bad!" Instantly the car stopped, without a shudder, as if a giant hand had rested on the roof and said, "Enough." We were exactly in the lane, although headed back toward the school.

I was awestruck and grateful. We were shaken up but not hurt. Cathy and I shared a grateful prayer to Jesus who saved us. Cathy's faith at five years old was pure and inspiring to me. She had absolute and automatic faith in Jesus' care for us. But I believe that morning's intervention, in what would have been certain disaster, was a miracle. If we had skidded another two feet, if we had encountered another car during the wild swings from side to side, the outcome would have been horrible.

The experience became a touchstone for me in moments of doubt. It became the foundation for greater faith and dependence on our Lord, whose tender care is always with us. He answers our prayers.

Janet L. Smith   *Gainesville, Virginia*

I Have Forgiven Her

My friend Jane was suffering from breast cancer. She had already been through a mastectomy and also through a programme of chemotherapy and radiotherapy. She was told that her returning cancer was of a particularly aggressive type. Although she was not a Catholic, Jane believed in God. She had two young sons, aged four and six, whom she desperately wanted to see grow into manhood.

In addition to her cancer, Jane was suffering from a greater pain. Two years earlier she had agreed to have an abortion. Her pregnancy had been quite advanced when she was told during a routine ante-natal visit that her unborn son would be born with Down's Syndrome. At the time, her life was already riddled with stress—she was trying to run a business, raise two young sons and cope with an unsupportive husband.

When Jane told her husband about their unborn baby, he insisted that she have an abortion, even though her child was beyond the legal term for one. Faced with the prospect of a baby who would need high levels of help and support, and knowing that she would not receive any help from her husband, Jane reluctantly terminated her pregnancy. Soon afterwards, she arranged a burial service for her child, whom she named Jack, and tried to get on with her life.

It was then that Jane's cancer returned. During her treatment and therapy, her thoughts turned to her unborn child and the decision she had taken to terminate his life. She saw her cancer as a punishment from God for what she had done. A visit to a freelance *faith healer* confirmed this view—he told her that she had committed an evil deed and that God was indeed punishing her.

Jane was devastated and sank even deeper into a sense of guilt and remorse. As she continued her treatment (and also tried to run her business and be a good mother to her sons) her sense of guilt escalated and she became desperately unhappy.

As a way of helping my friend, I asked a priest I knew if he would talk to her about her abortion and assure her that despite what she had done, God still loved her very much and was waiting to forgive her. We arranged a day and time for her to visit the priest. On the way to pick her up, I popped into the Catholic Cathedral Church in the centre of Birmingham (St. Chad's).

The church was empty but I sensed God's presence. I didn't have much time, so as fervently and devoutly as I could, I closed my eyes, joined my hands in prayer, and asked God if He would please forgive Jane for the abortion she had agreed to, and take away her guilt.

It was then that I heard God's voice clearly say, "I have forgiven her." At first I was shocked. Could it be that I had wanted God's forgiveness for Jane so badly that I had imagined His response? No, I knew it was God Himself speaking to me, and I know what I heard that day. I clearly heard God telling me that He had forgiven Jane.

I took her to see the priest in his beautiful spiritual retreat of Chez Nous (House of Prayer) in the heart of the Worcestershire countryside. He spoke with Jane at length, and prayed with her. Then he blessed her and told her that her unborn child, Jack, was now an angel and she must pray to him, not for him. She was at last able to receive God's forgiveness through His servant, Fr. Denis.

Jane said she felt a real sense of release and freedom after talking with and being blessed and prayed for by Fr. Denis. She truly experienced God's love and felt liberated. That day, God released her from her heartache and took away her guilt. However, He did not take away her cancer. Three months later she died in the local hospice, the day before her youngest son's fifth birthday. May she rest in peace with Jack.

Patricia M. Greene   *Birmingham, West Midlands, England*

Proof of God's Love

Our first daughter, Abigail, was born handicapped because of a bad delivery. It was at this time that I came to know Jesus and to pray every day for healing and guidance. I would pray over and over, "Oh God, be merciful to me a sinner." This simple prayer strengthened and carried me through the many difficult days of caring for her. Abigail died when she was almost two.

Nine months later, I gave birth to another little girl whom I named Anne. Besides this mercy prayer, I had prayed to St. Anne every night, and promised her that if everything were well, I would go to the shrine of St. Anne in Quebec to thank her for this gift of new life. Little Anne was born with perfect health. As I had promised, we went to St. Anne's shrine in thanksgiving for her and again after the birth of our son, Thomas.

When Thomas was eighteen months old, I accidentally backed up our car over him. I called out to Anne, who was seven at the time, and asked her if I had hit something. She told me I had hit Thomas!

I immediately drove forward, and there he was. He had just eaten a banana and the banana was everywhere. I pleaded with God to spare his life because he wasn't moving. I carried him upstairs to call 911.

All I could pray during these desperate moments was "Oh my God have mercy on us." I said this over and over again.

I carefully wiped the banana off his face and then suddenly he opened his eyes. He was all right.

I remind myself of this event whenever I lack faith, as proof of God's love for us. I haven't told this story to many people because it is so incredible to me.

Patricia W. Coleman   *Winnetka, Illinios*

"Next time you're praying while you drive, I think you can skip bowing your head and closing your eyes."

God's Karate Class

With my youngest child in his teens and almost ready for college and my daughter's wedding coming up, I knew I needed to end my years of volunteer work and do something that would bring in a salary.

Catholic Charities hired me to do home and hospital care for people who needed help. They trained me well and I loved my work. After a few years though, the Visiting Nurses of New York asked me to work for them. It was at a time when Catholic Charities was letting go of some services, so I accepted their offer.

Working for Visiting Nurses was very fulfilling also, and I loved each patient in a special way. However, caring for some of them was physically or emotionally exhausting, and sometimes both. I took my work to heart, and felt the pain of those I cared for. What upset me the most was when their insurance plan would not cover them anymore and they still needed help. I knew I was not supposed to take their suffering personally, but I did. I wasn't able to disconnect from their pain.

I started feeling depressed, and my work was becoming very heavy for me. My ten-year battle with depression had begun. Living in that dark, deep hole felt like the pits of hell. I couldn't imagine hell being any worse. Medication, therapy, and working didn't help much.

I prayed morning, noon, and night but it seemed like God was absent from my life. I was convinced that He couldn't take this pathetic excuse for a human being. I still called out to Him though, begging Him to "please, please, take me home if you aren't going to intervene and make me better." I wanted to die so badly, but didn't want to kill myself because of the pain it would cause my family.

After a few years, a new doctor prescribed a different medication and I was finally physically able to go to daily Mass again. This helped make my pain more bearable, but it was far from gone. It brought me to a point where I didn't feel like I wanted to die, but I certainly wasn't alive either. With so many people praying for me, I thought I should have been all better by then. I wanted my life back. "Jesus, help me!" I cried.

One morning, after another Mass of desperate pleading with God, I went home a different way. I happened to see an exciting looking advertisement in a storefront window and decided to go in and check it out. The young man behind a desk welcomed me to try out his three-month karate special.

"Karate? You've got to be kidding. I'm forty-five years old." I thought.

I watched a class that was in progress and noticed that there were people of all different ages in it. There were men, women and young adults in the class.

"I can do that," I thought to myself. I was a tomboy growing up, and still had it in me to run, jump, and do physical activities. And my new medication had given me some extra energy; enough to get more house work done. I didn't need to sleep and hide during the day as much.

I signed up for the three-month trial classes and soon discovered that the thirty-minute workouts were very strenuous. We did push-ups, sit-ups, jumping jacks and much more. I felt like I was in boot camp and was tempted to quit. It was way too hard. But, since I had already paid for the three months in advance, I felt compelled to make an effort. I talked to God more in that class than I did in my kitchen at home!

Learning the techniques of karate and practicing them on people took a lot of discipline. I learned self control, respect, meditation, and developed a total awareness of my surroundings in and out of class. I learned to stop short of contact on strikes and kicks when I practiced with another person, and had to make decisions as if it was a real attack against me. At times this practice felt very real.

As I climbed to the highest rank of belt order, control skills became more difficult. There were times of accidental contact that caused me or another person injury. Sometimes I had to resist the urge to hurt someone who hurt me, and I found that I needed to pray harder to maintain self control in those circumstances. By exercising this control, I felt confident that if I encountered someone who wanted to harm me or someone I knew in my personal life, I wouldn't lose control and hurt, maim, or even kill them without thinking.

Before every class we meditated for ten minutes. If someone didn't have a "higher power", they could focus on nature, the ocean, or whatever helped them to be one with their souls. Centering ourselves helped the class to develop a bond.

By the time my three-month trial period was up, I was hooked on karate. I signed up not only for the classes, but for another hour of intense training after the classes. By my sixth month of karate, my depression was gone and I was able to stop taking the antidepressants. I lost over thirty-eight pounds, and gained a lot of muscle.

Learning how to meditate was the most important technique I mastered, and it was during those solemn ten minutes that I glorified and thanked God over and over for saving me from a fate worse than death in an unconventional way. The breathing techniques I learned also helped save me spiritually, mentally, and physically, and continue to do so any time life becomes a challenge. Whoever thought one could meet God in a karate class?

Connie Andretta   *Denver, North Carolina*

Let us go and wake up the universe...and sing his praises.

Blessed Mariam Baouardy

When the soul seeks God, and seeks him alone, when it tends towards him with all it energies, when it clings to no created thing, God fills it with joy.

Blessed Columbia Marmion

God Sent an Angel

I was twenty-one years old, married, and teaching. Soon I was pregnant, and within the next six years, I had given birth to five baby boys. That was the end of teaching for me!

After my second child, then my fourth, and finally two years after my fifth son was born, I went into deep depressions and underwent many shock therapy treatments and required some hospitalizations. My dear husband, along with other family members, carried the load and prayed for me.

When I was young, I had often been taught to fear God and His eternal punishment. As I was battling my debilitating depression, I was almost paralyzed by my fear of God, but I prayed anyways. I begged Him to heal me and to set me free from my illness. My parents, who were very faith-filled, also prayed deeply for me. Then a miracle happened.

In 1972, a newly ordained priest who was assigned to our parish heard my confession. He was very kind and offered to come to my home and help me. He taught me all about the love that Jesus has for me, and encouraged me not to be afraid of Him. This priest was an angel.

As I learned about God's love, I felt so comforted that I slowly let go of my fear and depression. Gradually I began to hope and was finally able to surrender and completely trust our Lord. As I was healing spiritually, I saw a psychiatrist who prescribed an antidepressant medication that I continue to take to this day.

For the past fifteen years I have felt better than ever before. With the continued guidance of my spiritual director, plus the right medication, I was released from my deep suffering and now embrace a healthy freedom in God's tender and everlasting love and care.

Every day I pray to Jesus from my heart and I know He is near and wants only the best for me. I praise Him for blessing me with a loyal, hardworking husband who stood by me throughout the years, and for sending the angel of a priest—who still comes to my home—to lead me from despair to trust.

Noreen M. Mater   *Dunnville, Ontario, Canada*

Learn to pray to God in such a way that you are trusting him as your physician to do what he knows is best. Confess to him the disease, and let him choose the remedy.

St Augustine

Prayer can no more be divorced from worship than life can be divorced from breathing. If we follow his impulse, the Holy Spirit will always lead us to pray. When we allow him to work freely, he will always bring the Church to extensive praying. Conversely, when the Spirit is absent, we will find excuses not to pray. We may say, "God understands. He knows I love him. But I'm tired... I'm so busy... It's just not convenient now..." When the Spirit is absent, our excuses always seem right, but in the presence of the Spirit our excuses fade away.

R. T. Kendall

The Candy Factory

Growing up in a family of eight children with only one income, I was accustomed to living a simple life. We had no car and my father had to use someone else's boat to get to work. We children wore hand-me-down clothes—especially me, being the seventh child. But we never considered ourselves poor, and we never went hungry, having fresh food from our garden, and deer meat during hunting season.

Nonetheless, I dreamt of where, when I grew up, I most wanted to work so that I could enjoy a life of luxury such as my family could never afford. I remember often praying on Sundays and during daily Mass for a particular place where I wanted to work when I was old enough.

As my childhood years went by I continued with schooling, outdoor sports during the summer, indoor sports during the winter, helping my mom with chores, fighting with my siblings, attending Sunday family picnics, and visiting relatives across the lake—going by boat during the summer, and walking on the ice during the winter.

All this time I worked hard outside of school. By the age of ten, I was continuing the family tradition of selling Christmas cards door-to-door as a means of earning some extra family money for Christmas. As a teenager I did babysitting and waitress work. After graduating from high school in the early 1960s, I followed my older sister to the big city and completed a business course.

While I was job hunting, my applications to doctors' and lawyers' offices were turned down due to my lack of experience so I lowered my expectations and eventually got a job in the accounting department of a candy manufacturer.

Several years after leaving that first job I suddenly remembered something I had been praying for when I was a child: The job of my dreams and prayers had been to work in a candy factory! In my very first job as an adult, God had answered my prayers from childhood.

The sad part is that I didn't remember this at the time. But the impact of the realization, when it finally came back to me, has stayed with me ever since.

Yes, God does answer our prayers—sometimes without our realizing it. And He continues to do so in my life, more than fifty years after that first prayer for employment. I am now in my 60s, and I have two children and two grandchildren. I am so very blessed with all that really counts in life. I certainly had humble beginnings, and I experienced many rough spots throughout my life. But I have finally realized that when I put all my troubles in the hands of God, life is so much easier and wonderful. God Bless!

Helena Cody   *Lunenburg, Nova Scotia, Canada*

Let this be thy whole endeavour, this thy prayer, this thy desire,--that thou mayest be stripped of all selfishness, and with entire simplicity follow Jesus only.

Thomas a Kempis

If you are having difficulty loving or relating to an individual, take him to God. Bother the Lord with this person. Don't you be bothered with him - leave him at the throne.

Charles (Chuck) Swindoll

Ten Minute Meditation

One of the most exciting things about being a Christian is that you don't have to be *in charge* for wonderful things to happen.

In fact, with Christians, the more we surrender to *not* being in charge—the more wonderful things happen.

Today, imagine that you have an old country style mailbox along the side of the road. It's an old metal box with a lid that pulls down and a little red flag you push up when you've put a letter inside and you want the mailperson to take your letter.

As you walk up to that mailbox, do so with the expectation that God is opening up a new door for you.

Are you open to whatever that might be?

Prayer when time is completed:

Jesus,
help me to realize
that my walk with you
is meant to be new
and challenging
and exciting.
Help me to say yes
even when the new thing
in my life may not seem
so wonderful at first.
Amen.

M
E
D
I
T
A
T
I
O
N

Mary's Intervention

When I was twelve years old, my dad inherited a granary, and my mom began helping him run it. In the evenings, my siblings and I were left in the care of a Mexican-American Catholic woman. Being raised in a fundamentalist Christian faith, I was quite curious because I had heard all these fantastic stories about their *false* faith.

Our babysitter would answer all my questions, and there were many, because I was perplexed by her tales of miracles and other unexplainable things. I was especially enthralled with the mysterious visitations by the Virgin Mary to people and the apparitions and visions of her. I found myself really questioning if these things could possibly occur.

One night, in my childish faith, I asked God to please show me, in my sleep, a vision of Mary, and that's exactly what happened! I saw her standing, with hands open and palms out at her sides, as if in welcome. She was dressed all in white, with a white veil. She didn't speak a word.

I awoke with a certainty that the Catholic faith was real, and that Catholic was what I needed to be. Of course, I also knew it would have to wait, because my parents would never allow me to attend a Catholic church or to become Catholic.

As I entered young adulthood, I forgot this promise to myself, and I even forgot the dream. By my mid thirties, I already had two sons through failed marriages and was struggling to stabilize my life after a series of faulty choices.

Fortunately, while attending college, I had a course in Spanish with a Catholic professor. I became friends with him and two other students. Once more I asked questions about Catholicism. One of my friends gave me a book that gave direct answers to fundamentalist questions: why infant baptism, why prayer to the saints, and so on. As part of my studies I spent six weeks in Mexico, during which time we toured the Shrine of Our Lady of Guadalupe, where I witnessed many pilgrim Catholics seeking intersession through Mary in answer to various prayer needs in their lives. Some even crawled on their knees to the shrine, across the stone plaza. All of this made a strong impression on me.

A few months later, after graduating, I became pregnant with my third son. I began attending an RCIA class at a local church just to further my understanding of Catholicism. At that time I had not yet made up my mind to become Catholic.

At about three months into my pregnancy, I began to bleed and had to rush to the hospital, where it was discovered I was hemorrhaging and in danger of miscarriage. I was confined to bed at the hospital for several days to see if that would stop the hemorrhaging and prevent loss of the baby.

I had been struggling within myself over feelings of panic and despair concerning the pregnancy, wishing I hadn't become pregnant and sometimes wanting to pray I would lose the baby because of the circumstances surrounding its conception and the problems this would add to my life. But on the verge of actually losing the baby, I found myself wanting nothing more than to have that baby. My mind was in such turmoil, though, that I couldn't pray coherently.

One of my close college friends asked if she could bring over a priest and pray for me, and I eagerly accepted. They brought rosaries and prayed a rosary over the baby and me. I was so deeply moved and impressed that I asked if she would please give me the rosary so I could pray it as well. For me, prayer to Mary or any other saint was a huge hurdle to my acceptance and understanding of the Catholic faith. I must have prayed a hundred rosaries or more after they left, before I fell into a deep, restful sleep.

The hemorrhaging not only stopped, but the section of the placenta (which had begun to separate from the wall of the uterus) healed completely, and after a few weeks of bed rest, my pregnancy continued without incident and without limitation to my activities. I gave birth to a 9 lb. 8 oz. healthy boy at full term. All this was thanks to Mary's intervention, and I then proceeded to come fully into the Church.

June B. Cornish   *Quinlan, Texas*

God's Calling Plan

My daughter was upset because her husband, Mike, is deployed in Iraq and they rarely got to speak to each other. When they did, the connection was very bad. So, one day when I was on my way to morning Mass at St. Patrick's, I told my daughter not to worry because I was sending my guardian angel to whisper in Mike's ear to call her, and I was going to pray for the phone connection to be good.

When I got out of Mass, I checked my voice-mail and there was my daughter's happy voice saying, "Mom, he called! We talked and I told him you sent your guardian angel over to Iraq to whisper in his ear to call me."

Well, Mike couldn't believe it, so I continued doing it. Each time after I prayed, I would call my daughter and tell her I sent my angel to Iraq, and sure enough Mike would call and the connection would be good. We were so excited that I started telling everyone about it and my whole family got involved.

One day, my daughter and I both sent our angels over and he called twice, which is a miracle in itself since he can usually call only once a week. Mike was getting a kick out of what was happening.

John Paul the Great once said, "Solidarity and prayer wins wars." We started thinking that if we sent our guardian angels to whisper in the ears of the enemy, telling them to stop the war and love as Jesus does, there could be a huge conversion of hearts!

Through this experience, I learned to never underestimate what our guardian angels can do for us. Thank God we have such a gift as an angel to watch over and protect us. Please pray for our troops!

Judi A. Eichhorn   *Columbus, Ohio*

A Special Sign

In January of 1995, one of my three sons, Don, age twenty-seven, was killed in a snowmobile accident. Compounding this tragedy was the fact that he had not always gone to Mass on Sundays.

I was just devastated and could not think of anything else, even long after the funeral. I had a thirty-six-inch statue of Our Lady of Fatima, and I talked and cried to Mary every day.

In April of that year, I wrote a note to Mary, asking: "You remember when Jesus was preaching in the temple, and you thought he was lost? You searched until you found him, and you were so upset. So you should know how upset I am. I just have to know that my son is going to be with Jesus some day."

I asked Mary to intercede for me to Jesus, and give me a sign that somehow Don was saved. The sign was to have someone give me a rose (or several), for some unknown reason. Then I too could be at rest. I sealed the note, locked it in a safe, and told my family that I had asked for a special sign from Jesus, and if it ever happened, then I would get my note out and show them.

For months, there was no sign. But on August 25, which would have been Don's 28th birthday, a florist called and asked if I was going to be home to receive a delivery. It seemed like the strangest thing, because I never received flowers on Don's birthday.

The florist later delivered one rose and two blue carnations! I figured the rose was from Jesus, because that is what I asked for, and the two carnations were from the Blessed Mother, so I would know it was her doing. Never before had I felt so excited, and I have been at peace ever since that day.

It turns out that the person who sent the flowers was formerly a nearby neighbor, and her birthday was one day before Don's. I later asked her why she sent the flowers, and she said she really couldn't say why; it just seemed the thing to do at the time. I told her my story and how I figured Jesus used her to bring this all together. Even if I am all wrong in my thinking, it worked for me at that time in my life, and I didn't have to spend the rest of my life worrying.

I have come a long way in my faith since then. If this were to happen today, I would simply trust Jesus to take care of my son. Looking back, I feel a bit foolish that my faith was so weak. But I thank Jesus for the peace of mind he gave me at the time.

Marion M. Klokow   *Helenville, Wisconsin*

Give me one hundred preachers who fear nothing but sin, and desire nothing but God, and I care not a straw whether they be clergymen or laymen; such alone will shake the gates of hell and set up the kingdom of heaven on earth... God does nothing but in answer to prayer.

John Wesley

Sometimes it seems that we have been praying a long time and still do not have what we ask. But we should not be sad. I am sure that what our Lord means is that either we should wait for a better time, or more grace, or a better gift.

Julian of Norwich

The Parking Spot

When I read "Seek and you shall find. Ask and you shall receive. Knock and it will be open for you," I trust God at His word.

I have always prayed in my car. They are usually old, rehabbed, even totaled cars, which many people are surprised are still running. Sometimes I have to pray for the car to start. Most of the time, though, I pray for an open parking spot, either silently or aloud.

I can't recall when I began this practice, but I have been doing it for several years. It began while I was working with the elderly. I almost always pray for the Lord to find the parking place for me in shopping malls, at Wal-Mart, and downtown. My prayer is very simple: "Lord, where would you like me to park?"

A dear friend of mine, who is Jewish, commented that she had never seen anyone get better and closer parking places than I do. She had never heard anyone ask the Lord for a parking place before, either.

After suffering a broken arm, I received a temporary handicap tag for my car. One night when my friend and I were driving, I did not pray for a parking place; I simply looked for one. After I found one, my friend began to laugh, because it was the farthest from the door we had ever parked since she has known me, even with the handicap option!

I immediately replied, "I did not ask the Lord where He wanted us to park tonight."

The locations of our parking places are actually significant because my friend has arthritis in her back, and she is always in pain and at times can barely walk. I tell her that the fact that we almost always find a parking spot near the door is the Lord's favor to her and shows His compassion for her.

I had not realized that this is a special favor from the Lord to me as well, because I simply pray this prayer whenever I park. My friend had to point it out to me. I was humbled to realize the Lord was listening to such a mundane prayer when He has so many, much more important things to do.

Lola J. Wink   *Spokane, Washington*

The great people of the earth today are the people who pray. I do not mean those who talk about prayer, nor those who say they believe in prayer, nor yet those who can explain about prayer; but I mean these people who take time and pray. They have not time. It must be taken from something else. This something else is important, very important, and pressing, but still less important and less pressing than prayer. There are people that put prayer first, and group the other items in life's schedule around and after prayer.

S. D. Gordon

Even if we speak with a low voice, even if we whisper without opening the lips, even if we call to him only from the depths of the heart, our unspoken word always reaches God and God always hears.

St. Clement of Alexandria

Ten Minute Meditation

Expand your world. We all know people in particular who need miracles of healing and reconciliation. We know family members who need help financially or in other ways but I believe that God wants us to reach out even beyond the circle of contacts we have.

With prayer we can reach out across the world to help people in need. I remember in my own life an experience in which I felt that someone was praying for me—someone whom I did not know. It was a very dark time in my life and I was at the lowest of lows and somehow God was able to break through my darkness to bring me hope.

I believe that break through came through prayer. Be a ray of hope to someone today. You will be amazed how your world will expand in love and joy and good things. No act of kindness ever goes unrewarded.

Prayer when time is completed:

Jesus,
I ask you to bless
with love, joy
and miracles
someone who is most in need
of your love today.
Amen.

M
E
D
I
T
A
T
I
O
N

Saint Anne's Oil

In the mid 1940s my six-year-old brother was diagnosed with Perthes Disease of the hip. My parents took him to some doctors who put him in a cast from mid chest, down one leg and halfway down the other. He was confined to a hospital bed for about three months. Since this procedure didn't seem to be helping him, it was suggested we take him to a specialist, and there was only one of those in our town.

The specialist told us that my brother might never completely recover from this disease. He was put into a full leg brace on the side of the leg that was affected, and he wore a cork shoe on the other foot. We were also told that he would always have a limp. He was in the brace for two years.

My parents had non-Catholic friends who made a pilgrimage to St. Anne's in Quebec, Canada, and brought back some precious St. Anne's Oil. My mother and brother would rub the oil on his hip every night and say special prayers to St. Anne. Also during this time, my mother was in constant touch with the director of St. Anne's, and they continued to send us the oil.

Two years later, during a checkup at the specialist's, x-rays showed a complete absence of disease in my brother's hip, and he didn't even have a limp anymore! We had to get verification from other doctors, which was given.

We were told it was a miracle, and that whenever we got a chance, we should bring his brace up to St. Anne's and it would be hung on a center column where other crutches are hung.

It wasn't until 1957 that we were able to visit St. Anne's and bring my brother's brace and cork shoe. We thought they might not be placed on the column until after our short stay of just a few days, but on our second day, when we were saying prayers and walking around the column, we spotted his brace and cork shoe.

This had an indescribably profound effect on me. In fact, I started shaking and couldn't stop. How awesome—the wonder of God's love for us!

When my brother became a young man, he served in the US Air Force, and is currently in very good health.

Thank you, heavenly Father, for allowing us to have the saints to intercede for us.

Bernadette M. List   *York, Pennsylvania*

If we truly love people, we will desire for them far more than it is within our power to give them, and this will lead us to prayer: Intercession is a way of loving others.

Richard J. Foster

Give me, good Lord, a longing to be with you.

St. Thomas More

There is a general kind of praying which fails for lack of precision. It is as if a regiment of soldiers should all fire off their guns anywhere. Possibly somebody would be killed, but the majority of the enemy would be missed.

Charles Haddon Spurgeon

God's Travel Plan

One of my most beloved family members, Aunt Ethel, was stricken with polio as a teenager and had to endure long hospitalizations and procedures. She was left partially paralyzed and needing a long brace on one leg for the rest of her life. She was the most beautiful and graceful woman I knew.

Aunt Ethel converted to Catholicism late in life and loved Jesus and our Blessed Mother dearly. When her sister was dying, my aunt came from her home in Connecticut for visits and attended daily Mass. One rainy day I drove her the short blocks to the church for Mass, and that was the beginning of my own conversion to Catholicism.

After a battle with cancer, Aunt Ethel died. I was informed at seven thirty on a Thursday night that the funeral would be at eleven o'clock the following morning. How could I get from Orlando, Florida, to north of Madison, Wisconsin, in just a few short hours? How would this be possible?

I felt compelled to at least try to see what was available as far as flights and rental cars go. I started up the computer and checked all the airlines I could think of. Nothing would work out. The arrival times would get me there too late, and no rental cars were available. It was getting late and I had to go to work in the morning, so I woefully thought that it wasn't meant to be and that I would have to accept it.

My husband and I went to bed and I lay there praying and crying and feeling very frustrated. My husband got out of bed saying he was going to try something else and turned the computer back on. Then I suddenly recalled a small airport not far from Orlando where an out of town guest had once landed. So we pulled up that airport on the internet and boom, an airline there had a direct flight to where I needed to go! Plus, the cost was only sixty-nine dollars each way compared to all the other flights that were six to eight hundred dollars because of the short notice. It would leave at eight the next morning and arrive at nine fifty, giving me an hour and ten minutes to deplane, rent a car, and get to the church on time.

I found out that the drive time to the church from the airport was one hour and twenty-two minutes, twelve minutes too long. I told myself that if the wind was just right, maybe the plane would arrive a few minutes early. And maybe there wouldn't be much traffic at that time on a Friday morning. I could feel my spirits lift. God is a God of miracles!

As I started to book my flight, my husband suggested that I ask my mother to go with me. I knew full well that although she loved Aunt Ethel too, she abhors funerals and would not want to go. Oh well, I thought, what did I have to lose by calling? With only five minutes left to book the ticket before I'd have to start the process over, I decided that, okay, I would call Mom. It didn't take long to convince her to go.

Mom and I were up and packed at four o'clock the next morning. We drove effortlessly to the Sanford airport and arrived there by six o'clock when they were just opening. We breezed through security, got coffee, reminisced about the life of my Aunt Ethel, and studied the driving directions. As the plane was boarding, we briefed our stewardess on our predicament and asked if we could sit in the first row of seats if they weren't occupied. She graciously allowed us that luxury.

After we landed we hit the deck and walked quickly toward the rental car stand. Ughh. Ohhh. The sign said, "Be back in five minutes." Didn't these people know we were in a rush here? "Oh, thank you Jesus," I said as the attendants returned to the stand. They must have been on the last sixty seconds of their five-minute break. Thank you, thank you.

We waited impatiently as the clerk generated the computer paper contract. Then we hurriedly signed our life away as we looked at the local map that would get us out of there. During all this, Mom and I alternated our restroom break so as not to slow the clerk down. At last, we were ready to maneuver ourselves out to the parking lot, find the vehicle, and drive through the exit. We were finally on the road, headed for the church.

"Oops," I thought as I drove. I hoped that the first turn was correct. "I better keep driving. Okay it was." I breathed a sigh of relief and we continued on our way. I drove slightly over the speed limit and prayed to be invisible to all law enforcement that might have been around. Up we went over a hill, down through a small valley, and, in light traffic, we finally drove around the last corner into town. Up another hill we went, and around the curve to the *empty* church parking lot. It was eleven fifty-nine. "What do we do now?" we wondered. "Call the church. Okay, now where is the cell phone? Here it is. Oohh…" There was no cell phone service available.

Long story short, I had been given the wrong information and the funeral was actually scheduled for the next day! We weren't upset about the mix-up; we were just happy that we could attend the funeral.

People said we would not find a place to stay because there was a children's sports event in town and there would be "no room at the inn." Sound familiar? Well, the Lord found us two beautiful bed and breakfast homes to stay in that truly beat any hotel or motel room. And they were the same price!

God can do anything! His goodness is even better than we could ever imagine. He made it possible for my mother and me to say our farewells and pay our last respects to my Aunt Ethel. The way she lived her life and her unshakable faith continue to inspire me in my journey to live as Christ wants me to live.

Deanna D. Hobby   *Kissimmee, Florida*

God did not tell us to follow him because he needed our help, but because he knew that loving him would make us whole.

St. Irenaeus

The soul is in God and God in the soul, just as the fish is in the sea and the sea in the fish.

St. Catherine of Siena

Rejection Changed My Life

"We know that God makes all things work together for the good of those who love God and are called according to His decree." (Romans 8:28)

Many years ago I realized how true this scripture is, but not before I experienced disappointment and shed quite a few tears. It was at an extremely difficult time in my life when I desperately needed a job with benefits.

Prior to this, the Lord had answered my prayers for employment and provided me with a part-time government job with no benefits. I was most grateful to Him for that opportunity, but I continued to look for full-time employment that offered housing, retirement, medical, and insurance benefits.

A position finally opened and I applied for it but was not selected. The fact that I was the second choice out of sixty-five applicants wasn't much consolation. My loss was the same as the person who had ranked sixty-fifth.

I really couldn't understand why God didn't answer my prayers when He knew how much I needed another job. I cried and cried, and prayed and prayed, and then I cried and prayed some more. A dear friend tried to console me, telling me that when one door closes, the Lord always opens another one in His perfect time. It was hard to believe her, but truer words were never spoken.

Shortly thereafter, I applied for another job that became available and was hired. Praise the Lord! Eventually I was promoted and became the head of the entire unit. According to government regulations, if I had been selected for the first job I would not have been eligible to apply for the second job, which ended up being the turning point in my life.

Hindsight has shown me that even that many years ago, our dear Lord was taking care of me and securing my future. The first job that I wanted so badly would have been a dead end street for me. God knew what His plan was for me so I had to continue to love and trust Him as I waited for His answer to my prayer. I have thanked God ever since for not answering my prayers for the first job. That rejection changed my life and gave me a bright and secure future in which He continues to walk with and lead me. Thank you Lord!

Anita J. Oberholtzer   *Clearwater, Florida*

Nobody ever got anything from God on the grounds that he deserved it. Having fallen, man deserves only punishment and death. So if God answers prayer it's because God is good. From His goodness, His lovingkindness, His good-natured benevolence, God does it! That's the source of everything.

A. W. Tozer

Oh, how few find time for prayer! There is time for everything else, time to sleep and time to eat, time to read the newspaper and the novel, time to visit friends, time for everything else under the sun, but - no time for prayer, the most important of all things, the one great essential!

Oswald J. Smith

I Never Pray Alone

In December of 1988, my good friend and Franciscan pastor, Fr. Luis Baldonado, OFM, offered a series of four workshops on "Centering Prayer." At the time, I was awaiting the birth of my first child who was due very soon. Not quite sure why I was attending, I faithfully waddled into the church for the four consecutive weeks of the workshop.

Each week we studied the practice of centering prayer. We began with "Lectio Divina," where we reflected on sacred readings, and then twice in the session we sat quietly for twenty minutes, surrendering ourselves to Christ. We learned about the "sacred word," which is a tool that helps us quiet our minds so we will be better able to open our hearts and fill ourselves with the mystery of Christ. I chose a simple word as my prayer word, and that helped me to refocus myself during my prayer time.

My first child was born shortly after the workshops ended. In my early years of motherhood, I was plagued by a series of difficult and painful miscarriages and major surgeries. Throughout those challenging times, I continued with my centering prayer and remained rooted to my discipline of seeking quiet and surrendering to God daily. While centering prayer is quite simple in theory, the actual practice can be difficult at times. However, I never gave up on it. Using my prayer word helped me stay focused, and the books I devoured on contemplative prayer encouraged me to stick with this peaceful way to pray.

As my oldest child began to walk and talk, his sleep habits changed. He would often rise with me in the morning after my husband had gone to work and ask if he could sit next to me to "do centering prayer." We would sit companionably together, savoring our silence.

After becoming pregnant with my second son, I had the good fortune to attend a centering prayer retreat by the retreat master Fr. Basil Pennington. I will never forget him stopping me one evening, exclaiming with surprise over my six months pregnant and protruding belly. He exhorted me to remember that when a pregnant mother centered, her baby in uteri centered with her. His words profoundly encouraged me to continue on in my practice of Lectio—studying scripture for a few minutes, and the practice of centering; letting go and being open to God's grace for twenty minutes, twice a day.

In 1994, I became pregnant with my third son. Eight months into my pregnancy and with two small children, my husband and I transitioned through a major move to the Midwest. This time in my life was often hard, lonely, exhausting, and difficult. I faithfully continued with my daily centering prayer, and it became a period in my life when I truly experienced God as my friend in a deeply profound way.

In 2001, after four miscarriages and one near fatal ectopic emergency, I became pregnant again. Although it was difficult, the pregnancy was an amazing joy and blessing. I was close to forty years old and sick, and I was busy trying to keeping up with my three children. My oldest was thirteen, my middle child was eleven, and my youngest was seven years old. I continued with my centering prayer practice as I had through the years, twice a day on most days, once a day if that was all that time permitted.

Despite the times of desolation, aridity, and absolute emptiness that plagued me, I continued to *show up* for my time of prayer, rising to greet my Friend. Like the very bottom current running along the cold rocky floor of a deep river, the *presence* was still there. And at moments, that presence was quietly, fleetingly evident, but always calling me to continue.

Two years after my fourth child was born, we experienced another difficult move that was even more painful than our previous one. This forced move catapulted us to northern Illinois and dissolved the roots we had painstakingly cultivated over nine years. My husband left immediately to begin working in the new location, and I stayed behind with our four children for nine months in order to sell our house. At times, my struggles seemed overwhelming. However, I continued to rise to my centering time and to seek solace, even as solace eluded me.

It is now nineteen years later. My youngest, who is six years old, always asks me to wake him up so he can lie next to me while I pray early in the morning. My twelve-year-old also wakes up early often, climbs up next to me wrapped in a blanket, and lies quietly with me for twenty or twenty-five minutes. We all treasure our grace-filled mornings together.

Looking back, I realize that in being faithful to my prayer time over the years, I have succeeded in letting go of my own agenda. By seeking God's will on a daily basis, I have become increasingly aware of God's divine plan in the smallest as well as the largest events of our lives. I will continue to show up for my centering prayer time with emptiness, aridity, and gratitude twice a day as faithfully as possible.

Deborah A. Armenta   *Round Lake Beach, Illinios*

Don't let a day go by without praying a little! Prayer is a duty, but it is also a joy because it is a dialogue with God through Jesus Christ.

Pope John Paul II

Prayer enlightens the mind: man cannot directly fix the eye of his soul upon God, who is the light, without being enlightened by him.

St. Robert Bellarmine

My Mother's Prayer

Nearly fifty years ago when I was approaching my mid twenties, I worked during the day and attended college in the evening. I was studying to be a teacher.

I was the youngest sibling and had been a bridesmaid at least seven times. I didn't lack dates, but I never developed a relationship serious enough for a lifetime commitment. My mother was concerned because she felt God's plan for me was to be a wife and mother. She went to church and prayed to St. Anthony for his intercession in finding me a kind and loving husband.

Across the street from this church was a book publishing company where an air force veteran worked at night. During the day he attended college. He had his share of dates, but had not decided if any of those young ladies would be a good choice for a wife. As his graduation day approached, he dropped by the church on his way to work to pray for discernment about who he should marry.

Well, lo and behold, my mother and this veteran had a mutual friend. Her name was Mary; she also worked evenings at the book publishing company. Mary was a match-maker, so when I met her at the wedding of a friend, she arranged a double date with the veteran and me.

That is how my husband and I met. One year later we became engaged at midnight Mass in the front row of that very same church where my mother had prayed. We were married six months later.

Eleanor B. Crafa   *Northport, New York*

Ten Minute Meditation

Today's meditation is about letting go of control. Take a slow walk in your garden and look at the flowers growing there. Which one do you most like today?

A rose, a tulip, a sunflower?

A lily, a snapdragon, an orchid?

Pick a flower—any one will do—and think about what you like about that flower. Talk to the flower and tell it what you find special about it. It's color, its shape? How does it make you feel when you look at that flower?

Simply enjoy the flower.

That flower is true to its nature. If it's a dandelion you could yell at it to be a rose, or weep over it to be a lily, or smile at it to be a sunflower, but you know it is always only going to be the flower that God made it to be.

Is there anyone in your life you are not happy with being the way they are?

Prayer when time is completed:

Jesus,
thank you for creating
beautiful flowers
for me to enjoy.
Thank you for the variety
of them all happily blooming
in my special garden.
Amen.

M
E
D
I
T
A
T
I
O
N

The Green Scapular

My husband Danny and I recently celebrated our thirty-fifth wedding anniversary on October 7, the feast of the holy rosary. I didn't know about that feast day until many years after we were married, and now that I know about it, it adds wonders to everything that has gone on during our marriage.

My mom was an amazing Catholic convert who loved her Catholic faith like no one else I have ever known. When Danny and I decided to marry, she was concerned because Danny was not Catholic. However, he did attend Mass with me on weekends and said he had no problem with our future children being raised in the Catholic Church.

One night before our wedding, I began to feel a bit uneasy and questioned him about things. I said, "Danny, you know that it is important to me that when we have children I must raise them in the Catholic faith. You told me that you would be fine with that, but how do I really know you mean it?" Danny had never lied to me and had always been true to me, so I felt good about his answer.

He said, "I don't have a problem with that. I love you and if that is what you want to do, then our children can be raised Catholic. And if I ever join a church, it will be the Catholic Church."

I asked, "How do I know I can believe this? Why do you say this?"

"The history, Suzanne. The Catholic Church has all of the right history!" he answered.

It was such a surprise to hear him say that, and the sincere way he said it touched my heart and mind. Then, he pulled out his wallet, opened it, and there inside was a little square piece of cloth with a religious picture on it and a green border around it. I didn't know what it was, but I knew I had a similar brown one as part of my little first Holy Communion packet that was given to me years prior to that. I knew it was something Catholic.

He said his sister had given it to him before she married a Catholic. She had never given him anything so simple before, but he loved her and was the type to accept any little gift and cherish it. He told me he didn't really know what it was. All I can remember was thinking that this was a precious brother who would put that in his wallet. A sort of surge went through me, almost as if someone were telling me that everything would be okay.

I never discussed this incident with anyone else and went on to marry Danny. I knew my mother was still concerned about us, and I believe she must have been praying her heart out daily. I attended weekend Masses with friends or my folks at times, but it would get lonely without my husband there, and I would complain.

Unfortunately, I had problems getting pregnant and it was almost nine years before I delivered our first child. This birth was an answer to many long days of prayer. I reminded Danny shortly after Maria's homecoming (my mother asked me to name the baby Maria after the Blessed Mother, and so we did) that she should be baptized into the Church soon. He agreed with no problem.

I began to encourage my husband to attend Mass on Sundays with Maria and me because it occurred to me that if she realized that only I was taking her, she might turn away from the faith. At first he didn't go to Mass with us because she was so young, but eventually he did start going with us on Sundays.

I would like to say that Danny soon began to take instructions to become a Catholic but that was not to be. It took awhile, but he finally did go. Prior to starting the classes, he continued going to Sunday Mass with us, and my parents and I continued our prayers for his conversion.

When our first daughter, Maria, received her first holy Communion, the three of us were able to stand together and receive our Lord in the Eucharist. Danny had entered fully into the Catholic faith the weekend before, which was Holy Saturday night.

To this day, my heart swells and my eyes fill with tears of joy and thanksgiving when I think about this. I know my mother's prayers—and mine—were heard. My husband has been a faithful, dedicated Catholic for about twenty years now. We feel blessed that our wedding day was on the feast of the holy rosary, and we now know that the small piece of cloth that was in Danny's wallet from so long ago was a green scapular—a little sacramental of prayer for the conversion of someone to the Catholic Church!

Suzanne L. McConnell   *Bloomington, Indiana*

Ask God to give you the grace of prayer,…ask him ceaselessly. It is an alms that you beg of him. It is not possible, if you persevere, for him to refuse you.   St. Vincent De Paul

The angel fetched Peter out of prison, but it was prayer that fetched the angel.

Thomas Watson

We forget that God sometimes has to say No. We pray to Him as our heavenly Father, and like wise human fathers, He often says, No, not from whim or caprice, but from wisdom and from love, and knowing what is best for us.

Peter Marshall

"And take care. If anything
happens to you we're sunk!"

A Baby For You

When I became a bride at age twenty-six, I wanted to become a mother immediately. My husband and I prayed for a baby. Over a year went by, and still I was not pregnant. After several approved medical tests, it was determined that I could not have a baby. We then applied for adoption. More time passed, and we heard nothing from the adoption people. We wanted a child very much. Then we went to the Blessed Mother. We just knew, if it were God's will, that she would find us a baby to love. At the National Shrine of the Immaculate Conception in Germantown, Pennsylvania, we made a nine-week novena. Faithfully, we went to the shrine each week and prayed for a baby. Four months later, on the exact date that we started the novena, we heard those beautiful words, "There is a baby for you."

We were thrilled. God gave us a baby boy. This happened forty-one years ago. I am a widow now. I am so grateful to the Lord for giving me a wonderful husband, a good marriage, and a lovely son.

Maryann Kolod   *Bensalem, Pennsylvania*

Do not be frightened or grieve, or let your heart be dismayed. Am I not here, I who am your mother? And is not my help refuge?

Our Lady to St. Juan Diego

For Those Left Behind

I had been lost and away from the Church for a long time. During much of that time, I belonged to an Eastern Meditation cult group led by a demanding and controlling *guru*. Through a chain of events which I'm sure was the work of the Holy Spirit, I returned to my beautiful Catholic faith.

I began praying for the others who were left behind in the cult (spiritual, idealistic people with the best of intentions who continued to be misled by the guru).

I prayed often that he would let them go.

As it turned out, he died. When I prayed that the guru would let his followers go; I certainly hadn't intended for him to die, but that's what happened. I had been very careful not to wish him ill. I was hoping he'd just disband the organization.

I spoke to a priest about it in confession because I felt strangely responsible. The priest assured me that the man's death was a blessing for his misled followers. He also added that it was "a tough one" and to pray for the deceased guru, which I did. I realize now, after seeing his followers, that no matter what choices they make for themselves they really are better off. They have regained their free will.

Rosalie Marschall   *San Francisco, California*

Angel Chariot

My son, Patrick, had been home on leave from the army and was preparing to go back to complete the last part of boot camp. He was to go by bus to St. Louis and then board a plane for Aberdeen Proving Grounds in Maryland.

He called the bus station to ask about getting a ticket to St. Louis and was told that the bus scheduled to leave at one in the morning would get him there in time for his nine-thirty flight to Maryland. He asked if he needed to go to the station and purchase his ticket in advance and they said that no, he could just buy his ticket that evening when he got there. They said that the one a.m. bus was hardly ever full, and he wouldn't have any difficulty getting a ticket.

He thought everything was working out well. At eleven thirty that night, two of his buddies drove him to the bus station which is about forty miles from our home. I had to work the next day and didn't want to be up that late if I didn't have to. Little did I know that I wasn't going to get any sleep anyway.

When they got to the bus station, the ticket agent told them that there were no more seats available on the bus to St. Louis. Needless to say, Patrick was very upset and worried. He explained to the agent that he had to get to the St. Louis airport to catch the nine thirty flight the next morning or he would be late getting to Maryland. If that happened, he would be considered AWOL (absent without official leave) and would be in a lot of trouble.

They called and told me what was going on. The ticket agent suggested that they wait and see if someone on the bus would give Patrick his seat and then take a later bus to St. Louis. Unfortunately, no one could exchange seats with him because they all had important commitments too. Patrick was devastated. He knew he was in for a court martial.

They called me again and explained what had happened. The only solution we could think of was for his friends to drive him to St. Louis. I told them to come home and use my car because they had driven to the bus station in his friend Matt's pick-up truck, and Matt didn't think it would make it that far.

After the first call, I called my daughter to ask her to pray for a seat to become available. I had awakened her, but she didn't care. We both prayed the rosary, and I also prayed every other prayer I could think of. I especially asked for the intercession of St. Christopher, the patron saint of travelers, and St. Jude, the patron saint of impossible causes. Heaven was bombarded.

As I was drowsily saying my prayers and rosary, the phone rang another time. I wasn't expecting another phone call; I was waiting for them to get back to my house to get my car. Matt called this time to tell me that Patrick was on a bus that was going to Fort Leonardwood, Missouri, which is the army base where he had taken his basic training. They were going to pick up some soldiers there and then travel on to St. Louis.

I breathed a big sigh of relief, called my daughter with the news, and went back to my prayers. This time I prayed in thanksgiving to God for providing for and protecting my son. However, it wasn't until a couple of days later that I found out just how much He had provided.

From talking with Pat and Matt, I found out the details of what had transpired that night. Matt told me that they had just picked up Pat's duffle bag and luggage, preparing to come and get my car, when this other bus pulled in. The driver said he had received a call telling him to go to Fort Leonardwood, pick up some soldiers, and take them to St. Louis, and that he was to stop by the Springfield bus station, where my son was, on the way.

Pat then called and told me his part of the story. He said he boarded the bus and they drove to Fort Leonardwood. When they arrived, nobody knew anything about any soldiers going to St. Louis. So they drove on to St. Louis with Patrick being more than a little confused and in awe because he was the only passenger on the bus the entire way. He reached the airport in plenty of time, flew to Maryland, and finished his boot camp.

Once in awhile I ask my son what he and his "angel" driver talked about on the way to St. Louis, and if his "angel chariot" was comfortable.

Donna Wimsatt   *Monett, Missouri*

Faith in a prayer-hearing God will make a prayer-loving Christian.

Andrew Murray

A newborn child has to cry, for only in this way will his lungs expand. A doctor once told me of a child who could not breathe when it was born. In order to make it breathe the doctor gave it a slight blow. The mother must have thought the doctor cruel. But he was really doing the kindest thing possible. As with newborn children the lungs are contracted, so are our spiritual lungs. But through suffering God strikes us in love. Then our lungs expand and we can breathe and pray.

Sadhu Sundar Singh

Prayer is surrender - surrender to the will of God and cooperation with that will. If I throw out a boathook from the boat and catch hold of the shore and pull, do I pull the shore to me, or do I pull myself to the shore? Prayer is not pulling God to my will, but the aligning of my will to the will of God.

Eli E. Stanley Jones

Saint Theresa's Answer

It was two o'clock in the morning on October 8, 1984, when I was awakened by my husband Archie telling me he couldn't feel his legs. He had been suffering for over a week with terrible back pains, and we had visited three different emergency rooms. Each one sent him home with Valium and instructions to rest. They said he had just sprained his back.

That morning he tried to get out of bed and to the bathroom and landed face first on the floor. I immediately called 911. Our children were all home, so I was unable to accompany him to the hospital. I felt so helpless.

The next morning after the kids went to school I immediately drove to the hospital. The doctors couldn't tell me what was wrong; they only said that it didn't look good. He seemed to be paralyzed from the waist down and many complications could arise. He was only forty-five years old, but because he was a heavy man it was hard for them to pinpoint what was causing the problem.

Archie and I had started our marriage late in life and we often told each other that our marriage was predestined by God. Both Catholics, we had strayed from the Church in our twenties, but in our thirties we returned. It took awhile, but as we grew closer, our spiritual life did also. We often attended daily Mass, and I developed a special devotion to St. Theresa the Little Flower. When I was at the hospital, I immediately found the chapel and started a novena to my favorite saint. As you may know, if she answers your prayers she will send you a rose.

The days continued with my husband fading in and out of a coma. When I visited him he was either unconscious, or awake and talking nonsense. I was frightened as I continued my novena asking St. Theresa to save his life.

Finally, a neurosurgeon met with me and said it was not likely that Archie would live. They had found a blockage in his spinal cord and could operate to try to remove it, but the odds were that he wouldn't make it off the table. I was beside myself.

My mom was watching the kids so I could keep vigil at the hospital. I spent a lot of time in the hospital chapel praying rosaries and continuing my novena. I had a strong feeling that St. Theresa would help me.

The morning came for the doctors to try to remove the blockage. I spoke with Archie beforehand, but he was out of it. The doctors told me to go home because the surgery would take several hours, and they said they would call me when he was in recovery. I said no, I wanted to be there if he didn't make it. My mom was with me and we sat near a nurse's station where I continued to pray.

They wheeled him in the operating room at around ten o'clock that morning. At around ten thirty the nurses were all at the desk and I heard one of them say, "Where did this yellow rose come from?" No one knew; no one had seen it being delivered—not even my mom or I, who had been there the whole time. The nurses brought the rose over to where I was sitting. There was no card with it and they wanted me to have it. I started to cry and knew my prayers had been answered.

I looked up and saw them bringing Archie out of the operating room already. I ran to the doctor and he said they didn't operate because when they put the instrument in him to look for the blockage, it was gone. They were baffled, but I knew it was because St. Theresa had answered my novena.

Archie returned home in a wheelchair in April of 1985. He lived the next nineteen years in constant pain, but he never complained. We were both blessed to have each other, and we thanked God and St. Theresa every day we spent together. Unfortunately, I lost my soul mate Archie on February 7, 2004. He was tired and it was his time to go. I still feel that he is here with me, and that he is praying for me every day.

Carol G. Spoor   *Assonet, Massachusetts*

Ten Minute Meditation

Today look for an area that is a *hot spot* for you. Something that triggers your emotions in a negative way. A comment that makes you boil, an action someone does or doesn't do that gets you upset, a look, whatever.

What is that hot spot?

Talk to Jesus openly about this hot spot. Ask him why that button is such an easy mark for you.

Wait for Jesus to answer.

Prayer when time is completed:

Jesus,
you are my friend
and healer.
Help me to bring
my wounds
to you
for healing.
Give me the humility
to accept
being healed.
Amen.

M
E
D
I
T
A
T
I
O
N

I'll Be Okay

I was busy taking care of my mom who lived with me and was also taking care of my mother-in-law who was in her nineties and living by herself. My mother-in-law had lost all her children through the years, so I was the only one left to care for her. She had a few health problems like a colostomy and heart palpitations, so I went to her house every day to check on her and to make sure she had taken her meds.

One cold winter day I got a call from a neighbor of hers saying that my mother-in-law had been wandering around the streets wearing only her bedroom slippers and a dress. They had called 911 and she was taken to the hospital. When I got there, I found out that she thought it was 1905. She was in that state of mind for three weeks, and the doctor told me that she could no longer live alone.

I couldn't take her home with me because I had my mom to take care of, so I was forced to put her in a nursing home. Well, she had always told me not to ever put her in a home, and when she came out of her stupor and her mind seemed clearer, she was really mad at me.

My mother-in-law called me every name under the sun every day, and I went home crying after every visit. I prayed, but the weeks went by and things got worse, not better. She was so angry that she told me she was praying that God would get me for what I had done to her.

Once after I had gone to see her I did not sleep all night. I kept praying the same thing over and over again, "Please Lord, make her understand that this is her home now and she will be okay."

The next day I went to see her like usual and she had a big smile on her face. She shocked me when she said the exact words that I had prayed all night long. She said, "This is my home now and I'll be okay." She lived to be one hundred and never talked about how she hated me and what I had done to her again. I still get goose bumps when I talk about it. The Lord had truly answered my prayers.

Lorraine Christman   *Pepperell, Massachusetts*

Prayer is the most powerful weapon a Christian has. Prayer makes us effective. Prayer makes us happy. Prayer gives us all the strength we need to fulfill God's commands. Yes, indeed, your whole life can and should be prayer.

St. Josemaria Escriva

One way of recalling the mind easily during prayer and of keeping it more tranquil is not to let your mind race during the day, but to hold it close to the presence of God. Being in the habit of coming back to him from time to time, you will find it easy to remain peaceful during your prayer time, or at least to bring your mind back from distraction.

Brother Lawrence

The right way to pray is to stretch out our hands and ask of One who we know has the heart of a Father.

Dietrich Bonhoeffer

No One Spoke to Him

Our daughter-in-law's mother passed away and she was very concerned about her younger brother who might show up at the funeral home and cause trouble. He is a mentally ill young man who lives in a group home run by the state. In the past he had threatened our daughter-in-law's life, and no one knew what might happen if he showed up at the wake or the funeral. My husband and I prayed that Allen (not his real name) would not make any trouble at this difficult time.

He came to the wake with two guardians and a caregiver, and as he came in, not one person—sibling, relative or friend—greeted him. There was a sharp hush all through the room and the tension was very great as we all wondered what he might do. We could tell that Allen had been sedated for the trip; he stood almost motionless in a corner staring at some pictures of his family and mom.

No one approached him and no one spoke to him. I felt so bad for him. Before he had become so troubled, I had enjoyed talking to him at family gatherings. He used to talk to me about the Catholic Church and what it meant to him.

All of a sudden, the Holy Spirit moved me, and before I knew it, I was approaching Allen. I touched his arm gently and said hello. I asked if he remembered who I was and then repeated my name. I reached over and gave him a small hug and told him how sorry I was about his losing his mother.

He stammered for a few moments and glanced toward the casket where his mother was. I asked him if he would like it if I walked up there with him and he nodded. When we got close to the casket, Allen began to cry, and he told me how bad he felt. I asked him if he would like for me to say a prayer with him, and he nodded again. We both knelt down on the kneeler and I said the Lord's Prayer and a Hail Mary. We both blessed ourselves and he stood up. Allen thanked me, and just then a friend came in from his high school and they went and sat down to talk.

The tension in the funeral home seemed cut now, and people began to talk again. I spoke to his caregiver and she told me that he had been making great progress and was concerned that no one would speak to him. She said he had gone back to Mass and never missed a Sunday. He also had a small part-time job and was doing well. In a time of sorrow and bereavement, the Lord turned a sad situation into a miracle. I praise God and the Holy Spirit for using me as a vessel.

Judie J. Kolloen   *Shelby Township, Michigan*

The more you pray, the more you want to pray. It's like a fish that starts by swimming near the surface of the water, then plunges and goes on swimming deeper and deeper. The soul plunges, is swallowed up, loses itself in the delights of conversation with God.

St. John Vianney

Then I saw truly that it gives more praise to God and more delight if we pray steadfast in love, trusting his goodness, clinging to him by grace, than if we ask for everything our thoughts can name. The best prayer is to rest in the goodness of God.

Julian of Norwich

Three Hail Mary's

I belong to a God-fearing family of five children, and I lost my dad when I was only sixteen years old. My mom, a widowed housewife, raised us well despite the pain and hardships she endured. Throughout my life, I was always a very outgoing and fun person with a positive attitude.

I married my husband eight years ago, and every moment of every day has been a nightmare, especially when he's drunk. He is unable to hold down a job because of his drinking problem, so, at one point after a lot of prayers, God was merciful and I was offered a job that paid me more than enough to survive on. Because I knew I would be put to shame in public if I didn't give my husband money, I did so even though he took me for granted and used it to buy alcohol.

I have been tempted to run away from my situation rather than face it, but I always felt too ashamed to follow through with it because of my little daughter. I almost lost my senses, but I was determined not to give up.

I eventually quit my job thinking that my husband would take up the responsibility, but he simply did not bother. As the situation worsened, my faith in God grew even stronger.

At one point my husband worked for a company and quit without informing them. His salary was not deposited, and moreover, there was no money to buy food, clear the bills, and so on. I became panicked, worried, and unable to sleep. To whom should I go to for help?

As I was looking through St. Mary's Magazine, I read about many petitions that were granted through the "Three Hail Mary" novena. I prayed the novena devoutly and asked my husband to check his bank account to see if the company had deposited his last paycheck. Nothing. I prayed it again; he checked his account and came home saying there was no credit to his account yet. I still didn't give up and sent him back to the bank the next day. By then it was almost two weeks since he had quit his job.

After that third trip to the bank he came home saying there was no use sending him back there to check his account again and again. In spite of all this, I did not give up hope. With a strong will, I personally went back to the bank with him. I prayed and pleaded to our Blessed Mother, placing my situation in her hands and begging her not to disappoint me.

When we got to the bank, I sent my husband to check his account one last time while I pleaded with our Blessed Mother to aid me at this exact moment. I prayed the "Three Hail Mary" novena with tremendous faith and conviction, and wow! A true miracle happened.

My husband could not believe his eyes when he saw five figures in his account. With tears in his eyes he came running to me and we were both filled with joy. Together we praised and thanked our Blessed Mother who really heeds our petitions when we approach her with faith. It was a miracle that happened to a person who did not believe in miracles and who had little faith.

I pray to our Lord, not for wealth and money, but for my husband to stop drinking, for our daily bread, and for peace, love, and contentment in my life. I keep Christ as the head of my house and pray to our Blessed Mother to be with me always in whatever I say or do and wherever I go. I pray that God will guide and guard my family and keep us all away from mortal sin. I often visit the Blessed Sacrament to pour myself out to Jesus, asking Him to lighten my cross.

To this day, my husband continues to drink, creating a huge mess in my family. I pray that he will have the will power to stop drinking because it is the root cause of my family's destruction. Hence, I also pray that all of you who read this keep me in your prayers.

Celia Lourdes Cardozo   *Hubli, Karnataka, India*

The Power of Simple Prayer

I have long awaited an opportunity like this to glorify God for His miraculous healing of my boil. I am so happy to share this and pray that God will grant me the serenity of heart and mind to share this in honesty and sincerity. I hope that this piece will touch many hearts and help them to believe in the power of simple prayer and in the healing power of God.

In December, 1989, I had a boil on my neck during my school vacation. The swelling was big and painful. My aunties tried in vain to burst it with local herbs. As children, we used to visit our aunties and grannies for pesewa and toffees on Christmas Day. I remained at home because of this boil and watched my siblings go on these joyful visits. I stood in our window and saw other children singing joyful Christmas songs as they passed by our house on their way to their visits. Those who knew me waved as they passed by.

It was painful and I had no other choice but to allow my tears to flow.

I walked away from the window and went straight to my father's bedroom and stood in front of his wardrobe, which had a big, long mirror fixed on its door. As I stood in front of the mirror and looked at my boil I said, "God I want you to heal me and if you heal me I will not sin again." Just after this short prayer, I saw a white fluid oozing out of my boil.

I quickly ran to my mother and exclaimed the news to her. She was struck and said nothing for a moment. Then my elder brother entered and I narrated everything to him thinking he would share my joy, but he did not.

He doubted and called me a liar. His words pierced my heart like a two-edged sword with all its pain. It was unbearable and I spoke cruel words to him. My heart ached for days and still does whenever I remember this incident. Realizing that I had broken my part of the covenant, I cried bitterly and prayed to God for forgiveness. I believe God has forgiven me.

Augustus Mensah   *Cape Coast, Ghana, Africa*

A Difficult Prayer

My faithful Catholic husband of twenty-four years was diagnosed with an aggressive brain tumor when he was fifty-four years old. The youngest of our five homeschooled children was six at the time. The medical establishment had little to offer as treatment for this particular tumor, so my husband underwent an intense alternative treatment consisting of around-the-clock intravenous administration of a liquid medicine. My son called this, "the bags."

After surgery, "the bags" seemed to be working for several months. The tumor was gone, but my husband and I were exhausted from the intensity of the treatment. Then we discovered that the tumor had reappeared. I was devastated, but my husband did not seem overly troubled by this development.

Since the tumor was growing very slowly, we decided to take a break from the treatment and planned a pilgrimage to the Shrine of St. Joseph in Montreal, Canada. Our family had been praying throughout this eight month ordeal and because of our French Canadian heritage, we felt a special closeness to blessed Andre Bessette, the founder of the shrine.

April 8, 2003, a week after my husband's fifty-fifth birthday, seemed to be much like the days and weeks before. But my husband told me twice that day that he thought he was dying, and that he would miss me. I dismissed his concerns; after all, he was pretty much the same as yesterday and as last week. He did have a terrible sore throat, but he could walk and talk and care for his own personal needs. Yet he held my hand and whispered to me twice that he thought he was dying.

As our youngest son was preparing for bed, he spoke softly to me, "Mom, I'm afraid that Dad is dying."

I replied, "No, he has a bad sore throat, but the tumor is stable and not growing very fast. He is okay."

213

Later, when tucking my son into bed, he thoughtfully gazed up at me and said, "Mom, if the bags are not working anymore, wouldn't it be better for us to pray for Dad to go?"

I was taken aback and could not answer. Eventually I said, "Yes, I suppose it would be."

How could I say that, you may ask? Well, don't we teach our children that this life is but a preparation for our real home, for a life of love with the Holy Trinity? Don't we teach our children that heaven is a better place?

He then asked, "Why don't we pray that prayer right now?" I could not do that; I could not pray for my husband's death. I remained quiet, as did my son. After several still moments, I lay down beside him until he drifted off to sleep.

Three hours later, my husband died. There was no medical explanation for why he died that night. When the agony and confusion of this time had somewhat lessened, I asked my son if he had prayed that prayer, the prayer for Dad to go. He said yes. The father who gave himself completely to God and to his family, the father who underwent alternative treatments for my sake, the father who was so loved by his children, was prayed into eternal life by his youngest son, thereby saving him from further earthly suffering. God hears and answers all of our prayers, but I will never forget the power of a child's prayer.

Today, four and a half years later, my son does not remember this story. I told him about it as I was writing this and he said, "Well, I don't remember that, but it must have been the Holy Spirit in me that made me pray that way." The Holy Spirit indeed.

Fae D. Presley   *Hersey, Michigan*

A Hedge of Protection

About four years ago I had some very strong, unsettling thoughts of our adult son Robb being in a car accident. I kept telling myself it was just a horrible thought being he had been in a near fatal accident when he was sixteen.

For two to three days this thought kept popping into my head. I imagined our daughter-in-law calling us late at night to tell us he had been in a car accident. I figured it must be the Holy Spirit prompting me to pray extra hard for Robb's safety since he drove many miles a day for the company he works for.

Every time the thought came into my mind, I prayed. I asked the Holy Spirit and our Blessed Mother to form a hedge of protection around Robb and his car and to keep him safe as he drove. I also prayed a lot of Hail Mary's for him. There was such a heavy feeling in my heart that I could feel it in my stomach at times. It was something that cannot be explained; you just feel it so strongly in your soul.

About a week later, just after ten o'clock at night, I was getting ready for bed when the phone rang. It was our daughter-in-law and she was very upset. Robb had just called her from his car—he had been in a horrible car accident and was upside down in a ditch, hanging from his safety belt. He was only a half a mile from home so she loaded the kids into her car and hurried to where the accident was.

When his wife and children arrived at the scene, they saw the fire rescue people pulling Robb out of the car through the back window with the jaws of life, a hydraulic machine that cuts through metal to rescue accident victims.

Our son is six feet and five inches tall and was driving a mid-size company car. He had made the terrible mistake of checking his cell phone messages as he was driving home. It had been raining all day and it was

215

very foggy out. As he took his eyes off the road, he hit a rural mail box and the car flipped. Because he had his safety belt on, the only cuts he got were from when he was being pulled through the broken glass.

A few days later, we went to see the car and as I looked inside, I saw that the roof had been flattened except for a pocket where he said his body had been cradled like a womb. When I told Robb about what I had been experiencing prior to the accident, he got tears in his eyes. He was very thankful for the Holy Spirit working through his mom for his safety.

Two and a half weeks after the accident, Robb's oldest daughter made her first holy Communion. As we sat in Mass that morning, I just couldn't imagine him not being there for that wonderful moment. I give praise and thanks to the Holy Spirit who I know without a doubt was responsible for prompting me to pray for that hedge of protection for our son.

Judie J. Kolloen   *Shelby Township, Michigan*

We follow him and he draws us to himself by love. Prayer makes the soul one with God.

Julian of Norwich

It is such a folly to pass one's time fretting, instead of resting quietly on the heart of Jesus.

St. Therese of Lisieux

Prayer is not merely an occasional impulse to which we respond when we are in trouble: prayer is a life attitude.

Walter A. Mueller

Ten Minute Meditation

Turmoil. Imagine that there has been a big storm that hit your garden. Heavy rain, hard wind, thunder and lightening. As you go into your garden after this weather disaster, you look about and you can't believe what a mess it is in.

Reflect.

Could you have stopped that storm from happening?

Could you have prevented lightening from hitting your favorite tree?

Could you have stopped the wind from blowing that tree down?

The storm is over. It has hit hard, but…

Now notice the sun is shinning. You notice the flowers are starting to lift themselves a bit; a squirrel is delightedly investigating the sunflower that has broken off and is in delicious easy reach for munching.

Look, the sun is now reaching a part of your garden where it never did when the tree was there. Perhaps a new kind of flower can be planted there? A flower that needs the sun.

Prayer when time is completed:

Jesus,
open my eyes
that I may see
the Love
that you have
for me
even in times
of trouble.
Trouble that often times
opens the door
to new opportunity.
Amen.

M
E
D
I
T
A
T
I
O
N

217

The Missing Art Work

Years ago when my daughter was in junior high, she had a project to do for a class and asked to take some of the artwork from our walls to help illustrate it. We have some art that is worth quite a lot of money and those, of course, were the pieces she needed.

The day her project was due, off she went with her large bag full of expensive art. I prayed when she left the house, asking God to please keep her focused and aware of that bag she was carrying. I had total faith in God that He was watching over her and I wasn't really worried about it getting lost.

Then home she came without it! She was in tears and had no idea where the art was. I began to pray for its return, asking God to please help us find it. I also prayed for anyone who might have stolen the artwork, asking the Lord to change the heart of any possible thief. I prayed, "Lord, please give anyone who has those pictures a heart of repentance and a desire to return them to us." I felt very stressed and know I stressed my daughter with my great desire and need to find those expensive things.

Weeks went by with her checking everywhere and with everyone, and no pictures surfaced. Finally, one day a light came on in my head and I prayed, "Lord, these are only material things. You have blessed us with so much, I let go of these pictures, I let go of the importance I have given them. Thank You and praise You Lord for all that You supply in abundance." I felt a total release and relief, and so did my sweet little girl. I told her not to worry about it for one more minute, and told her that she was far more important than any material thing.

The very next day my daughter walked into a classroom and there were all the pictures lined up on the edge of the board in the front of the room! My daughter rushed up to the teacher and claimed them all immediately. She was overjoyed to see them!

The teacher explained that he had just that day come upon the bag and because it did not have a name on it, he thought he would try displaying the pictures to see if anyone would claim them.

She was so happy and proud to be able to bring those pictures home. The Lord had in fact answered all our prayers in His time and in His way. He had used this whole situation to teach me a lesson I have never forgotten.

Debra J. Ishii   *Kent, Washington*

Work as if you were to live a hundred years, pray as if you were to die tomorrow.

Benjamin Franklin

If the heart wanders or is distracted, bring it back to the point quite gently and replace it tenderly in its Master's presence. And even if you did nothing during the whole of your hour but bring your heart back and place it again in our Lord's presence, though it went away every time you brought it back, your hour will be very well employed.

St. Francis de Sales

Pray, and let God worry.

Martin Luther

Thanksgiving Every Day

We live in Florida and our daughter, Stephanie, lives hundreds of miles away in Canada. In 1989, the doctors found a lump in our daughter's breast that would require surgery. She made it through the surgery fine but a few weeks later a blood clot that had evidently traveled from her breast during the lumpectomy operation to her brain caused a serious bleeder, a stroke.

We received a phone call from St. Mary's Hospital in Canada informing us that our daughter had had a serious stroke and was completely paralyzed on her left side. They told us we needed to come as soon as possible. It was five days before Thanksgiving and when we called the airlines their flights were so full they couldn't help us until one week later.

We were so saddened and felt almost helpless to handle the situation that was ahead of us. My husband and I, though, are fervent prayer warriors, and believe in trusting the Lord. At the time, we were involved in our church with an online prayer ministry team. We notified everyone on the team to start praying.

When we finally arrived at the hospital, we found Stephanie's room and stopped outside the door and prayed for Jesus' healing power to take over her body. When we went in our poor daughter had a twisted face, no movement in her left arm, and no speech. The gleam in her beautiful eyes was gone.

The neurologist spoke with us and told us that Stephanie would never be able to live alone or possibly work again. He explained that our daughter was one lucky girl to even be alive.

We told the doctor it was not luck that kept her alive; it was the Lord. We went back into the room, prayed and anointed her whole body with blessed holy oil from church.

Stephanie was allowed to go home in two days and there we made the best Thanksgiving dinner ever. Stephanie tried to speak to let us know how much she loved us for being with her during this hard time. We had to feed her, as she couldn't eat correctly because of the twisted angle in which the stroke left her face and mouth. However, what was important was that we were all together as family, Stephanie, me (her mom), her dad, and our two grandchildren, Joey and Nina.

My husband had to go back to the states to work; I stayed behind in Canada with Stephanie for eight weeks while I helped her as she went through heavy duty physical therapy. At first, she was not able to do much, but as the weeks went by, she began to speak slowly, one word at a time and tried to smile again.

She went through several depressions (which is normal for a stroke of that magnitude) but finally there came a time when she wanted to visit a few friends. This was a breakthrough as she was ready to go out in public again.

Around the fourth week of therapy her healing became more evident. Bit by bit, piece by piece she made progress. She could lift her hand and arm with my help; she could feed herself and digest solid foods much better.

Although expressions of face and mind have not come back, nor her singing voice (her vocal cords were depressed by the stroke), Stephanie progressed to the point where she could go back to work. Today she can move her whole left side and even drive a car. She must live with someone to help her out with more structured things in life but be we feel that God has truly been merciful in allowing our precious daughter to be healed, part by part and piece by piece.

This is why it is Thanksgiving every day in our lives. We dedicate daily through prayer our four adult children and four grandchildren totally to Jesus, Mary & Joseph (The Holy Family). God gave us mercy and the ability to pray no matter what prognosis is heard.

As I write this, Stephanie is almost forty-two years old and works as a dental assistant five days a week. She loves the Lord, and doesn't hesitate to let people know who healed her from the stroke.

Doreen K. D'Angelo   *Boca Raton, Florida*

Tina's Boo Boo

For twenty-four years I was a teacher's assistant for the Head Start program in Tarentum, Pennsylvania. One day a little girl and boy were fighting over a toy. The boy insisted that it was his turn to play with it, and the girl was not ready to give it up. Not knowing what else to do, Freddie (not his true name) came toward Tina like a thrown javelin and bit her on the top part of the palm of her hand. This behavior was out of character for him.

Tina let out a high-pitched scream and we ran to her assistance. Sure enough, he had bit her skin deep enough to cause a laceration and it was bleeding. It looked like she would need a few stitches.

After talking about it with the other staff person, I took Tina to the adjacent room where there was a first-aid kit. As I comforted this little four-year-old, I talked silently to God, asking why He allowed this to happen to her. Her family had all kinds of problems and her dad had died the week before. Oh, how I wished I had been bitten instead of her.

With overwhelming grief in her little heart, Tina cried over her boo-boo. The compassion in my heart ran so deep that I knew it wasn't all mine, and I cried with her.

As I applied a butterfly bandage to the laceration, I prayed for God to help her and heal her. Then I covered that bandage with a regular one, and sat and talked with her as I applied pressure to her hand to stop the bleeding. Finally, it appeared to have stopped, so we walked back to the classroom. In most cases we would have called the parent, but we knew her mother was finishing up at work and would be there in thirty minutes, so we didn't call her.

It was nap time and as Tina lay on her mat, I checked the outside of her bandage to see if there was any sign of bleeding. After checking it twice, I told her to come to me if she saw any blood on it.

Soon her mom appeared in the doorway. Tina jumped up and ran over to her saying, "Mom! Mom! Freddie bit me!" We explained to her mom what happened and Tina showed her the hand. She pulled off the bandage and said, "See Mom." When we looked at her hand, there was nothing there. Nothing at all.

We all looked at each other, and Tina's mom must have thought we were a little nuts. Tina just kept looking at her hand in search of the wound. She even checked her other hand. There was nothing. Not believing it, I also looked at both of her hands. The bite was so big, how could we be missing it? Tina just kept saying, "Uh huh, Mom, he did bite me. He did bite me, Mom!"

We knew he did; we had seen it too. I knew I had prayed for her healing, but I never expected a miracle! To think it was that easy. I just prayed from my heart and God did the rest!

Judy V. Krantz   *Tarentum, Pennsylvania*

Prayer is not only asking, but an attitude of mind which produces the atmosphere in which asking is perfectly natural.

Oswald Chambers

Since God knows our future, our personalities, and our capacity to listen, He isn't ever going to say more to us than we can deal with at the moment.

Charles Stanley

Nothing Wrong With Me

One day I suddenly felt some sort of pain in the lower part of my stomach. I did not consider it important, but rather just a passing inconvenience. But then the pain returned, at first every week and then every couple of days. Then it was there every day, and eventually it was constant. The intensity of the pain fluctuated from a dull pain to a sharp, knife-cutting pain. After a couple of months, it became my constant companion.

Being Catholic, I had learned about the saints and knew this was a great opportunity for me to offer up my suffering as they did. However, after six months I couldn't handle the pain any longer, so I made an appointment with my doctor. I had a feeling there was something very seriously wrong with me, like cancer.

I am part of a charismatic prayer group that was declared the intercessory prayer group by Sr. Bridge McKenna. She is well-known all over the world for her gift of healing and had visited our prayer group once. The day before my appointment, I asked our prayer ministry to pray over me and with me. I told them what my problem was, but because of my discomfort, I wasn't able to pray too hard.

They prayed for fifteen to twenty minutes and nothing happened. I was not feeling well, so I went home. When I had asked for prayers, I was more concerned about receiving strength and not being afraid to see the doctor. That was Wednesday evening. Thursday morning I woke up and started doing my chores. Suddenly I noticed that I had no pain!

My first thought was that it couldn't be true and that the pain would return soon. An hour passed and I started getting nervous and excited as I waited for the pain to return. I was pretending that I was doing some chores around the house but in reality I was anxiously waiting for what was going to happen. Well, nothing happened! The pain was gone! I waited the whole the day and it didn't return.

I was embarrassed to go to the doctor since I had made an emergency appointment, giving them my sad explanation about my awful pain, and now it was gone. But, I decided to go anyway. The doctor found nothing wrong with me and I wouldn't be surprised if she thought I was a hypochondriac. The next few days I was still nervously wondering if the pain would return and it didn't. That happened ten years ago and the pain has never returned.

Halina Acca Makowski   *Chicago, Illinois*

None can believe how powerful prayer is, and what it is able to effect, but those who have learned it by experience. It is a great matter when in extreme need to take hold on prayer. I know, whenever I have prayed earnestly, that I have been amply heard, and have obtained more than I prayed for. God indeed sometimes delayed, but at last He came.

Martin Luther

Beware in your prayers, above everything else, of limiting God, not only by unbelief, but by fancying that you know what He can do. Expect unexpected things above all that we ask or think.

Andrew Murray

It was not going well.

God's Cancelled Flight

"Lord, I miss my husband so much," I prayed. "You can do all things, so will you stop his plane for me?" My prayer request sounded so absurd.

My husband works part-time and is also working on his master's degree. He had been studying in New York City for the last five weeks, and we missed each other so much. We have two children, a two-year-old son, and a fourteen-month-old daughter, and it was hard on all of us for him to be away.

That weekend he had a business trip to New Orleans from New York City, and had a thirty minute layover in the Atlanta airport, which is the one closest to our home. Atlanta's airport is so big that thirty minutes isn't even enough time to get through security and back to the gate, let alone visit with anyone.

I started having a simple conversation with God, telling Him how much I appreciated having a faith-filled husband. I told Him how much it would mean to the kids and me to see daddy even if it was only for a few minutes. I also asked a friend, whose husband also travels, to say a prayer or two for us. Having prayer warriors assist us never hurts.

On the afternoon of his flight, I told my husband that I would check to see if his flight from Atlanta to New York was full so if it was, he could ask to be bumped to a later flight and maybe we could see each other. When I went to the airline's website though, I could not check for seat availability like I had in the past for other flights. In fact, the flight wasn't even showing up at all. I had to run an errand, so I decided to check back later.

As I got into the car, a funny feeling washed over me. It was then that God placed a message in my heart that I would see my husband that night.

When I got back from my errand, I tried to check on the flight again, but the information still did not appear on the website. I proceeded to call the airline, and the representative told me that the flight had been canceled. I called my husband right way to tell him the news so he could book another flight. When he called me back, he said he was going to be able to spend the night at home because his flight was now the next morning! I was so happy that God had answered my absurd prayer request!

Kristin A. Sommer   *Fayetteville, Georgia*

The essence of meditation is a period of time set aside to contemplate the Lord, listen to Him, and allow Him to permeate our spirits.

Charles Stanley

The wish to pray is a prayer in itself.

Georges Bernanos

There come times when I have nothing more to tell God. If I were to continue to pray in words, I would have to repeat what I have already said. At such times it is wonderful to say to God, "May I be in Thy presence, Lord? I have nothing more to say to Thee, but I do love to be in Thy presence."

O. Hallesby

The Perfect Substitute

Let me start with the beginning. For three years I had been a classics teacher: Latin, Greek and ancient culture. I love what I do and I try to be a good Christian in fulfilling my duties as well as possible. My hero and inspiration in this is St. Giovanni Bosco, the Italian priest who took care of so many poor children in nineteenth century Italy.

I love my job. I also love my husband and God blessed our love with a child which was due to be born in August. My pregnancy was going well so that it was no problem for me to keep fulfilling my duties at school, which in the Netherlands, ends in July. So I reasoned that with my pregnancy-vacation, combined with the nursery-vacation and the summer holidays I would have a total of three months to be home with our baby—I wouldn't have to go back until December.

My only concern was for the children in my school. I would miss them but more than that, I had been working hard so that they would be able to do Latin and Greek in the first half of the next year. Classics teachers are very few here in the Netherlands, let alone good classics teachers.

So I began praying for a miracle, a miracle that I would find a substitute, a good substitute that would be able to teach them Latin, Greek and ancient culture.

In my prayers, it was very funny, but I felt like when I was eleven years old and wanted a beau-ti-ful Barbie-doll so much. I kept saving, and saving, and saving my pocket money, so sure that mom and dad would take me to the toy store one day, when I would have enough. I kept raving about it. Sure enough, finally, I got the Barbie-doll! It was the most beautiful doll I ever had, and there was never anyone happier than me that day.

So it was that though I completely trusted in Jesus, I felt like that little eleven-year-old girl and kept bringing up the subject to Jesus, again and again. I couldn't keep quiet about it. It was something that moved me so much; my strong desire that I wanted such a good education for those children. "Please God, let the substitute be as good as me, or, preferably, even better!"

Now normally I am the laziest person I know, but this problem motivated my prayer life in such a way, that I truly felt the Holy Spirit was definitely at work. "Ask, and you shall receive."

I was not used to praying novenas because I thought that I would be no good at it, that I wouldn't have the discipline to keep it up for nine days in a row. But this was so important to me that my mom bought a novena candle for me (I was broke) and on Sunday I started a novena to the Sacred Heart.

I took the candle home and had it burning whenever I, or my husband, was around. Praying turned out to be much easier than I had thought. That alone felt good, and I wondered about the huge sense of security and trust I came to feel when the novena was almost done. I had never felt that before. No solution whatsoever in sight, but knowing, not rationally, but spiritually trusting that Jesus was there and taking care. It felt great, and it made me let go.

After nine days, the candle was only half burnt but the novena prayer was done. That Friday night, was the end-of-the-school-year dinner with all the teachers of my school. I went and half way through, the geography teacher turned and asked me if there was any progress in the substitution case. "Well, Someone's working on it…" I replied. My colleague may not have noticed the capital in my answer, but the statement immediately proved true. He said: "Oh well, in case you still should need someone, the wife of a friend may be interested in the job." Of course I asked him, begged him, to contact the woman and let me know.

The next week she turned out not to be interested. "Too many hours," she wanted to have more time with her kids. Sigh. To add dramatic effect, later that week I spoke to a friend, a director at another school who was also looking for a classics teacher. He confirmed it was "almost impossible to find a good classics teacher nowadays." (Yes! Thank you, Wim Kokx—I needed that!)

Can you imagine how I felt by then? I still had the candle burning and I wasn't desperate, but when anyone asked, "What are you going to do about getting a substitute?" the only thing I could do was fall silent because I didn't know.

Shortly after that it was time to work on the next year's program. I suggested that as an emergency solution, we could opt for periodical education; no spare lessons the first half year and double the amount (or somewhere near the double amount) of lessons when I would come back. The day after I put that suggestion forward, I read in the Old Testament about Sara being impatient and encouraging Abram to sleep with Hagar (complicating God's plan) just because she thought the miracle she wished for wouldn't happen!

That story gave me back my courage—I felt I should be bold and trust that God would give me the exact thing I had wished for. Knowing that the candle was still burning, I thought, "Let's see what happens when the candle has burnt up."

That afternoon, the phone suddenly rang—my direct colleague, Hanna was practically jumping up and down with excitement, "We may have found a substitute!" she exclaimed. She went on to explain that the German teacher had all of a sudden remembered his old neighbor, who was a retired classics teacher with many years of experience, and who had used the exact books we were using, might be interested! "I've called the fellow," she told me, "but he wasn't home. I'm going to try again tonight."

A couple of days later, the candle was almost gone. In fact it was just a soft glow when I got home at six, about two hours late in comparison to normal Tuesdays. It was the Feast of Thomas the Unbeliever, and that day I had seen my substitute with my own eyes. He was everything I could have ever wished for. He had many years of experience, wasn't looking for a full job, proved a good contra-weight for my loquacious, sometimes bull-dozering colleague, who still liked him very much, nevertheless!

I was so excited that I practically glowed for days. In fact, I'm still raving about this wonderful experience. I feel like those blessed people in Jesus' time who, after he had performed a miracle for them, couldn't keep quiet about it no matter how much he asked them to!

The final blessing of the story is that on the eighth of August our beautiful daughter Rosa was born. She's almost two weeks old now and absolutely lovely. I've never heard my husband singing as much before as he does now.

Ria Post   *Den Haag, Zuid-Holland, Netherlands*

Why is it so important that you are with God and God alone on the mountain top? It's important because it's the place in which you can listen to the voice of the One who calls you the beloved. To pray is to listen to the One who calls you "my beloved daughter," "my beloved son," "my beloved child." To pray is to let that voice speak to the center of your being, to your guts, and let that voice resound in your whole being.

Henri Nouwen

The value of consistent prayer is not that He will hear us, but that we will hear Him.

William McGill

Prayer may not change things for you, but it for sure changes you for things.

Samuel M. Shoemaker

Ten Minute Meditation

Courage is being open to taking a new pathway if it opens before you.

Imagine you are walking in your beautiful garden. It is early morning, and the sun is just starting to rise and send fingers of rosy light onto the path before you. As you walk along you notice that the pathway is going into an area you have never seen before. Hmmm?

Should you follow it? You have never gone that way before. You look ahead and you see that Jesus is ahead of you on this pathway.

A new adventure, a time of discovery for you. Will you continue?

This pathway may be a new way of looking at someone, an insight on a relationship you have been closed to. Ask Jesus today to reveal to you the new path he has opened before you.

Whether it is a path of new prayer, new direction or new hope, go forward with joy and excitement, because Jesus is going before you.

Prayer when time is completed:

Jesus,
every day
presents new possibilities
of growth.
May I always
be open to your
guidance.
Amen

M
E
D
I
T
A
T
I
O
N

233

Pushed to the Edge

My story is one of many years worth of prayer which led to an answer I never expected, but one that completely changed my life for the better. When I was young, I had big dreams of someday working for a large corporation, having a house, family, and pets; the typical American dream, so to speak. I have a degree in accounting and wound up working as a teller for a local bank in town. Not exactly the dream job for a college graduate but it was a start. My husband, a writer for the local newspaper, and I struggled as together we barely made $20,000.00 a year. We had two children by the age of twenty-eight and our little apartment was bursting at the seams.

We made the decision to buy a house. With barely enough for a small down payment, we moved into our new house when my son was just six months old. My daughter Gina was three.

As always, when you first move into a house, there are several expenses that you never bargain for. Not to mention, my health was not that great as I had recurring stomach problems since my teen years as well as several allergies. As our bills grew, so did the balances on our credit cards. I prayed over and over for a solution to our money problems. We would just get ahead and some new disaster would happen. My son, Marcus, was stricken with an immune system deficiency when he was two years old and was in and out of the hospital on a monthly basis for treatments.

At this young age, my husband was not always the most understanding person in the world, and my timidity and fear of confrontation led to me hide the fact that we were getting into more and more debt.

I just kept praying for an answer. In the mid 90s, our church opened up a Eucharistic adoration chapel. I went there on a weekly basis and prayed for help with financial problems.

I received many promotions over the years with the bank but with each salary increase, came more bills. Soon the children were attending Catholic school and there was tuition to pay, uniforms, lunches, etc. Still, I continued to pray for a solution.

I had risen to the level of branch manager with the title of Assistant Vice President of a large corporate bank in the local area. Job pressures were intense and not only was I now praying for financial relief, but for relief of the mental stress as well. Faithfully, I went to chapel each week and prayed for an end to all this mess.

Unfortunately, I decided to take matters into my own hands, thinking that God would help me through it. There was a customer that I had taken care of who needed a large sum of money refunded to their account. I refunded this money, but as it turns out, our corporate area also refunded the money as well. When the customer called to alert me to the situation, I took this as a sign from God as a temporary solution to the problem. I took that money and used it to pay for some of our bills. It went unnoticed. As time went on, things similar to this had occurred, and I would take advantage of the situation.

I would pay the money back in small amounts in the same, unnoticed manner.

Eventually, I came up with the idea to ask my aunt, who had great credit if we could use her line of credit to help pay down some of our bills since she wasn't using it. She agreed reluctantly over the phone and assumed I'd be bringing papers by for her to sign.

I didn't do that. I signed her name to the papers myself and paid off several thousand dollars worth of our debt with her money. Still, even through all this bad stuff, I continued to pray. I made regular payments on her account as I said I would but eventually it all caught up with me.

One day, the auditor came to look at our books. The funny thing is, she caught me in the act of actually helping out a customer in need rather than myself. After the bank investigated and found this to be misappropriation of funds, I was fired from my job.

Of course, my husband had no idea any of this was going on. When I was fired, he blamed the bank because I led him to believe it was all them and not me. Then one day, I got a call from the local police department. I knew I had to tell him what had happened. In the mean time, it had only taken me one month to obtain a new job at the local college where I had gotten my degree, Franciscan University of Steubenville. They of course also had no idea of why I had lost my job either.

Eventually, my guilt got the best of me and I went to the police and confessed, then I went to my husband and confessed, then I went to my priest and confessed.

I felt as if I had ruined the lives of everyone around me. I was seeing a therapist and was planning suicide. I had written a letter to a dear friend whom I had known and trusted for years. I told him the story of what had happened and how I felt that everyone would be better off without me. In this friend, as well as in the people with whom I worked, finally came the answer to my years of prayer. By now it was mid 2004. I had been praying for nearly ten years for relief from the financial burdens and the mental stress.

This friend, this angel called and said that he was planning to take care of the money that I owed the bank and this would greatly help my chances in court of staying out of jail. I couldn't believe my ears and I didn't want to accept his offer until he told me why he was doing it. He said that God told him to. That God told him that he could save me if he did this. I asked how I could ever repay him and he told me to lay all my burdens down at the foot of the cross. He said to just love myself and love my family and that was his repayment.

I was so full of love and gratitude. God also let me know when the time was right to talk to my bosses at the university and they too were very understanding. In fact, the human resources director hugged me and said, "We all make mistakes. You can continue to work here as long as you want."

Eventually, my husband forgave me as well.

I was placed on three years probation with the courts and I was able to keep my job, my house, and best of all, my family and friends.

The conversion I experienced was incredible. Just as Jesus paid the debt for all of our sins, so this friend paid the debt for mine. Now my life is simple. I am a secretary for the University. My husband, children, and

I lead a simple life and we always tell each other everything now. My top priority is to please God and to do his will and his work always.

I continue to keep that same hour of adoration in our Eucharistic adoration chapel. I no longer have to pray for relief from those types of problems, but I will never forget the wonderful answer which God gave me to those prayers.

Kathy A. Giannamore   *Toronto, Ohio*

Kathy Giannamore is the author of At the Foot of the Cross, *a true life story of her conversion of which this story is but a small part. A wonderful, encouraging book for anyone who has ever made a "mistake" and wants to know how loving, powerful and ready God is to bring them though it.*

Every morning lean thine arms awhile
Upon the window-sill of heaven
And gaze upon thy Lord,
Then, with vision in thy heart,
Turn strong to meet thy day.

Thomas Blake

How can God speak to us if we don't take time to listen? Quietness is essential to listening. If we are too busy to listen, we won't hear. It takes time and quietness to prepare to listen to God. Ps. 62:5

Charles Stanley

Prayer is where the action is.

John Wesley

Something for Myself

Fibromyalgia seems to have become an umbrella term that encompasses numerous intermittent aches and pains, especially those with unknown causes. To those of us who have it, the pain is real and inescapable.

Having fibromyalgia combined with arthritis and another possible hereditary degenerative disease, I have various discomforts off and on throughout most days and nights. This wasn't the case a few years ago.

My pain was much worse a few years ago, and I spent the greater part of most days in pain. It was bad enough that I'd been put on several medications that included muscle relaxers, antianxiety and antidepressant drugs, something to help me fall asleep, something to help me stay asleep, something because I wasn't getting enough sleep, a pill for acid reflux, and this and that for stress. All that, plus vitamins. I had to start carrying a pillbox with a beeper to remind me what to take and when. This all changed within three seconds.

I was sitting at my computer reading e-mail from friends. A wonderful group I am part of sends prayer requests when necessary, and we also circulate special prayers we find. I must have come across a prayer I particularly liked, so as is often the case, though not often enough, I started praying right there at the computer.

I prayed for a lot of things I wanted for my family and friends, the families of my friends, and the friends of my family. The list was pretty long and I felt bad for asking for so much, but I kept on. There was plenty I wanted for several people. Some were people I know and love; others were loved ones of loved ones. And some were strangers from the prayer requests I received from friends. When I finally finished, I was feeling fairly selfish and greedy for asking for so many things. I know He can handle it all; I just don't like praying as if I'm handing God a *to do* list.

But God doesn't see things the way we do. Immediately I heard a loving male voice, soft yet clear, say, "Since you ask nothing for yourself." Almost before I could finish my thought of "Nothing for myself?" a feeling started at the base of my back and began moving up. It felt exactly like something warm being lifted out. It was a physical sensation of relief. I plainly felt the pain being peeled out of my body, right out the tops of my shoulders and away.

I sat stunned, amazed at the sudden realization that not only had I really heard the voice, but had just been healed of the symptoms of at least two incurable diseases in my back. How magnificent is God's mercy! It felt fantastic! I also somehow understood that while my back pain was gone, the diseases that had progressed to that point were still part of my cross to bear. I was not cured, but had been given a much-appreciated respite. I stopped to recall what I had prayed for, and though I had prayed for things I wanted, I couldn't think of one thing I had asked for me.

It is coming back now, mild pains and discomforts. These I offer for the holy souls in purgatory in the hope that it gives them some relief or blessed release. I'm grateful for their intercession and appreciate the additional years that I've been able to do more with my family and friends. I'm thankful that God sees better than we do. Oh, and all those prayers I asked? He's said "yes" to most of them and I'm grateful for that too.

Deborah F. Flynt   *Foxworth, Mississippi*

Nothing tends more to cement the hearts of Christians than praying together. Never do they love one another so well as when they witness the outpouring of each other's hearts in prayer.

Charles Finney

2x4 From Heaven

"Hi Spike, do you have a moment? I need to talk with you."

Spike was one of the priests at St. Francis Xavier Church where I attended Mass. He got his nickname because his hair changed with the phases of the moon. Spike had been a dentist before becoming a priest and I thought the combination of his medical knowledge and spiritual occupation might come in handy when I asked his advice about being hooked up to an insulin pump to manage my type 1 diabetes.

"Sure, I'm just finishing up in the sacristy, meet me here."

I had called all the references that the doctor had given me for patients who used insulin pumps. All the patients positively endorsed the pump. Most of them had nightmarish diabetic stories to tell. To me, they all sounded much sicker than I was. The best I could deduct from their stories was that it was better to be a pump user than have to take multiple injections everyday. I still had my doubts.

"I'll meet you at the church in ten minutes," I said as I kissed my husband, who was bathing our two young sons, good-bye.

"I am having serious reservations about being hooked up to a machine for the rest of my life," I said to Fr. "Spike."

"Will it make living with diabetes better for you?" he asked.

"All the patients I have contacted say they are better off with the pump. I just don't know if I am willing to take this step. I will never be able to be normal."

"How long have you been diabetic?" He waited; obviously this was a rhetorical question. "If this will make controlling your blood sugar easier and your doctor recommends it, then I think you should go for it."

"Thanks, I needed to hear those words from a friend."

I had just lied to a priest. My dilemma was that Spike's words had not calmed my paranoia of wearing an insulin infusion pump. I had wanted Spike to say that there was a miracle cure. I wanted him to tell me how I could conjure, through prayer or pilgrimage, a miracle that would release me from my thirty-year daily grind of diabetes. I wanted a miracle to cure me so that I didn't have to sacrifice each moment of each day to a disease. I wanted a big smack on the forehead by the preacher pronouncing me, "Heeealed."

I went home disappointed and sat in the basement recreation room of my house, surrounded by the scent of dog and graham crackers. I waited for the noises of the house to settle. When all was quiet, I began pacing feverishly around the room to work out the pent up venom I felt in my gut. Finally, the festering tirade to God, who in that moment had disappointed me so severely, broke loose.

"What is this? Now you want me to be hooked up to a machine? While I sleep? When I shower? Will there never be a moment of peace from this nagging disease? I was churning and pacing, shaking my fists at God, knowing and not caring that I was breaking all protocol in approaching my Creator.

"They told me thirty years ago there would be a cure. This insulin pump is no cure. It's confinement. I'm supposed to have the faith of a mustard seed? How much faith does it take? Obviously, a lot more than I have."

I couldn't stop. I kept going like a spoiled child. "How much more will you take from me. Now my kidneys are spilling protein. Is it dialysis next? Another drug? What else is it that you want from me? I am so sick of this. I hate you and your silent demands and your tests to prove how much I love you. Are you that insecure?"

The ranting started to take the form of a lovers quarrel; the more mature partner quietly letting hysteria spin me to exhaustion. I collapsed in tears on the couch, the curses and pleas still silently playing in my head. Finally, I went up the stairs to the bathroom to brush my teeth for bed.

"How can I do this? I can't be hooked to a machine for the rest of my life."

I was standing in the small bathroom adjusting my pajamas. As soon as the words had formed in my mind, it felt like a large baseball bat hit me on the back of the head, literally propelling me face first to the floor.

241

I lay on the tiles for a moment, dazed. I picked myself up and sat on the edge of the bathtub. I gazed around the tiny room and looked behind the shower curtain for somebody holding a club or a two-by-four.

I touched the back of my head. No bump. No pain. I looked at my fingers, no blood. I stood and looked in the mirror; no mark appeared on my cheek where my face had hit the floor. I quickly tested my blood sugar to see if I had experienced a hypoglycemic episode. Seventy-two flashed on the glucose meter's screen, a little low but not *pass out* low.

Suddenly, I was filled with a sense of peace. "You're fine," skimmed across my mind. No spoken voice, just a smack to bring my hysterical self back in line. I had been smote by the two-by-four of heaven; a loving tap to get me back on the path of gratitude. All reservation about insulin pump therapy left me. I was filled with the assurance that everything would be okay.

"Thank You." I whispered.

Maureen F. Regulinski   *Richmond, Virginia*

There is a difference between believing that prayer is important and believing it is essential. 'Essential' means there are things that will not happen without prayer.

Dee Duke

He who runs from God in the morning will scarcely find Him the rest of the day.

John Bunyan

Always Under His Care

All my childhood I had prayed for a cat. Any cat would do, but what I dreamt most was of an Abyssinian cat. My husband made that dream come true with Snolea Nutmeg Tokay, my first Abyssinian.

When the Air Force sent us to Belgium, we went happily with our three children, one on the way, and our seven cats. Our cats were well loved, as were the kittens born to them. Every single person who took one of our cats came back and said it was the best pet they had ever had.

For the first few years, our male cat bred European females, but it got to the point that bringing strange cats into the house upset the other cats, so we made the decision to stop breeding. Then a Belgian woman called whose cat we had bred before, and I began forming the words in my mind in Flemish to tell her we didn't breed cats anymore. When she finished talking, the words that came out of my mouth in Flemish were, "Sure, bring her over."

When I got off the phone, I told my husband I had no idea why I said that, and that I would call her back if he wanted me to. Michael said it would be okay with him if we bred the cat one more time, so we did.

Less than a month after breeding that lady's female cat, our home was destroyed by a fire and we lost all of our precious cats. Material things were inconsequential—our whole family mourned the loss of our cats. Thankfully, when the woman found out about our fire, she said she would save two kittens for us.

I consider it a miracle that God had different words come out of my mouth than I had intended to speak when the woman called to see if we would breed her cat. If He hadn't, we would have never had Timmy and Tommy to love and remind us of our dear sweet babies awaiting us in heaven.

We no longer breed cats, but take in homeless ones in the names of the cats we lost. This miracle that God gave me has made me realize that He does anticipate our needs, and that we are always under His care. I have no fears about the future because I know God can and will take every tragedy and bring good from it.

Deborah M. Turner   *Yorktown, Virginia*

A day without prayer is a day without blessing, and a life without prayer is a life without power.

Edwin Harvey

There is not in the world a kind of life more sweet and delightful than that of a continual conversation with God.

Brother Lawrence

Effective prayer is prayer that attains what it seeks. It is prayer that moves God, effecting its end.

Charles G. Finney

Rich is the person who has a praying friend.

Janice Hughes

Ten Minute Meditation

Roadblocks. Sometimes it seems that you cannot move forward. When this happens, do you feel a sense of panic?

Perhaps this is a time to change directions for a time. Roadblocks usually offer alternate routes. A detour may take us out of our way for a bit, but eventually we will reach our destination if we can accept it and go peacefully with it.

Today, imagine that you have come to a closed door in your life. Try and try as you might the door will not open. Stop, look around, and prayerfully ask God what other direction you might go that will still help you to continue forward.

Prayer when time is completed:

Jesus,
I always have a roadmap
of the direction
I think I should be heading towards.
Help me to relax
when roadblocks happen.
Help me to see that a detour
does not mean
I will not get to my destination.
It may take longer,
but the new route
will open up new possibilities
I have never explored before.
Help me to be open
to see them.
Amen.

MEDITATION

Something Good is Going to Happen

My friend Craig lives in Los Osos, California and has type 1 diabetes. In March of 2007, he ended up with double pneumonia after riding a motorcycle in driving rain to see his mom and step-dad in another state. He was experiencing so much pain just trying to breathe that he would hold his chest while walking up the steps.

Craig's diabetes was out of whack as well, and he was experiencing weekly seizures. I could tell he was starting to give up. He was almost sixty years old, had a great wife, two daughters and three grandchildren, but was starting to tell me, "If I die, I've had a good life."

I didn't want to hear that death talk and told him, "Taylor (who is his oldest grandchild) really needs you and so does the rest of your family. I'm going to pray and put you on my prayer list and something good is going to happen."

I belong to an e-mail prayer group that includes Fr. John Vaughn, the former Minister General of the Friars Minor, the retired Franciscan sisters in Marian Residence of Santa Maria (the prayer powerhouse of the community), Baptist relatives in Canada, and an evangelical missionary sister-in-law in Peru, as well as family and friends. I completely believe in the power of prayer, and in connecting people to pray together.

I left for Delaware in April to help my daughter who was having her third child, and was gone for two months. When I returned, Craig told me his miracle story.

A couple of weeks after I left Los Osos, he went to the doctor for a cat scan. Craig had smoked for twenty years, but had stopped the year before. The doctor knew how sick Craig had been and was expecting to find black, diseased lungs.

The doctor called Craig in for a second cat scan, saying, "We think we did something wrong and need to take a second look at your lungs." The doctor couldn't believe the results.

After the second cat scan, the doctor told Craig, "I am amazed. You have the clear lungs of a baby." Craig was amazed too, and so thankful to the people who had prayed for him. After some adjustments and a new type of insulin, Craig is no longer experiencing seizures. He told me this story again on his sixtieth birthday on September 29, 2007.

Carol M. Valine Zarek   *Los Osos, California*

Prayer is not asking. It is a longing of the soul. It is daily admission of one's weakness... It is better in prayer to have a heart without words than words without a heart.

Mahatma Ghandi

You may pray for an hour and still not pray. You may meet God for a moment and then be in touch with Him all day.

Fredrik Wisloff

Our prayers should be for blessings in general, for God knows best what is good for us.

Socrates

The Grace of Baptism

I had never had any children though I had always wanted them, so after my husband's biological children were almost grown, we adopted first one baby girl and then another. Unfortunately, three days after the second baby came into our lives and our hearts, her biological mother asked for her back. Since hers was to be a private adoption, we had no choice but to return her.

Two months after we gave back our baby, the phone rang one morning and we were asked if we still wanted the baby. Of course we did, so we drove immediately to get her. When we arrived at the house to which we were directed we found a terribly sick infant, so we took her first to our local parish to have her baptized and then to the emergency room at our hospital. The baby was seen by our family physician who told us that he was afraid there was nothing much to do for her but to take her home and love her, so we did. This occurred on a Saturday.

The following Monday she was no better, so we arranged an appointment at the doctor's office on Thursday.

Over the next few days we determined that she must be blind and deaf because we were unable to elicit any response to sounds close to her ears or things in her line of vision. Her life consisted of crying, eating, crying, sleeping, and more crying. Her little body seemed so tense it was almost rigid.

The earliest appointment that we were able to arrange was for five days after we took her home. That Thursday morning, as my husband, my sister, and I were drinking coffee, the doorbell rang. The priest who had baptized her was at the door and asked to see her. This was very surprising because we had not spoken to him since her baptism, and he had never been in our home. We told him that she wasn't doing well and that we had an appointment with the doctor within the next two hours.

He asked if he could hold her, so I took her from the crib and handed her to him. The moment he took her in his arms she became calm and quiet. The tiny little body relaxed as if she were at total peace. He wanted to pray for her, so he laid hands on her and prayed over her. His prayer was one of the most beautiful prayers any of us had ever heard. He then left so we could get to her doctor's appointment. At the doctor's office she was seen by a physician's assistant, and when he examined her she was a perfectly healthy, normal infant. She is now twenty-four years old, intelligent, in good health, and possesses a profoundly deep faith in God. I truly believe that God cares for her deeply and that He has a special purpose for her life.

Thanks be to God, who always hears our prayers.

Virginia Schmuck   *Portales, New Mexico*

When God speaks, oftentimes His voice will call for an act of courage on our part.

Charles Stanley

Prayer requires more of the heart than the tongue.

Adam Clarke

Seven days without prayer makes one weak.

Allen Vartlett

Key to Forgiveness

In 1991, I became the guardian of my youngest sister's three girls, Rachel, Gemma, and Bianca, because of the instability of their parent's lives. I knew the kids needed a family lifestyle and I tried to give them one.

A court investigator had told Rachel, who was sixteen, that I was wrong for not allowing her more freedom, which led to the day Rachel disappeared. She called me in the evening to announce she was going to the movies! I told her to come home *now*. She came into the house furious and verbally exploded in my face.

Rachel was so out of control I had to call the police, who took her to a mental health facility because she threatened to kill herself. Her parents were angry with me and the family splintered. Devastated, I turned to a daily prayer of "O my sweet Jesus! Please put this family back together."

Just before Easter, 1992, Rachel was at another facility and her therapist wanted a family meeting with my sister, her husband, and me. It was like mixing gasoline with lighted matches.

The tension in that small room was as if a mosquito buzzed loudly inside my head. I needed to focus; I needed to be at peace. My little prayer was my only comforting thought. Over and over I repeatedly told myself: "O God! This family needs to be healed! Let me be the door through which forgiveness enters this room and the hearts of those who are hurting!"

I did not realize that my sister was the *key* to this door; without her mercy, the door would stay locked; maybe forever.

After a volatile session, we were all exiting the building when my sister suddenly turned and hugged me, sobbing that she loved me.

A tremendous cloud of peace enveloped me and I felt as if I was standing on air. Then I turned around and threw my arms around my brother-in-law. I could hear the loud gasp of the therapist. I knew Jesus had touched us. Through my sister, the key had found the lock, turned, and the door to forgiveness was thrown wide open. All the hours of praying for my family had been answered. We were whole again; we were healed.

Someone once said, "To raise your own children is to walk with nature; to raise someone else's children is to walk with God." Truer words were never spoken.

Martha Dolciamore   *Soquel, California*

Be thankful that God's answers are wiser than your answers.

William Culbertson

What we usually pray to God is not that His will be done, but that He approve ours.

Helga Bergold Gross

Love him totally who gave himself totally for your love. His beauty the sun and moon admire, and of his gifts there is no limit in abundance, preciousness, and magnitude.

St. Clare of Assisi

Ten Minute Meditation

Time moving too fast? Maybe today is the day to just *look* for your ten minutes. Find a nice quiet place—hopefully cool—and just look and listen and enjoy.

Prayer when time is completed:

> *Jesus,*
> *to spend time*
> *with you*
> *doing nothing*
> *is everything.*
> *Amen.*

M
E
D
I
T
A
T
I
O
N

Unexpected Blessings

"I thank God every time I remember you." Philippians 1:3

The poem "Holland" talks about an artificial amalgam of tulips, windmills, clogs, Edam cheese, greenhouses and the traditional costume of Volendam fishermen. It also talks about New York and its tall buildings, art galleries, museums and other historic sites. This analogy between Holland and New York compares the birth of a normal healthy baby and a special needs baby and how differently a person reacts to the two places and situations.

Rolando Adriel was born on March 1, 1978. His birth took our family to Holland instead of New York. Our journey to Holland began during delivery. He was born with cerebral palsy due to complications. From the beginning, Roland, as we called him, was a fighter and full of God's light. God graced our family and our community with fourteen years of his presence.

Literally speaking, he was not a giant in linear measure but rather in the measure of his character and impact on our lives. As days passed and turned into years, I realized that the beautiful baby I held in my arms would never be able to do what other normal children did. He never walked, spoke a word, or took care of himself but his beautiful brown eyes spoke a thousand words. Roland taught our family how to pray without ceasing, to empathize with the needs of others, to accept the will of God and to understand how God loved us. He manifested all the gifts of the Spirit such as love, kindness, charity, peace, joy, fortitude, perseverance in prayer, understanding and wisdom.

It's been fifteen years since Roland's death and I can truly say that I understand profoundly that although Holland is not New York, Holland is a wonderful place with its own beauty and uniqueness. Roland was a lesson in God's love, and in his helplessness, he was larger than life to me.

Azalia C. Perez   *Hebbronville, Texas*

Note: Below is the poem, "Welcome to Holland" by Emily Perl Kingsley. This is the original poem although the poem "Holland" remembered by the author (Azalia C Perez) was about planning a trip to New York rather than Italy. I received permission by Emily Perl Kingsley to share with you her poem. It is so beautiful and I can see why it has been adapted to so many different places—which is how Azalia discovered it.

Welcome To Holland
By
Emily Perl Kingsley

I am often asked to describe the experience of raising a child with a disability - to try to help people who have not shared that unique experience to understand it, to imagine how it would feel. It's like this......

When you're going to have a baby, it's like planning a fabulous vacation trip - to Italy. You buy a bunch of guide books and make your wonderful plans. The Coliseum. The Michelangelo David. The gondolas in Venice. You may learn some handy phrases in Italian. It's all very exciting.

After months of eager anticipation, the day finally arrives. You pack your bags and off you go. Several hours later, the plane lands. The stewardess comes in and says, "Welcome to Holland."

"Holland?!?" you say. "What do you mean Holland?? I signed up for Italy! I'm supposed to be in Italy. All my life I've dreamed of going to Italy."

But there's been a change in the flight plan. They've landed in Holland and there you must stay.

The important thing is that they haven't taken you to a horrible, disgusting, filthy place, full of pestilence, famine and disease. It's just a different place.

So you must go out and buy new guide books. And you must learn a whole new language. And you will meet a whole new group of people you would never have met.

It's just a <u>different</u> place. It's slower-paced than Italy, less flashy than Italy. But after you've been there for a while and you catch your breath, you look around.... and you begin to notice that Holland has windmills....and Holland has tulips. Holland even has Rembrandts.

But everyone you know is busy coming and going from Italy... and they're all bragging about what a wonderful time they had there. And for the rest of your life, you will say "Yes, that's where I was supposed to go. That's what I had planned."

And the pain of that will never, ever, ever, ever go away... because the loss of that dream is a very very significant loss.

But... if you spend your life mourning the fact that you didn't get to Italy, you may never be free to enjoy the very special, the very lovely things ... about Holland.

It Makes a Difference

As soldiers, my buddies and I experience a lot of spiritual things before we step onto the battlefield every day; it's the way we get focused right before we leave. I kind of go into my own little place, taking a few minutes to talk to God. I'll say something like, "Hey, give me the strength to lead these men, and give me the strength to do the right thing out there."

Everybody takes a few minutes to focus like that. Then, right before we step onto the field we'll say, "Okay, let's make sure this is a good one." That is always a very, very spiritual moment for me.

A lot of split-second decisions have to be made while we are in the midst of battle. At those times my prayer will be something like, "Hey, watch over me, make sure I'm taking care of my men and the boys, and make sure we're doing the right thing out here. And keep us safe." There's a lot of that type of praying going on during combat.

Once, about the eighteenth or nineteenth day during my second tour to Iraq, my prayers were answered in a big way. We were finishing up from being on patrol, and some of our trucks arrived to load us up. We were coming out of several houses that we had been in.

The trucks pulled in and the first group loaded up. All was fine. Then the second group went to load up. I was making sure we were getting our final counts right when, Pow!, A sniper suddenly shot and hit a guy who was next to me.

When that first shot rang out, we returned fire on the sniper. Then we started taking fire from another area. At one point I remember looking through my scope, but something wasn't making sense. I knew what I was shooting at, but I wasn't hitting my target. I thought, "Ah, I'm not shooting at the right thing; I guess I need to shoot over here."

I remember thinking that I wasn't seeing correctly as I watched my rounds impact. It was sort of unreal, and everything was slowing down for me. I knew something was wrong with my gun, but I didn't know what. I figured that at least I was firing, so I kept on aiming and shooting the best I could. In times like that, there is a lot of adrenalin pumping through your body and you just keep moving.

We assaulted the first house, and when we were done clearing it, we started for the second house. We cleared a lot of buildings that day and pushed through the neighborhood to make sure it was all secure.

It was during one of the funny little pauses we have when nothing is really going on when one of the guys poked at my gun and said, "Oh yeah, you might want to take a look at this." And then he said, "Hey, take a look at that! Your scope is done!"

I looked at it and my mouth must have dropped about a foot! A huge hole appeared in the scope of my gun. A bullet had been aimed at my head and missed me by a mere inch. All's I could say was, "Ah geez, here we go!"

When I got back to camp, my boss took a look at my gun and said, "You've definitely given up one of your nine lives today." I just looked at him and smiled, "Yeah, that one was pretty close." Then everybody started making comments like that.

Afterwards, when my adrenalin slowed down, I felt a huge sense of relief. I definitely felt very fortunate. I called the guy who got shot to make sure he was okay, and he was. I was so happy!

You know, we get a lot of religious support from back home. It's like a lot of people come out of the woodwork to keep us in their hearts and prayers, and look after us. We are thankful for the support we get from the people back home: family, friends, and churches. It makes a difference.

Sonny Mott   *Norfolk, Virginia*

The Coach Mechanic

In 1997, I led a group of pilgrims to the House of Prayer in Achill, County Mayo, Ireland. We were about two miles from our destination when suddenly our coach came to a halt. The driver informed me that the acceleration cable had broken.

At that point, we were stranded in a fairly remote location with no mobile phones to rely on. I knew we needed the help of our Blessed Mother, so I asked our group to join me in the rosary.

Towards the end of the first mystery, some of us noticed a rainbow. Then a car pulled up in front of the coach and a man with bright red curly hair jumped out. "Hello there! Has your bus broken down? I am a coach mechanic, can I help you?"

Wow, a coach mechanic! Our Lady had answered our prayer a thousand fold. Tom, our guardian angel, spoke with our driver for a minute and then lifted a floor panel in the aisle of the bus. He asked the driver to steer the bus at his command while he pressed a throttle, and before we knew it, the bus was back on the road.

We arrived at the House of Prayer just in time for Mass, and the priest gave thanks for the help we had received through the power of prayer. As an extra bonus, Tom finished repairing our coach while we attended Mass. The rosary is truly a powerful prayer.

Paula C. Hagan   *Skelmersdale, Lancashire, England*

Holding His Hand to Heaven

I've decided to write down my experiences with God. I guess I'm afraid that in time I may forget. After all, it's through the death of my son Jason that I've come to truly let Jesus into my heart. I have a family here and I can't always be thinking of Jason and what he went through or I will quit living for the people I still have. I know I will see Jason again and my heart aches for that time, because it will be then that I will feel complete again. Until then I struggle with going on.

My mother got sick when I was seven years old with Hodgkin's disease. I didn't know at the time how serious it was; I just knew she had to go to the hospital a lot. I went to Catholic grade school at the time. In religion class I remember being told that if you obey the Ten Commandments, prayed and went to church, God would give you what you asked for. So I would ask him to make my mother better, but she kept getting sicker.

When I was around ten years old my brothers and I got all our money together and walked up to the church to light a *magic candle* because those requests went straight to God. My mother lived through the surgery she was having at the time and we just knew it was because of the *magic candle.*

Then my mother got sicker and died when I was thirteen years old. From that time on for years I figured God didn't answer my prayers or He didn't hear them. I thought he was mad at me. I must have done something wrong, especially because after that my dad started drinking a lot. So I cooked, cleaned and took care of my bothers who at the time were nine, twelve and thirteen years old. As far as church went, I felt as though God didn't want me there. He told me that by taking my mother. When I had bad times I would talk to God in case he had forgiven me and might want to start listening. I was afraid not to believe in God but I really had my doubts. I believed he didn't want me.

When I graduated from high school and my friends were going off to college and looking for money, all I wanted was to get married to a great guy and have children, so that I could have a family, traditions and happy memories that I didn't have growing up. We didn't have to be rich. All I wanted was to be together in love.

I met Bill and we had three beautiful children and all my dreams came true. I thanked God everyday for my blessings and also for starting to hear my prayers again. It felt so good to have God as my friend, I kept thanking him everyday. My father no longer drank the way he did when my mother died and we became very close. Jason became the son that my dad couldn't enjoy while we were growing up, because he had so many hardships back then.

Then Jason got sick with leukemia and my world fell apart. I asked God, "Now what did I do. I'm so sorry for whatever it was. Please make him better." The doctors told us he would need a bone marrow transplant. That the best donor would be that of a sibling and that there was only about a twenty-five percent chance of that happening. We all got tested and as we waited for the results, I prayed like I have never prayed before. I prayed for forgiveness, even though I had no idea what I had done. I prayed for strength and for Jason's health. I prayed, "Please let one of the other children match." When we got the results back the doctors were shocked and amazed. Not only did one child match but they both did. The doctors told us they had never seen anything like this before. It was as if we had triplets.

I gave the credit to God. From that point on, I believed that God was listening and this was his way of letting me know he wasn't going to take Jason. I would tell people, "God knows how much Jason means to me, I couldn't live without him. He's not going to take him and God is going to make him better."

Jason was able to come home for two months before the transplant. Everything was going great and his body was responding to the oral chemo they had him on. All of our spirits were up. We truly believed we were going to beat this disease. While we were home, we made sure we spent a lot of family time together. Then one night something happened to me that was so frightening. I was alone, lying on the couch and praying. I must have fallen asleep when I was awakened by this harsh, cruel voice yelling, "Why are you believing in someone you have never seen?" I jumped up to see who it was, but the room was empty. I was so afraid and although I didn't see anyone, I felt someone was there. I said, "Because it's all I have. I can't go through this alone. I need God." Then I heard this wicked laugh and it faded away. I just sat there too afraid to move. I never heard that voice or laugh again. I couldn't figure out what that was all about then, but now I believe it was Satan trying to pull me away.

I remember the day Make-A-Wish came to pick us up for Jason's wish. He was so excited we were going to Lone Star in a limo for lunch, then downtown for a computer. We had so much fun watching the excitement in Jason that day. When he came downstairs from getting dressed he had his Levi shirt, blue jeans, cowboy boots and cowboy hat on. Jason loved country; he listened to country music all the time. That day he was looking like a real cowboy. I told him how great he looked. Out of nowhere he looked at me and Bill and said "If I don't make it through the transplant this is what I want to wear in the casket." I was so shocked by that. I told him, "Jason every thing is going great. You're not going to die. Don't even think that." He just giggled and we all shrugged it off.

BJ wanted to be the donor. He was eleven years old. The doctors were leaning towards him anyway because he was a male. BJ was so happy that they picked him. If he was afraid he never told anyone. He had to have four days of injections right before transplant day. They were very painful for him because it made all his bones hurt. Then during the transplant he had to keep his arms extended for four hours and not move them. He did great and I was so proud of him. He never complained or changed his mind. Jason was so touched at seeing how much his brother loved him. Jenni went from BJ's room to Jason's visiting with them and seeing if there was anything she could do. I was so touched by seeing all the love that was going on between the three of them. After B J was done we all went into Jason's room. We watched BJ's marrow go into Jason. It felt as if God was right there with us. They needed ten million cells from BJ and he gave them forty million. Once again the doctors were amazed;

they had never had a donor so young donate so many cells. They were so thrilled and excited for the outcome. I continued to thank God for his blessings. Everything was going great.

About a week after the transplant, things started going wrong and Jason was showing signs of grafting. He started getting sick and continued to get worse every day for the next five days. The doctors had to put him in the ICU. He was put on a respirator and sedated into a coma. Our nightmare began all over again. The doctors were telling us he might die, that he has graft viruses host and it has destroyed his gut. He was also showing signs of liver problems. Jason finally stabilized about two weeks later and they started bringing him out of the coma. I prayed constantly asking God over and over, "Please let me keep him."

Jason started waking up enough to whisper to us. He was still on the respirator, but they were working on getting him off of it. One day Jason asked me what heaven was like. I told him, "I don't know, but I hear if you think of the happiest you have ever been and ten times that, that's how happy you are in heaven." Jason just smiled and nodded his head. Then he asked if he was going to die. I told him, "The doctors told us you were going to, but you're getting better now." Jason's eyes filled with tears. I asked him what was the matter and he said, "What would happen to you if I died? You always said that we were your world." I said, "Ahhh honey, I don't know, but when they told us you were going to die I knew I couldn't do anything to keep you. It was up to God. So I just prayed and thanked God for giving you to me for nine years, because if I would have never had you, I would have never had those nine years of happiness."

Bill asked him if he wanted us to say the Lord's Prayer. Jason nodded his head, so we started to pray, about half way through the prayer Jason turned his head away from us and was looking across the room. When we finished the prayer, Jason looked at us and asked us if we could see the angel standing over there. We said, "No." He said, "She is right over there, she is standing there with Jesus." I got scared because I had always believed that you never see the face of Jesus till death. I started to pray to myself real hard. "Please Jesus don't take him yet. I know he is not mine to keep and I promise I will give him back to you, but I need for him to know how much he's meant to me. I want to make sure he is not afraid to go to you. Please hear my prayer. I beg you." Then I asked Jason if he was sure it was Jesus with the angel. He said, "Yeah, it was that man on the cross and he had the word God above His head so that I would know that it was Him, but they are not there anymore."

I sat and watched and hoped that Jesus heard my prayer. Jason fell asleep and when he woke he said that the angel that was in the room earlier smiled at him and kissed him on his head. I asked him if Jesus was with her. He said no, but that the angel was so pretty. Jason said that he has seen her before, but that he couldn't remember where.

Jason slowly started to improve and they moved him from the ICU to a regular room. While we were there I asked him if his angel came with him. He said "Yeah, she's real nice, but I can't figure our where I have seen her before." I just told him not to worry, that it would come to him. A couple of weeks had gone by, and as he was lying there watching TV and I was sitting next to him looking through an angel book, Jason asked me what I was looking at. When I told him, he just looked at the pictures as I was turning the pages. I came to one page and he said, "That's the halo my angel has." It was a picture of an angel that had strands of pearls for a halo. I was surprised because I always envisioned angels with a stream of light around their head. I asked, "Is her halo just like that?" Jason said, "Yeah, its jewelry." I told him that they were called pearls. Then I asked him if it was the same angel that was in the book. He said, "No, just the halo is the same." As I continued to flip through the pages, at one point he said, "Wait, back up." So I flipped back some pages and he had me stop on one particular page. He said, "Let me see that picture close up." I held the book closer to him and he said, "That one looks a lot like my angel." It was a picture of a woman with two cherubs above her shoulders. I said, "But she doesn't have any wings." She had short dark hair and thin facial features. I asked him if his angel had wings. Jason said, "Yeah, but the face here looks a lot like my angel's face, but not exactly." We looked at more pictures to see if we could find the kind of wings she had, but we couldn't find any. Jason said that all the wings in the book were pointed and that his angel's wings were rounded.

Later on when Jason woke up from a nap he asked if when my brother came in from Erie, could he bring the picture he has on his bookcase of my mother. He had finally figured out where he has seen his angel before. "It's that picture; my angel is your mother." He said that he was going to ask her next time he saw her. I said, "Isn't that wonderful, maybe she is your guardian angel." Jason said, "No, Jesus made me and he knows I don't like to go anywhere alone. She is going to hold my hand to heaven." Well that threw me off guard. At the time, Jason was slowly improving and I believed he was going to get better. So I said to him, "Jayce, you're getting better, you're not going to die." He just shrugged his shoulders and said nothing.

I'm not sure if it was the same day or a couple of days later because when you are in the hospital for weeks like we were, you lose track of days and nights. Jason looked at me and said, "I asked my angel if she was your mother and she told me she used to be. Then I asked her if she was my grandmother and she told me she would have been." Then a sense of peace came over him. Although I never saw her, he continued to tell me how she would come to him in his dreams or stand by him in the room. One day, I asked him if she talks to him. He told me, "Sometimes." I asked him what they talked about and he told me I wasn't allowed to know. When I asked him why I wasn't allowed to know, he said, "Because you're going to be left behind." I couldn't accept that because even though Jason wasn't improving as fast as the doctors would have liked, he wasn't getting any worse. I still believed he was going to get better.

On June 22 at around 3:00 a.m., something happened that I have never been able to forget or erase from my mind. We were all sleeping and Jason called for me. I woke up and I couldn't figure out why Bill wasn't waking up. Anytime Jason called for either one of us, we both got up. I believe now that this time the Lord didn't intend for Bill to be a part of the experience. I went over to Jason to see what he needed and he told me he had to poop. When Jason pooped, because of the problems with his gut, it would sometimes be painful and he would have to squeeze my hand. I asked him if he needed to squeeze my hand and he told me no. I said that I would be right back that I was just going into the bathroom to get soap and water to clean him when he was done. Jason wasn't able to get out of bed because of the drugs he was on. He couldn't stand and his range of motion was very limited. He would just go to the bathroom in his pants and then we would clean him because it was less painful for him that way. When I got back I was sitting on the bed until he was done. I opened his pants to change him and my heart feel to my stomach, there was blood everywhere. As I was leaning over him and looking at all this blood, the first thing that came to my mind was, "My God, you're coming to take him aren't you? He's not going to get better and I promised I would give him back to you if you would get him out of ICU so that I could talk to him. That's what you did, didn't you? The doctors aren't making him better. Please! Please! Take this fear from my face because Jason doesn't know and I don't want him to see how frightened I am." Then I looked up at Jason and the look on his face was something to this day I can not describe, but in my heart I knew at the time that Jason knew what was happening. Neither one us said anything. I changed him and sat with him, holding his hand and stroking his head. Just loving him so much. I was so afraid of what was going to happen.

The next week was horrible and Jason took a turn for the worse. He was suffering with so much pain. The doctors kept running tests on him to try and find out what was causing all the bleeding. They worked on regulating his pain medicine. I was so afraid and sick inside, the feeling of helplessness was unbearable. The doctor kept saying, "It will be alright and he will be fine." But that sickening feeling in my heart kept telling me I was going to loose him, I didn't know when, but I knew; I just knew he was going to go to heaven.

We wanted to bring him home and on July 8 we did. His liver was not functioning and he was still bleeding but the doctors could do nothing else to save him. At home, we gave him pain medicine and fluids. He was getting platelets every other day and for the most part he was comfortable. Most importantly, he was constantly surrounded by the love of his family. No more hospital, tests or doctors.

Jason was home for about two days when he asked to look at all our picture albums. I was uncomfortable with this; after all, they were full of happier times, but I sat on the couch as he laid there and flipped through all the pages. Some pages he would linger on and others he just flipped on by. I remember BJ commenting on a picture or two and Jason looked at him and said, "Shhh." He didn't want anyone to talk to him as he looked at these albums. I couldn't tell what he was thinking and I was afraid to ask for fear it was something sad. Jason didn't look sad; it was almost as if he was memorizing them. When he was done he said, "Okay, you can put them away." Then he went to sleep. He never did say anything about the pictures.

One morning, Jason wanted us to put him in his wheel chair and take him outside. When we got outside, he wanted to face the back yard where he sat for a couple of hours just looking. Whenever Bill or I would say anything he would say, "Shhh." I asked him if it gave him a headache or something when we talked. He said, "No, I'm just listening." So I started to listen for whatever. What I began to hear amazed me. I heard the pool filter, birds chirping, the breeze blowing through the trees, dogs barking and cars in the distance. Then I began to realize what he was listening to. They were sounds that we take for granted and never really hear. After he was done outside he wanted to go into the house. He had us push him up to the front door which has a full view window in it. He sat there for about an hour the same way. He didn't want anyone to talk and he didn't say anything. Then he wanted us to put him back on the couch. He never did get back into his wheelchair again. We had the air conditioner on at the time, but I turned it off and opened the windows so he could listen. Now I will go sometimes by myself and just listen to the wonders of the world, like Jason taught me.

Shortly after all of this, Jason asked me if he went to heaven and didn't like it, could he come back. I believe the Lord spoke through me when I told him, "Yes, you can. Jesus doesn't make anyone stay who doesn't want to be there." I told him that I already talked to Jesus and he only takes people that are very special to Him. "You are so special to Jesus that he wants to show you His home. He knows that you are not sure you want to stay, so he is going to show you the places most important to Him. When he is done you can just say thank you, it is beautiful here, but I want to go back to my mom and dad. Then he'll send you back and you will get better and won't be sick anymore." Jason nodded his head and smiled, and he asked what if I come back and I'm in a casket? The Lord continued to speak through me and I said, "That won't happen because heaven time is different than earth time. Did you ever hear the saying; 'He ran the race in God speed time'?" Jason said, "Yeah, but I don't know what that means." I told him it means "Heaven time, its real fast. While you're seeing heaven, we will be here waiting for you to breath. We'll ask, did he breathe? Did you see him take a breath? Then all of a sudden you will start to breathe again and you'll get all better. It will be as if you were never sick." Jason nodded his head, then he asked, "Mom, next time you talk to Jesus could you ask Him, if while he is showing me heaven, could he have the angels take me to some of the places he is not going to show me? Then when I come back we can all look at them together." I said, "Sure, I'll ask Him that." The next day he asked me if I asked Jesus yet. I told him, "Yes, I asked Him, and he said no problem, that would be fine." Jason smiled.

Jason continued to get weaker everyday. Although the pain was under control, he was dying a little bit more every day. It broke my heart to see him this way. I would continue to pray. In my prayers, I found myself asking Jesus to please take him home, because I loved Jason so much I wanted him to live and have fun. I knew he wasn't really with us, and he wasn't with Jesus, he was in-between places. That is what I saw when I sat with him and continued to tell Jesus, "If Jason can not be the Jason he would want to be by staying here, please take him with you. I would take care of him for the rest of my life, but I don't want that for him. Please don't keep him here for me. Take him with you, where I know he will be happy. He will be able to run and play and do all the things he can no longer do here. He would no longer have pain. Please give me the strength to go on without him because I will miss him so much."

One afternoon BJ sat down next to Jason, he thought Jason was sleeping and he began to cry. All of a sudden, Jason opened his eyes and asked BJ, "Why are you crying?" BJ said, "I don't want to loose you, I will miss you so much." Then Jason looked at him and said, "BJ, don't cry. When I go to heaven I won't look like this anymore and I won't feel like this anymore."

There's something I have to tell you about this. Jason didn't know what he looked like. He didn't look the same. He had no hair, his face was swollen, and in fact his whole body was swollen. With his liver gone, he was completely yellow from head to toe. Even the whites of his eyes were yellow. There was one time while he was still in the hospital that he wanted to see what he looked like. I didn't have a mirror there and when I pulled the drawer out from under his tray the mirror was gone. Jason told me, "That's okay it didn't matter anyway." He never asked again what he looked like. So when he said that to BJ I was shocked because I knew somehow he must have known.

One day, I was sitting on the couch next to Jason. He motioned for me to come closer. I put my face next to his. It was hard for him to talk out loud. He would talk very little, and when he did it was just a whisper. I put my face next to his so I could hear him. Jason dropped his cheek up against my cheek. I went to pull away and he shook his head "no." About five seconds later I felt a current coming from his cheek. It felt so good, unlike any feeling I have ever felt before. I didn't know what it was. I said, "Jason, I feel something," and he nodded his head. Then I asked, "Do you feel anything coming from my cheek?" Jason nodded but he didn't say anything. Then I asked, "What is that? It was so nice. Jayce, is that your love?" He smiled and nodded his head. I asked him, "Do you feel my love?" Jason nodded again. I was so amazed that just by touching our cheeks we could feel each others love. I can't remember ever telling him after that, that I loved him. I would just put my cheek up against his and the current would come and he would smile. I miss that smile and I ache all the time for that feeling of his love.

Another day, I asked Jason if his angel had come home with him from the hospital. He said, "Yeah, it's your mother! Sometimes she's sitting right next to you." I looked next to me and asked, "Is she here now?" Jason said, "No, but she was there a little while ago." Then I asked him, "Why don't you tell me when she's here? I'd like to know if my mother is sitting next to me or is in our home." Jason just looked at me and said, "Why? She's not here for you, she's waiting for me. She's going to hold my hand to heaven." Again I was amazed by what was happening. I didn't know this could really be true. Here my nine-year-old son was teaching me about things I never knew.

269

From the time Jason got sick, Bill and I would pray the rosary to ourselves every day, sometimes four or five times in a row. Thinking back, I don't know what was going through my mind when I started saying them. Now I think it was probably because it is Mary's prayer to her Son. Being a mom, I figured she would understand my pain. I still pray at least one every day because it helps bring me comfort. Anyway, Jason would see us pray sometimes. Two days before he died, he asked us if we had said the rosary yet that day. When we told him yes, he asked us to say it again, only out loud this time. We didn't ask any questions, we just did it and Jason laid there and listened. He never told us why he wanted us to do that.

Later that night, I was sitting on the floor watching Jason sleep. He opened his eyes and looked at me and I laid my cheek against his and we felt the love current. Jason just smiled. We didn't say anything. His eyes were barely open at this point. Jason couldn't move any parts of his body except a little bit of his right arm, because he was so weak. I got up to fluff his pillows and reposition his legs and arms. When I went to move his right arm, I could tell he no longer could move it himself. I looked into his face and it was as if I could read his mind. He was telling me, "I can't move it anymore, but don't tell anyone." I just said very low, "I understand and I won't say anything." Then I put my cheek up against his for a while and we shared our love. I got a washcloth and wet it with warm water and I just kept wiping his face with it. Jason just lay there so still and I could tell how good that felt to him. I never did tell anyone that he lost the use of that arm until after he died. I knew Jason didn't want anyone to feel bad for him.

Jason kept seeing his angel. He had not spoken of seeing Jesus since the time he saw him in the ICU. He would talk about Jesus showing him heaven, but as far as we knew; his angel was going to hold his hand to heaven. The evening before he died, Bill and I were changing him. Jason looked at us and said, "Jesus is coming." I asked, "Did you just say Jesus was coming?" He said, "Yeah." Then Jason said, "You guys are the best." (He said that to us a lot from the time he went into the hospital). I said "Awe Jayce, you make it so easy because you're the best."

I was so afraid of what Jason had just said about Jesus coming. Then I thought of how the Lord spoke through me to him about seeing heaven then coming back. So I thought maybe, just maybe, that's what's going to happen.

About six hours before Jason died, he had a real bad pain spell. We got it under control and he was comfortable again but his breathing became very shallow. I sat next to him on the floor while he lay on the couch. Jason's eyes were barely open; we hadn't seen his eyes wide open for days. I could tell he was watching me, looking right into my face. I was stroking his arm and caressing his head, just remembering all the fun times we had shared in the nine years that he was mine. Remembering all the love we had for each other. Bill was sitting on the couch by Jason's feet. Then the thought came to me as if it were a voice in my head.

I believe now it was the Lord speaking through me again. I said, "Jayce, I think I know what you are doing. You're hanging on thinking if you refuse to go see heaven, Jesus is going to say, well Jason's just not going to come, so I'll have to find someone else." Jason nodded his head, yes. I said, "Honey, it doesn't work that way. You are going to stay sick until you go see heaven. Then you can come back and you'll get better." Jason let out a sigh and then I told him, "I already asked Jesus if I could go instead of you and he told me no. Jesus told me you're more special to him than I am and he wants you to see his home." Then Bill said, "We'll wait right here for you." Jason looked over at Bill then back to me. I leaned over and we touched cheeks, I could feel the love current. I whispered in his ear, "Thank you for loving me Jayce." Jason nodded his head. Then Bill said, "Let's ask Jesus to hold you in his arms and make you better." I immediately thought, "Where two or more shall gather in my name I will be there." Jason then took a breath and turned his head towards Bill. His eyes opened wide and he sat up. There was no way Jason could sit up by himself, but he sat up and his blue eyes were shinning so beautifully. He looked right at Bill then he turned his head and looked at me. He lay back down slowly and closed his eyes. I laid my head on his chest waiting for him to breathe and I touched my cheek to his only this time the current was gone. That is when I realized he wasn't coming back.

For days I would pray and ask God to please let me see Jason. I wanted to see him healthy and happy and having fun. I wanted to see him out of pain. Two weeks after Jason died, I had a vision. Nothing like this has ever happened to me before. I was sleeping and it seemed like a dream, but not exactly. I was seeing Jason die all over again the same way that it had happened. Bill was sitting where he was at the time, I was where I was at the time and Jason was looking at us while we were talking to him. I was trying to wake up and I remember yelling, "No, this is not what I want to see." But I could not wake up, so I shut up and watched. Only this time when Bill said, "Let's ask Jesus to hold you in his arms to make you better." These two perfect arms reached under Jason's back and lifted him towards this beautiful light that was shinning through his eyes. His solid body was coming back down on to the couch, but a lighter body was fading toward this beautiful light. The most amazing thing I have ever seen was this white mass right along the side of Jason. It didn't have a body, but I knew by seeing it that it was his angel holding his hand. Just like Jason told us she would. Jason was in Jesus' arms and holding his angels hand.

It wasn't until after Jason was gone and I was thinking about all of this that I realized Jesus gave me what I asked him for in the ICU. I wanted Jason to know how much he meant to me, which I know he did. I wanted to make sure he wasn't afraid, and I know he wasn't. Now I pray for strength and comfort, because I know I have to do what I told Jesus I would, I have to give Jason back.

Susie Nau

Treasure in Heaven

Have you ever demanded God to prove to you that He exists?
Barbara Parker did.

Barbara is a recovering cocaine addict at Epiphany House, a Halfway House for recovering drug addicts in the ghettos of Asbury Park, New Jersey. Every Tuesday evening I volunteer, conducting a drum circle and spirituality group with the women there. We come together with the twelve steps. We *beat out stress* on our djembes, congas and ashikos and experience the healing power of our Divine Musician.

When I first met Barbara three years ago, she had entered our program directly from prison. She related how at the age of ten she was made to steal cars in an effort to support her mother's alcohol habit. Her young life regressed downward from there. Today, Barbara proudly adopted her own twelve-year-old granddaughter to save her from a life of abuse.

While at Epiphany House, Barbara struggled for over a year with interviews and rejections before she was able to attain her first job at a local supermarket. Sadly, no one wants to give a second chance to an Afro-American with a prison record. Barbara's supervisor soon began displaying his prejudice by cutting her hours, barely giving her enough wages to pay rent—nonetheless food, bills or transportation. She could not make ends meet.

Despite overwhelming obstacles, Barbara has stayed clean from returning to the numbing world of drugs. How did she do it? Why did she do it? Where was God, her higher power, in all of this? What good did prayer do for her life of struggle and pain?

Barbara's prayer was a cry of desperation to God! She would attend Sunday Baptist services, and with the congregation cry out to God for the grace to become a *victor* instead of a perpetual *victim*. She pleaded in song, psalms and community prayers for God's help. Yet, Barbara continued to feel hopeless and abandoned by her creator. Privately, she'd pray morning, noon and night, with her granddaughter, crying out to God for help, but her world continued to crumble. Nothing was easy or going right. Support was hard to find...mercy was even harder.

I am an Associate of the Sisters of Mercy and one of God's Ambassadors of Encouragement. On the day Barbara graduated from Epiphany House to reenter the world of temptation, I prayed that God would allow me to be his instrument to help her whenever she was in need.

Being a faithful member of Fr. Thomas Keating's Contemplative Outreach, I'd sit for two periods of Centering Prayer daily. I'd make my intention to *be* with God and consent to His presence and action within. Then I'd wait for discernment. It wasn't long before I clearly heard God in my heart saying, "Whatever you do to the least of my brethren, you do to Me." The next week I heard, "Go and sell all that you have and distribute it to the poor, and you will have treasure in Heaven."

And so, whenever Barbara would call me: broke at the train station, at a corner store hungry, on a curb in need of a ride, in need of a new pair of shoes, a warm winter coat or a doctor bill to be paid—I never hesitated. I gave in the name of Jesus. I was happy to be His hiding place, His face of unconditional love and acceptance for her.

Last week, I was feeling very low. I was trying to be grateful but instead was wallowing in self-pity. Then I felt the hand of God lift me from the depths to raise me on high. Barbara's caseworker had sought me out, and with tears rolling down her cheeks, shared that Barbara had just gratefully told her. "I was the only evidence she had on earth, to prove *There is a God!*"

My own dark cloud immediately lifted. I smiled broadly and quoted St. Theresa's words, "Truly, Christ has no body but ours."

Barbara A. Woodzell   *Lincroft, New Jersey*

Please Hear My Prayer

I came from a very poor family in a small town in Tennessee. I was very shy but had a wonderful mom and dad, and two small brothers whom I loved dearly. Still, I was a very lonely little girl who desperately needed a sister in my life.

Brothers are wonderful, but a little girl needs someone she can grow up with and share her dreams and secrets. I was so faithful to God because I knew he was always there for me and he always answered my prayers.

I was taught to always believe, and I did believe, that our precious Lord would always be there for me. I was nine and a half years old when I found out my mom was going to have another child. I was so happy. I went into my bedroom and begin praying ever so hard to Jesus.

This was the prayer that I said every morning and all through out the day: "Precious Jesus, never have I asked anything of you that you didn't answer, because you love me with all of your heart. My mom is going to have another child. I need a sister so badly. Please give me a sister this time, as I am lonely for a sister's love. I will help mom with her and I will always try to protect her and love her with all of my heart. Please hear my prayers, sweet Jesus. Please Jesus, I need a sister so badly. I know you will give me a sister this time."

I said this prayer throughout the day. And when bedtime came I always prayed to Jesus. This was my bedtime prayer: "I know I'm just a child. But a child who always talks to you as if you're my best friend. I am shy, and have very few friends, but you love me the way I am. You hold my hand when I am scared and lonely. Before I close my eyes at night, I always trust that you are here with me during the darkness of the night. Please bless me with a little sister to cherish and to love. I love you, Jesus. Please hear my prayers."

Never once did I have any doubts that God would answer my prayers and give me a sister. The days, weeks, and months passed and my faith grew even stronger in God. When mom was seven months along, she went into labor and dad called a cab as we had no vehicle. Off they went to the hospital. I started praying so hard that my mom and baby sister would be okay.

I waited, it seemed, forever, as the minutes passed by so slowly, then the hours. I became frightened for my mom, so I prayed that God would please let them be okay. Finally, my dad came in the door and his face was so pale that it scared me.

I started to cry as I was afraid that maybe I shouldn't have asked Jesus so often for a baby sister. Maybe he didn't want that. Then as my tears flowed, my dad said to me, "Sissy, you didn't get one sister, God gave you two sisters! Twins!"

I was so happy. I remember asking my dad if mom was okay. He told me she was and that my sisters were very small but they would be okay. He said I needed to say a prayer for them as they were born too soon and were very tiny and weak.

I darted off to my bedroom where I knelt down on my knees and began thanking Jesus for this wonderful miracle. I knew he would let my sisters grow strong and that he would let me keep them.

The twins stayed in the hospital for several weeks. Then they came home to all of us. They were so little and so pretty. They didn't look alike so that made me feel even more blessed as I knew they would both be different and I would get to know each of them. They would have their own personalities.

I knew that this was just one of the miracles that God would bless me with throughout my life. Now I am fifty-two years old, and my sisters and I live two hundred miles apart, but we are always in each other's thoughts and prayers. We are very close. We see each other three to four times a year.

I was right about there being a very special bond between sisters.

Thank you, Jesus, for both of my younger sisters and my two brothers. Thank you, Jesus, for always hearing my prayers.

Juanita R. Wilbanks   *Hamilton, Tennessee*

Authors by Location

Africa

Ghana
Augustus Mensah, *Cape Coast, 212*

Kenya
Jane Wangari Muthoga, *Nairobi, 125*
Jackline Mukami Nyagah, *Embu, 150*

Australia
Gail L. Creswell, *Brisbane, Queensland, 122*
Grace R. Vega, *Cammeray, New South Wales, 75*

Canada

Nova Scotia
Helena Cody, *Lunenburg, 171*

Ontario
Noreen M. Mater, *Dunnville, 169*
Laurie Obidowski, *Brampton, 9*
Carol Lynn Thibault, *Ottawa, 155*
Heather J. Toutant, *Oshawa, 79*

Central America
Maria M. Fabro, *Buttonwood Bay*, *Belize, 81*

India
Sr. Ambika Mary F.I.H., *Kollam, 154*
Rowena S. Glasfurd, *Bangalore, 77*
Celia Lourdes Cardozo, *Hubli, 210*

Ireland
Helen M. O'Leary, *Munster, 62*

Mexico
Fr. Joseph Langford, MC, *Mexico City, 3*

Netherlands
Ria Post, *Den Haag, Zuid-Holland, 229*

United Arab Emirates
Della L. D'Cruz, *Abu Dhabi, 97*

United Kingdom

England
Bridget Donaldson, *Morpeth,*
Northumberland, 66
Patricia M. Greene, *Birmingham, West*
Midlands, 162
Paula C. Hagan, *Skelmersdale, Lancashire, 259*
Anne A. Jones, *Rushden, Northants, 106*

Wales
Josephine Stella Namatovu, *Cathays,*
Cardiff, 113

United States of America

Alabama
Emily A. Whitley, *Dadeville, 40*

Arkansas
Donna L. Skipper, *Mena, 42*

California
Therese C. Corsaro, *Palmdale, 104*
Martha Dolciamore, *Soquel, 251*
Sharon R. Friel, *San Francisco, 19*
Marilyn L. Larson, *Fresno, 49*
Rosalie Marschall, *San Francisco, 199*
Mary Louise Noroski, *Woodland Hills, 57*
Carol M. Valine Zarek, *Los Osos, 246*

Connecticut
Stacie A. Van Deusen, *Norwalk, 92*

Delaware
Leigh Ann M. Woodin, *Georgetown, 60*

Florida
Norma W. Coffin, *Melbourne, 139*
Doreen K. D'Angelo, *Boca Raton, 220*
Deanna D. Hobby, *Kissimmee, 184*
Marcella E. Kiesel, *Tampa, 24*
Mary L. Palmer, *Orange Park, 33*
Melvin Perry, *Jacksonville, 131*
Anita J. Oberholtzer, *Clearwater, 187*
Josie Zuniga, *Miami, 99*

Georgia
Kristin A. Sommer, *Fayetteville, 227*

Illinois
Deborah A. Armenta, *Round Lake Beach, 189*
Patricia W. Coleman, *Winnetka, 164*
Halina Acca Makowski, *Chicago, 224*
Evelyn Heinz, *McHenry, 108*
Regina M. Sabadosa, *Oak Lawn, 64*
Eleanor E. Waeyaert, *Moline, 28*
Susan M. Walker, *Wheeling, 14*

AUTHORS BY LOCATION

Appendix A: Authors by Location

Indiana
Suzanne L. McConnell, *Bloomington, 194*
Kathleen Delia Miller, *Chesterton, 89*
Ann M. Sabocik, *Hobart, 47*

Kansas
Kathryn Rohr, *Hays, 7*

Maine
Lisa Curran-Crimp, *Kennebunk, 157*

Maryland
Jackie M. Farrell, *Ft. Washington, 67*
Elizabeth Goral-Makowski, *Baltimore, 127*
Debra R. Kolodny, *Silver Spring, 5*

Massachusetts
Jo Ann Breau, *Leominster, 86*
Linda M. Cass, *Weymouth, 141*
Lorraine Christman, *Pepperell, 206*
MaryAnn Holak, *Beverly, 134*
Carol G. Spoor, *Assonet, 203*

Michigan
Judie J. Kolloen, *Shelby Twp, 208 & 215*
Fae D. Presley, *Hersey, 213*
Sr. Ann Shields, *Ann Harbor, 17*

Minnesota
Br. Kevin Brutcher, FSC, *Fridley, 137*

Mississippi
Deborah F. Flynt, *Foxworth, 238*

Missouri
Daniel E. Halley, *Hazelwood, 11 & 94*
Margaret A. Jensen, *Stark City, 129*
Donna Wimsatt, *Monett, 200*

Nebraska
Susan M. Phillips, *Omaha, 112*

Nevada
Celeste D. Lovett, *Henderson, 119*

New Jersey
Barbara A. Woodzell, *Lincroft, 273*

New Mexico
Virginia Schmuck, *Portales, 249*

New York
Anonymous, *Binghamton, 38*
Eleanor B. Crafa, *Northport, 192*

North Carolina
Connie A. Andretta, *Denver, 166*

Ohio
Judi A. Eichhorn, *Columbus, 176*
Kathy A. Giannamore, *Toronto, 234*
Sr. Georgene M. Golock, *Akron, 70*
Betsy J. Jackson, *Toledo, 117*
Katherine M. Komar, *Broadview Heights, 72*
Michael Scanlan, TOR, *Steubenville, 1*
Molly N. O'Connell, *Mason, 145*
Diane Parkhurst, *Boardman, 54*

Oklahoma
Coreen V. Marson, *Catoosa, 100*

Pennsylvania
Elizabeth L. Chabala, *Bridgeville, 152*
Maryann Kolod, *Bensalem, 198*
Judy V. Krantz, *Tarentum, 222*
Bernadette M. List, *York, 182*
Linda J. McCann, *Philadelphia, 148*
Roberta H. Sefchick, *Prompton, 91 & 143*

Rhode Island
Lillian J. DeOliveira, *East Providence, 22 & 51*

South Dakota
Lynda S. Lowin, *Blunt, 124*

Tennessee
Juanita R. Wilbanks, *Hamilton, 275*

Texas
June B. Cornish, *Quinlan, 174*
Susan M. DeFanti, *Euless, 87*
Dora C. Gallardo, *Uvalde, 115*
Jo Ann Mason, *Temple, 31 & 84*
Azalia C. Perez, *Hebbronville, 254*
Antonieta E. Tellander, *Laredo, 44*

Virginia
Sonny Mott, *Norfolk, Virginia, 257*
Maureen F. Regulinski, *Richmond, 240*
Janet L. Smith, *Gainesville, 160*
Deborah M. Turner, *Yorktown, 243*

Washington
Debra J. Ishii, *Kent, 218*
Lola J.Wink, *Spokane, 179*

Wisconsin
Marion M. Klokow, *Helenville, 177*

Index

Appendix B: INDEX

INDEX